TexaVegan

Low-Fat Vegan Recipes

by Deborah Brutsché

Texavegan. Copyright, © 2012, by GreenBelt Publishing. All Rights Reserved. Originally printed in the United States of America. No part of this book may be used or reproduced in any manner whatsoever without written permission except in case of brief quotations embodied in critical articles or reviews. For information, address GreenBelt Publishing, POB 200487, Austin, Texas 78720.

www.texavegan.com

Book Design by Stephanie Toal; Cover Design by Stephanie Toal
Photography by Rusty Brutsché

Library of Congress Cataloging-in-Publication Data

Brutsché, Deborah, edited by: Leslie Michaelis
     Texavegan / Deborah Brutsché
     ISBN-10: 0983361622
     EAN: 978-0-9833616-2-6
     Brutsché, Deborah. Author

First Edition: January 2013

Dedication

Dedicated with love to Rusty, Jen, Rus, Niki, Matt, Angela, Ella, Juliette, Mia and Jake. Thank you for sharing this journey with me and for bringing sunshine to my life everyday.

Acknowledgement

First and foremost, I must thank my publisher and son, Matthew, for his vision and tireless investment of time and energy into this project. Your enthusiasm and encouragement served as a genuine inspiration while your wise counsel kept the project on target. Thank you, Matt!

Without the kind persistence of my editor, Leslie, I would still be adding new vegan recipes. Your painstaking attention to detail and skillful editing successfully helped guide this manuscript into a tasty culmination of dishes. Thank you for your unfailing good humor and tenacity, Leslie. You have my undying respect as a person and as a brilliant editor.

Stephanie, thank you for contributing your amazing design talent to this project. Your creativity helped bring life to *TexaVegan*—inside and out. Thank you for investing your passion and support towards making this cookbook a reality.

Angela, thank you for the time, boundless energy and enthusiasm you put into this project. You patiently edited my words and helped pull the book together. You are a talented professional that I feel honored to have on my team and as a member of our family.

For the photography, I must thank my husband Rusty. You bring a deeper dimension of beauty to my life, and you've done the same in this book. You turned fruits and vegetables into a deliciously stunning display—exactly as I'd envisioned. Thank you for your ongoing support, assistance and encouragement.

I must also thank my daughter, Jen, for being so creative in arriving at the *TexaVegan* book title. And, thanks to you for devoting the time and energy into initial edits for this project.

Thank you to my little tasters, Ella, Juliette, Mia and Jake for taking a bite when I knew you really didn't want to. Many thanks to the big people testers, too, for being honest when enduring the recipes that didn't really work. I thank you all.

I also want to thank Rus, Niki, Jen, Angela and Matt for your favorite recipe contribution. They are delicious.

Thank you Mom, I was listening and watching!

With my sincerest gratitude, thanks to you all.

Deborah

Table of Contents

Transitions in Tradition	6
Choosing the Best Produce	7
Stocking a Vegan Kitchen	12
Salads & Dressings	23
Soups	59
Burgers & Sandwiches	81
Fresh Vegetables	99
Corn, Potatoes, Rice & Grains	155
Pastas & Pasta Sauces	189
One-Dish Meals	211
Tofu, Beans & Peas	227
Sauces, Dips, Gravies & Extras	249
Breads, Muffins & Breakfast	273
Fruits & Desserts	293
Index	339

Transitions in Tradition

Food is a strong part of who we are, and many of our memories are attached to the smells and tastes we have experienced throughout our lives. When I first decided to become vegan, I had a tough time moving away from the traditional meals on which I was raised—dishes that typically included copious amounts of butter and cheese. In 2006, I read about the effects of an animal-based diet in T. Colin Campbell's book *The China Study*, and became convinced that a vegan diet was the right decision for me.

Creating delicious vegan meals was much more challenging than I thought it would be (particularly during the holidays), but I became determined to create new, healthy traditions. Struggling to find recipes that were healthy yet appetizing, I eventually made my own collection of basic dishes. Many are adaptations of the meals my mother and grandmother used to prepare, incorporating the distinctive flavors of the Southern United States and Mexico without the use of dairy or meat ingredients, as well as some new recipes I created along the way.

I am blessed with a large family that consists of different cultures, beliefs and customs, and I love them all. While the eating habits of my children and their families vary, my kitchen welcomes all and serves enjoyable meals that are savory for everyone. Families who are looking for healthier cooking options will enjoy the simple, versatile dishes offered in this cookbook. If you don't know where to start, try the Mexican Red Posole soup (page 68), Stir-Fry with Soba Noodles (page 225), or Coconut and Banana Nut Cupcakes (page 329).

Choosing a low-fat vegan diet has been the right decision for me, but I do not claim to be an authority on its health benefits. If you are interested, I encourage you to read the works of T. Colin Campbell, Caldwell Esselstyn, Jr., M.D., Neal Barnard, M.D., John A. McDougall, M.D. and Dean Ornish, M.D. There are many talented authors who have also written helpful vegan cookbooks. Find these people, read their works, and have fun!

It takes courage to make changes. We all deserve the opportunity to modify our lifestyles in a way that will help us become as healthy as possible.

All the best,

Deborah

Choosing the Best Produce

Shoppers now have hundreds of choices of fresh fruits and vegetables from all over the world, often year-round. Remember when iceberg lettuce and a slice of pale tomato was a dinner salad? Now a salad can be can be a rainbow of vegetables, fruits and nuts full of health-promoting nutrients.

Since vegetables and fruit are the core of your vegan diet, knowing how to pick the freshest, tastiest produce will become a survival skill. Here I offer suggestions for recognizing the finest produce that nature and your local grocer have to offer. The best advice when buying produce is to follow the seasons. Buy organic produce from local farmers as often as you can—their tomatoes just cannot be beat!

ARTICHOKE
When buying an artichoke look for one that is dark green and feels heavy for its size. They can be boiled, steamed or grilled.

ARUGULA
Arugula, also called rocket, is a pungent, nutty green. It makes delicious salads but can work as a side or be added to soups. Large arugula leaves can be bitter, so try to use small baby and medium sized leaves.

ASPARAGUS
Look for crisp firm stalks. Avoid limp or shriveled spears. Green is the most readily found but white is also available at times and tends to be expensive. Place upright in a jar with water and keep in the refrigerator until ready to cook. To prepare for cooking, snap off the white woody part. Peel away the outer skin from the base to the tip. The thinner varieties do not need to be peeled. One pound of asparagus equals twenty stalks.

AVOCADO
Gently push the skin to determine the ripeness. The avocado will yield slightly to pressure when it is ready to use. Avoid the soft or mushy ones. If an avocado is hard, it will take 2-4 days to ripen. You can speed this up by placing it in a brown paper bag until ripe. Do not refrigerate until cut, just store them on the kitchen counter.

BEETS
Beets should have crisp looking greens, when attached. If just buying the bulbs, they should be firm with fairly smooth skin. Buy small or medium bulbs in any color. Wash but do not trim or peel the skin before cooking so the juices will not leach out.

BELL PEPPERS
Look for firm peppers with smooth skin. Avoid shriveled or ones that have soft spots or moldy stems.

BOK CHOY
Look for crisp, bright green leaves and stalks. Avoid any with brown spots or wilted leaves. Bok Choy is great to use in stir-fry or salads.

BROCCOLI
Look for bright green, crisp stalks, with tightly-closed buds not yellow. Can be steamed, roasted or boiled.

BROCCOLINI
A hybrid of broccoli and Chinese broccoli that should have bright green leaves and stalks. Avoid wilted and limp bunches.

BROCCOLI RAAB
Has a slightly bitter flavor. Look for deep green and crisp leaves not wilted or yellow.

BRUSSELS SPROUTS
Look for small, brightly colored without wilted leaves. Cook lightly until fresh, tender and brightly colored. Overcooked Brussels sprouts tend to get foul smelling. Fresh is better than frozen. One pound of Brussels sprouts equals four cups.

CABBAGE
Heavy, firmly packed heads with crisp leaves without discoloration are best. Many different varieties like Red, Green, Napa or Savoy. Cabbage can be braised, steamed, stir-fried or eaten raw in salads.

CARROTS
Look for firm, heavy, smooth-skinned carrots without cracks. Loose carrots are usually some of the sweetest, while those in plastic bags tend to be a little slick and rubbery. One pound of carrots equals three cups of diced carrots.

CAULIFLOWER
Look for a firm head with bright colored leaves of creamy white. Avoid wilted leaves or brown spots on the top edges of head.

CELERY
Select those with shiny and crisp stalks, avoiding any with yellow or brown spots.

CHILES
Choose chile peppers that are glossy and firm without shriveling or soft spots.

Jalapeños—Sometimes jalapeños will have a crack at the stem but other varieties should not.

Poblano—Sometimes mistakenly labeled *pasilla* in North America, poblanos are medium-hot peppers with a rich, sweet flavor. Delicious when stuffed.

Anaheim—Mildly spicy with a peppery flavor. They are good to stuff or when chopped and added to soups.

COCONUT
Look for a coconut that is free of mold and is heavy, with firm "eyes." Shake to make sure there is a lot of milk inside.

CORN
It is best to buy corn that is still in the husks. Look for green husks with plump kernels. Avoid corn that looks dried out. When you peel back the husks, the silks should look green and be a little sticky.

CUCUMBER
Cucumbers should be firm without shriveling or discoloration. Check the ends for firmness; they tend to get soft first. English Hot House cucumbers have a mild flavor, small seeds and thin skin that requires no peeling.

FRUIT
Apples—It's harder than it should be to find the "perfect" one. Look for a firm apple that is heavy for its size. No soft spots or shriveled skin. If possible, ask the produce person to cut one open and let you taste before you buy. Right now, my favorite is Jazz or Fuji. These varieties seem to be pretty consistent in quality. Tarter apples, like Braeburn, Winesap or Granny Smith, are great in pies and for baking. One and a half pounds of whole apples equals four cups of sliced apples.

Bananas—Avoid broken skin or moldy stems. Ripen at room temperature. When bananas are ripe, but aren't being used right away, peel and wrap them (sliced or whole) in wax paper, then foil and freeze. Three bananas equals one pound or two cups of sliced or one and a quarter cup of mashed.

Berries—Mainly blueberries, strawberries, blackberries and raspberries. Choose brightly colored berries without soft spots, discoloration or mold. If buying in a plastic container, make sure berries move around freely and do not stick together, which is a sign they could be moldy.

Cantaloupe—Choose cantaloupes that are heavy for their size, free of bruises or cracks. Sniff where the stem has been removed. A good cantaloupe should have an identifiable fruity aroma at the stem end.

Citrus—All citrus should be heavy for its size and fragrant at the stem, without soft spots, bruising, or mold. **Ripe grapefruit, limes, lemons, and nectarines** should be plump and give slightly with pressure; they should not be rock hard. All should have a sweet fragrance. Avoid citrus that appear shriveled or dry.

Grapes—Ripe grapes should be plump, fragrant and firm. Make sure stems are mold free and the grapes do not have soft spots.

Mango—Look for fruit that will give to light pressure. Avoid loose or shriveled skin.

Mexican Papaya—Look for firm fruit that gives slightly with pressure. Papaya has a sweet flavor with a slightly musky aroma. It is good simply served with a slice of lime.

Nectarines—Avoid bruises, tinges of green or shriveling. Look for nectarines that are plump and will give slightly with pressure, firm but not rock hard. They should have a sweet fragrance.

Peaches—Look for peaches that are plump and will give slightly with pressure, without being mushy. They should be fragrant with a peachy smell. Avoid any with bruises, tinges of green or shriveling. Three to four medium peaches equals one pound.

Pears—Choose fruit that is firm and fragrant. Pears are ripe when they give to gentle pressure. Ripen in a paper bag a day or two before serving if too hard. Avoid bruising and mushy, soft spots.

Watermelon—Whole watermelons should feel heavy for their size. Avoid cracks or soft spots. If the area where the melon sat on the ground is creamy yellow in color that indicates it was ripe when picked. If you are buying a slice of watermelon, the flesh should look dense and have a sweet fragrance. Avoid overripe melons where the flesh has pulled away from the seeds.

GARLIC
Buy heads that are firm, not shriveled or soft. Store in a dark, dry place.

GINGER
Ginger should be smooth and wrinkle free. Can be kept frozen for up to 3 months.

GREEN BEANS
Beans should be bright green in color, flexible when bent and should snap crisply when broken. One pound of trimmed green beans is equal to three cups of raw beans or two cups of cooked.

GREENS
Collard, Kale, Turnip, Chard, Mustard, Spinach
Choose brightly colored leaves with fairly stiff stems that free of brown spots or wilt. Approximately one pound of greens equals six cups of leaves.

LETTUCES
Romaine, Red Leaf, Boston, Iceberg, Endive, Arugula, Frisee, Escarole
Look for brightly colored leaves with fairly stiff stems; avoid brown spots or wilting. Romaine or iceberg lettuce is a good choice for when you are using a thick, heavy dressing that might be too heavy for a lighter lettuce.

LEEKS
Tops should feel crisp, not yellow or withered.

MUSHROOMS
There are thousands of varieties. Look for mushrooms free of soft spots or mold. Most varieties should be firm. Exceptions would be enoki, oyster and wood ear. To store, remove from plastic and place unwashed in a single layer on a sheet pan with a damp paper towel over the top and place in the refrigerator for up to a week. A few of the more popular ones are as follows:

Porcini—They look like button mushrooms only they are dark brown in color. They have a woodsy, earthy, meaty flavor. Choose firm ones without soft spots. Wipe clean with a damp cloth not in water because it toughens the flesh.

Morels—Morels are hollow-like mushrooms with a rich flavor. They should be washed in water to make sure all the sand is washed away.

Chanterelles—They are golden in color and smooth. They have a rich, earthy flavor with a hint of pepper.

Oyster—They have a mild great flavor with a velvety texture. Wipe with a damp cloth to clean.

Shiitake Mushrooms—Firm flesh with a meaty flavor. Discard stems and wipe with damp cloth to clean.

OKRA
Look for small pods about 3 inches long which are more tender and flavorful than larger ones. Avoid pods that look dull or stale or have brown spots. They should snap when broken in half. Okra has a short shelf life, they should be used sooner rather than later.

ONIONS
Green or Spring
They should have bright green stalks. Not dried out or shriveled.

Sweet
Onions should be firm without soft spots. Their necks should be tightly closed with no green sprouts. Four to five medium size onions equal one pound.

Vidalia—Tend to be sweet and crisp with a subtle aftertaste. Flat stem end and round at root with yellow skin.

Texas 1015 Sweet—Softball size with yellow skin.

Walla Walla—Large with yellow skin.

Maui—Grown in Hawaii and is large with white skin. They tend to be juicy and sweet.

Red Spanish Onions—Purplish-red skin with a mild, sweet taste. They are great to use raw.

Yellow Onions—Look for medium size firm onions. These tend to be juicy with a crisp texture and a sharp flavor. These are a great choice for a cooking onion.

Shallots—Look for dry, firm bulbs free of sprouts, soft spots or mold. Milder than an onion in taste. Great for cooking.

PEAS
English Peas—Look for the bright green, glossy pods. They should be heavy for their size and the medium pods tend to be sweeter than the larger ones. Do not purchase pods that rattle when shaken. Refrigerate immediately since their sugar content turns to starch after picking. Can be eaten raw.

Sugar Snap or **Snow Peas**—Look for crisp peas that are not limp or discolored. Remove strings before eating. Can be eaten raw.

Black-Eyed Peas—Commonly, black-eyed peas are found in a package of shelled, presoaked and partially cooked peas. Look for evenly colored peas without soft spots, discoloration or that feel slimy.

Crowder or **Cream Peas**—These are mostly often sold already shelled. Look for evenly colored peas without discoloration, soft spots or that feel slimy.

POTATOES

Russet Potatoes—Choose potatoes that are wrinkle free, without cracks, soft spots or sprouts. Organically grown Russets are a little sweeter. Three to four medium potatoes equal one pound.

Red Potatoes—Choose firm potatoes that are without cracks or sprouts. Red potatoes are low in starch, with firm flesh and hold together well in cooking.

Yukon Gold Potatoes—Choose firm potatoes without soft spots. Yukon potatoes tend to have a sweet flavor with a buttery, flaky texture. Do not need to be peeled.

Sweet Potatoes—Choose those that are firm and heavy for their size. Free of cracks and soft spots. There are many varieties of sweet potatoes with white or orange colored flesh. Garnet or Jewel are orange flesh varieties. Garnets are often called "yams" and are best used when mashed or in baking. They have dark red-to-purple skin with deep orange flesh and a sweet, almost caramelized flavor. Jewels have copper-colored skin with yellow-orange flesh. They tend to be sweet and moist.

RADISHES

Look for bright green leaves with smooth skin that are small for their size.

TOMATILLO

Tomatillos are not green tomatoes, but they are a member of the nightshade family. Look for dry, tight husks. They should be crisp and free from mold.

TOMATOES

Look for plump tomatoes that feel heavy for their size. Avoid bruises or discoloration. When fully ripe, tomatoes will yield to gentle pressure. Do not refrigerate until after they have been cut; tomatoes lose their texture and freshness a couple of hours after slicing, even in the refrigerator. A tomato should smell very much like a tomato, especially at the stem end. Some varieties you will easily find at the market are:

Beefsteak—Large, red, sweet, with rich tomato flavor. Great for slicing.

Cherry—Tend to be sweet with a rich, juicy flavor. You can find them in red or yellow.

Heirloom—They come in different colors, shapes and sizes and should be juicy, rich and sweet. Be picky and don't buy soft or bruised tomatoes. Heirlooms tend to be expensive and many times are not worth the extra money.

Hothouse—Usually attached to the vine, medium size with sweet tomato flavor.

Roma—Plum-shaped and less sweet than other tomatoes but useful for making sauces. Five to six Roma tomatoes equals one pound.

SQUASH, SUMMER

Crookneck & Zucchini

Look for young squash with firm skin without soft spots or shriveling. Choose smaller squash—they have a more delicate flavor than the larger ones. Edible skins. Do not overcook.

SQUASH, WINTER

Acorn, Butternut, Many Varieties

Look for firm rinds with no soft spots. The heavier the squash, the thicker the edible flesh it has inside. Squash should be peeled and deseeded before eating. Can be baked, boiled or steamed until tender.

Stocking a Vegan Kitchen

Cooks new to being vegan may have difficulty wading through the millions of products in their local grocery to find foods with no animal byproducts. Some substitution ingredients simply don't taste the way you would expect while certain products work well in some dishes and not so well in others.

Through years of following a low-fat plant-based diet, there are seasonings and ingredients that I have learned to rely on in my cooking. As a result this section includes a list the items that are most regularly needed in my pantry, refrigerator and freezer, along with some brands that have proven to be consistent and yield the best results.

This list is not intended to be a promotion of any particular brand or an endorsement of any manufacturer. There are so many new options available everyday. If an item here does not suit your personal taste, explore and experiment until you find one that meets your needs.

Read the labels when buying processed foods. It is amazing how many products are not vegan that should be. *Why should most taco seasonings contain milk? Veggie burgers? Soy cheese? Non-dairy creamer?* Recognizing animal products by the different names used in packaging is almost impossible. Here are a few names of additives that are dairy in origin: casein, caseinate, whey, lactalbumin, lactoferrin, lactoglobulin, lactose, lactulose, nougat, recaldent, ghee, paneer, caramel color or flavoring, natural flavoring, and solids. This is just the beginning. Research a product or its ingredients online before buying. Just remember if it has more than four or five ingredients listed on the label and you can't pronounce them, maybe you should just get an apple.

Vinegars & Sauces

APPLE CIDER VINEGAR
A mild, sweet cider flavor. Add it to almond milk to mimic buttermilk for breads and desserts.

BALSAMIC VINEGAR
Balsamic vinegar is aged in wooden barrels and has a rich, slightly sweet taste and is ideal for dressings and marinades.

CHAMPAGNE VINEGAR
Champagne vinegar is light and delicate and works well in light dressings.

HOT PEPPER SAUCES
Some of my favorites are Tabasco® by McIlhenny Co., Sky Valley Sriracha® sauce by Organicville®, and Sambal Oelek® chili paste.

MIRIN
A sweet, low alcohol rice wine for use in marinades, stir-fry and salad dressings.

RED WINE VINEGAR
Buy the best quality available. Try a Cabernet Sauvignon vinegar elaborated from a fine wine with added mint. There are many choices especially in red wine vinegars.

RICE VINEGAR
Rice vinegar is delicate in flavor which goes nicely in salads, marinades and dressings.

SHERRY VINEGAR
This or any flavored vinegar can add depth and a little sweetness to dressings and marinades.

SOY SAUCE or TAMARI
A salty condiment that comes in light and dark varieties that adds a salty, earthy depth of flavor to so many dishes. Tamari is soy sauce that is made with little or no wheat. The naturally brewed products such as San J and Nama Shoyu are standards in my pantry.

WHITE BALSAMIC VINEGAR
White balsamic vinegar has a milder taste and is good for light dressings and marinades. Alessi white balsamic vinegar is used in Roasted Garlic Hummus Dressing (page 27).

WHITE VINEGAR
Great old stand-by. White vinegar is usually made from grain, such as malt, corn or rice. Good quality white vinegar is a entirely clear liquid. There are many variations in acidity and mineral content. Choose a milder brand for most uses.

VEGAN WORCESTERSHIRE SAUCE
Worcestershire sauce is usually made with anchovies, so be certain to select a vegan brand, such as The Wizards®.

Oils

The less oil used to create a dish the better. When sautéing, try using only one tablespoon of oil, if at all, preferring to replace oil with vegetable broth, water or wine. When baking or roasting, try to use condiments like mustards, vinegars, pesto, soy sauce, or minced garlic. You will be amazed how little oil is missed in most dishes.

CANOLA OIL
Canola oil is ideal for sautéing or stir-frying when the flavor should be mild and as unobtrusive as possible. Brands such as Spectrum® or Whole Foods® Grocery 365 Brand® work well for this purpose.

ROASTED SESAME OIL
A thick brown oil with a very distinctive taste and intense nutty flavor, this oil makes marinades sing. However, it burns easily and should not be used for cooking, just for flavor. A little goes a long way.

EXTRA VIRGIN OLIVE OIL
Least refined olive oil from the first pressing and the purest of taste. Flavors can be lost when overheated.

PEANUT OIL
Peanut oil has a mild flavor and good in delicately flavored foods. Peanut oil can be used for frying because it doesn't burn easily at high temperatures.

WALNUT OIL
Walnut oil has a soft delicious aroma. Nut oils are for seasoning not for cooking. Use for dressings or to drizzle over greens. Keep refrigerated. Nut oils quickly go rancid after opening. It should always smell fresh and nutty.

GRAPE SEED OIL
Grape seed oil has the highest burn threshold so is good for sautéing and frying. It is clear oil that is light in taste and great to use in salad dressings.

COOKING SPRAY
Spectrum® brand canola cooking spray has given me the most consistent results.

Seasonings

Everyone has different tastes and many times it is the seasonings that can make or break a recipe. Try Deb's Seasoning (page 269), for a simple recipe that can be used in nearly everything. Deb's seasoning is mild and made without added salt, so that the amount of salt and heat in a dish can be easily controlled. There are so many vegetable and grill seasonings available, a little exploration will yield one you'll love.

GRILL SEASONINGS
A couple that are basic and easy on the palette include Simply Organic Vegetable Seasoning® and McCormick Spicy Steak®.

SEASONING BLENDS
For a change of pace, try Tony Chachere's Original Creole Seasoning®, but only when salt content isn't a consideration.

TACO SEASONING—Burritos® and Old El Paso Taco Seasonings® are brands that do not include milk in their list of ingredients. Try making your own mix starting with the recipe for Deb's Taco Seasoning (page 269).

FRESH JALAPEÑOS or SERRANO CHILES
Chiles are the perfect seasoning for the little kick they can give a soup or dish. Don't be afraid that jalapeños are too hot for you until you try them. They have been bred to be milder than they used to be. If you want more heat, use just the seeds and membrane from the center or substitute Serrano chiles which are usually hotter with a great chili flavor.

Dried or Fresh Spices

Having these spices available in your kitchen's arsenal will offer you the best chance to explore your creativity when cooking. Spices are how a dish often gets it character. When adding spices, be careful to go slowly until you get a feel for what tastes right. When a recipe recommends a "pinch or two," always try one pinch first to see whether the dish really needs the second one. *Hint: A tablespoon of fresh herbs equals about a teaspoon of dried.*

CAYENNE
From the cayenne pepper plant. Very hot and spicy, but great to use a sprinkle here and there.

CHILI POWDER
A pure lightly toasted ground powder that combines ground, dried chiles with spices such as cumin, garlic, oregano, and coriander. New Mexican chili powder is fragrant, sweet and a little hotter. Pasilla chili powder is milder.

CHIPOTLE CHILES
Jalapeño peppers that have been smoked. You can buy a small can with added adobo sauce. They are very hot but add a delicious smoky flavor to salsas, beans or soups.

CHIVES
A mild, sweet herb with a fine grass-like appearance and a flavor similar to an onion. Easy to grow in an herb garden and can be used in many dishes.

CILANTRO
A green, leafy herb, resembling flat-leaf parsley, with a sharp aromatic flavor. Use carefully when serving guests since cilantro's distinctive flavor can be unpalatable to some palates.

CINNAMON
Ground or in sticks.

CUMIN
A strong-flavored, tart seed that works well in spicy dishes. Use it lightly since it can overwhelm other seasonings.

CURRY POWDER
A spice blend available in a wide variety. Experimentation will be necessary to find blends which suit your personal taste. Freshness is the key word when choosing curries.

DILL
Fresh or dried.

FENNEL
An herb and a spice. The anise-flavored seeds add fragrance to dishes. Ground fennel can be found in Deb's Seasoning (page 269).

ITALIAN PARSLEY
Also called flat-leaf parsley, has more flavor than the common curly-leaf parsley. Sweet, fresh flavor. Fresh is best and can be grown at home year-round.

MARJORAM
A sweet, mild and aromatic herb that can be used in place of oregano which has a stronger and harsher flavor. Dried or fresh.

NUTMEG
Use whole nutmeg seeds so you can grind it yourself when needed because it loses its flavor fast after grinding. A fine blade zester works well for this.

ONION POWDER and **GARLIC POWDER**
Fresh onions and garlic are by far best for most recipes, but these bottled spices can be used when fresh is not available.

PAPRIKA
Made from dried paprika pepper and available in sweet, mild, hot and smoky forms. Flavors are used at different times through this collection of recipes.

PEPPER
Fresh ground is best, but a coarse grind of bottled pepper is best if fresh is not available.

RED PEPPER FLAKES
Coarsely ground flakes of dried red chiles, including the seeds. Use when a hot, spicy flavor is desired.

SAFFRON
The most expensive spice in this list, it adds a distinctive flavor and color to dishes.

SEA SALT
Coarse or fine, the flavor is stronger and more complex than iodized table salt. The grays or yellow salts supposedly have more unrefined minerals.

THAI BASIL
Hard to find, but if you have an herb garden you can buy seeds and grow it yourself. Milder and a little sweeter than regular basil.

THYME
A good addition to most dishes. Dried or fresh.

TUMERIC
A vivid yellow powder that adds color and has a mild, warm flavor.

Tomato Products

CANNED TOMATOES
Crushed canned tomatoes can make a soup or dish too sweet and thick; diced or whole tomatoes makes a lighter, thinner broth taste more like fresh tomatoes. Fire-roasted tomatoes can provide added depth to many soups and chilies.

TOMATO PASTE
Tomato paste that comes in a tube must be the best invention ever. Find it in the pasta section of the grocery store and keep it in your refrigerator for use a little at a time.

PASTA SAUCE
A great pasta sauce for everyday meals is 365 No-Fat Brand® from Whole Foods®. It's a simple marinara sauce made without any oil. Add capers, more garlic, olives or red pepper flakes to change the flavor for what you need. Muir Glen® also makes a no-oil mushroom marinara that is tasty, too.

RO*TEL®
RO*TEL® is a tomato and pepper blend when a little zip is needed in a dish. It comes in mild and spicy.

Canned Beans

Canned beans work well for soups and other dishes. I usually buy Eden Organic brand, which is salt free and helps control the amount of salt in my dishes.

CHICKPEAS
Excellent for hummus, soups, sauces and dips, it is a good idea to always have dried and canned chickpeas on hand.

BLACK BEANS
Also known as "turtle beans," black beans are known for their distinctive flavor and my personal favorite.

PINTO BEANS
A brown, mild bean that can be used in endless ways.

WHITE BEANS (NAVY)
A small, white, light-flavored bean perfect for baked beans. When cooked, they have a nice thick sauce that is really tasty.

SMALL RED BEANS
Often called Mexican red beans, these are also one of my favorites, as they tend to be milder than kidney beans.

Dried Beans & Peas

Always stay well stocked when it comes to dried beans and peas because they can be used for meals on a weekly basis. Some favorites include: Black Beans, Navy or white beans, Pinto beans, Lentils, Split peas, Garbanzo beans, Large Lima beans and Red beans. Be on the lookout for new varieties.

Rices

LONG GRAIN BROWN RICE
This is a favorite and can be found in recipes throughout this book. White rice may suit some recipes better, so both are always available in my pantry.

BASMATI
The most fragrant rice. Good for curries and pilafs.

TEXMATI
A brown rice that is grown in Texas and Arkansas.

JASMINE
From Thailand, jasmine rice is a floral rice with a silky texture.

ARBORIO
A short grain rice that is starchy and can absorb lots of liquid. Good for risottos.

WILD RICE
Surprisingly, a wild grass not a grain. For faster cooking, it's better soaked overnight to soften and then cooked like regular rice the next day.

Grains

QUINOA
A small grain that is high in protein but free of gluten. Can easily be used as a substitute for rice or any grain. Very good but don't overcook.

PEARL BARLEY
Mild and chewy. It is a good change from rice. Since the outer husk has been removed it is a little less nutritious than regular barley but much faster cooking.

MILLET
A small grain and the taste is similar to cornmeal. It can be used as a substitute to couscous.

BULGUR WHEAT or CRACKED WHEAT
Popular in tabbouleh. Can be used in chili to add a heavier texture. Soak in water until swollen and fluffy or just simmer until fluffy unless it is precooked.

COUSCOUS
Really a tiny pasta made from semolina, not a grain. It has a moist, nutty flavor and is easy and fast to cook.

Condiments

VEGAN MAYONNAISE
A popular brand like Veganaise® can be used in many things like biscuits to make them light and fluffy. Another brand, Wildwood Garlic Aioli®, can add zest to a plain sandwich.

OLIVES
Many varieties are available to suit various tastes; I tend to prefer French Nicoise® and Greek Kalamata®.

MUSTARD
Dijon and yellow mustards have different textures and flavors and each has its uses. Make certain that sugar is not listed as an ingredient or that the label states that the mustard is vegan.

CAPERS
A tangy addition to many dishes, from pasta sauces to roasted potatoes. I love the salty, briny flavor.

Sweeteners

I try to replace white sugar as much as possible with organic cane sugars, such as beet or cane sugar, raw sugar, brown sugar, maple syrup, agave nectar, molasses, barley malt and brown rice syrup. A concern for vegans in using refined white sugar is the way some products are processed with animal bones.

AGAVE NECTAR
A natural sweetener that comes from the agave cactus. It is low in sucrose and has a low glycemic index. It has slightly more calories than sugar by volume but is 25% sweeter, so you use less. It can be used in many desserts and in oatmeal. I use the brand Madhava.

BARLEY MALT
A low sucrose sweetener that comes from whole barley.

BROWN RICE SYRUP
As the name implies, this is a natural sweetener made from fermented brown rice.

BROWN SUGAR
Really just refined sugar with a little bit of molasses added back. Once again, check your brands to address concerns in processing.

MAPLE SYRUP
Great for baking and for pancakes.

MOLASSES
A thick robust-tasting syrup produced during the refining of sugarcane or sorhum, varying from light to dark brown. Sorghum molasses over Blackstrap is preferred.

CANE and EVAPORATED CANE SUGAR
Best for baking. Vegan refined cane sugar is available at natural food stores. Although a little less sweet, evaporated sugar is similar to white sugar with less processing.

CONFECTIONERS' SUGAR or POWDERED SUGAR
A combination of ground sugar and cornstarch useful for making icing. Be certain your brand is vegan.

STEVIA
A powdered extract from the stevia plant, stevia is a zero-calorie sugar substitute. It is much sweeter than sugar, but can be safely used in cooking. Some brands can have an aftertaste but many do not. One-half of a cup of sugar equals 3½ tablespoons of stevia.

TURBINADO SUGAR
A coarse, unrefined sugar sprinkled on cookies or cupcakes for a sweet crunch.

Pantry Items

ARROWROOT
Extracted from the roots of the arrowroot plant, this tuber starch stays clear when added to water and has a neutral taste. Good for puddings, pie fillings and cakes. It gives a silky gloss to the appearance of food.

BAKING POWDER
Look for a double-acting aluminum-free baking powder, like Rumford brand.

BAKING SODA
Not just for baking, baking soda can be used for cleaning and refreshing a freezer or refrigerator. Arm and Hammer is an old stand-by, but Bob's Red Mill Aluminum Free Baking Soda works just as well.

BROTHS
Rapunzel brand Vegetable Bouillon cubes (Sea salt with herbs and No-Salt added with herbs) are a favorite substitute for homemade. Mix it with 2 cups of water normally to create a base. Swanson Vegetable Broth also has light flavor and does not

change the taste of dishes. Not-Chick'n Natural Bouillon Cubes by Edward & Sons® is the broth used in the Vegetable Gravy on page 253.

BREADCRUMBS
Home-made breadcrumbs on page 270 add freshness to dishes, but if using prepared, try Ian's Panko Japanese Breadcrumbs which are very crunchy. These breadcrumbs are great for covering the tops of casseroles or tossing with vegetables before baking.

CEREALS
Vegan options for breakfast cereals include those such as Grape Nuts®, Post Shredded Wheat, Barbara's Bakery shredded wheat, and Vegan Granola with papaya cashew mix by Milk & Honey. Old-Fashioned Quaker Oats is also a popular morning staple.

CHOCOLATE
Ghirardelli® unsweetened is great for cocoa and semi-sweet or Double Chocolate chips for baking, as is Ghirardelli® Hot Chocolate in Mocha or Double Chocolate. Ah!laska Chocolate Syrup® works well for topping ice cream or desserts.

COCONUT MILK
Regular and light Thai Kitchen coconut milk in a can be used for a variety of purposes. Keep it in the refrigerator after opening.

COOKIES and CRACKERS
Health Valley graham crackers are good for puddings and for pie crusts. Back to Nature brand's Lemon Cookies, Chocolate Delight Cookies, Chocolate Chunk Cookies and Classic Creams are all vegan; Uncle Eddie's Vegan Cookies, found in the freezer section, are a crowd favorite. Brown Rice Snaps is a delicious snacking cracker by Edward & Sons®.

CORNSTARCH
This grain starch, made from ground corn kernels, has a cloudy appearance when added to water and a cereal-like taste when cooked. Can be used to thicken soups and gravies.

DIPS
It is easy to add packaged seasoning to non-dairy plain yogurt, sour cream or cream cheese. Try making Chili Peanut Dip on page 264 or Chive Aioli Dip on page 265. For an off-the-shelf option, try Guiltless Gourmet Black Bean Dip which does not contain added oil.

FLAXSEEDS
Ground flaxseeds have an earthy, nutty taste that can be used in many recipes and in oatmeal. They can also be used as an egg replacement in baked goods (see Baking Suggestions, page 294). Try the 365® or Spectrum® brands found in the vitamin section at Whole Foods® for a fresher taste than the bulk variety.

FLOURS and CORNMEALS
Bob's Red Mill coarse or medium ground cornmeal and Arrowhead Mills regular yellow cornmeal are the ones I use the most. Masa Harina De Maiz® is the masa I use for tortillas, to thicken soups or for masa dumplings. For baking, King Arthur bleached or unbleached all-purpose and whole-wheat pastry flour seems to work best, often mixing the two in equal parts.

HUMMUS
Making homemade hummus, like Roasted Garlic Hummus (page 87), is easy, but if you buy hummus, be certain to use brands that are oil-free.

MISO
Made from fermented soybeans and the malt of barley or rice, miso is used most often in soups. Milder tasting brands, such as Miso Master Organic Sweet White Miso, work best in most recipes. The darker miso have a heavier, stronger flavor.

NUTRITIONAL YEAST
A yellow colored yeast that comes in a flake form. It is good sprinkled on top of dishes, added to breadcrumbs for a topping or used in sauces. It has a "cheese-like" flavor.

PASTAS
With all of the different shapes and flavors of pastas available it's easy to have a pantry overflowing with pastas. Look to stock yours with a variety of rice, wheat or buckwheat.

PUDDINGS
The Dr. Oetker vanilla and chocolate pudding mixes can easily make a tasty treat. Simply use non-dairy milk, like unsweetened almond milk.

TAHINI
Smooth rich paste made from sesame seeds used in making hummus and sauces. Sold in the dairy section and in the bulk areas of natural grocery stores.

VANILLA EXTRACT
After trying different brands of Mexican vanilla extract, which is a very flavorful type of extract, I always seem to go back to Citlali brand for its complex depth of flavors.

Tofu

For tofu lovers, try the Wildwood Organics and Mori-Lite brands. Although most brands are pretty good, the refrigerated ones can seem fresher.

There are basically two types of tofu, silken and regular. Both can be found in different textures from soft to super-firm. All are made from soybeans, but some are processed differently to achieve different textures.

SILKEN
Silken tofu has a smooth, creamy texture and is used in making sauces, dressings, puddings and creamy pies. It is usually found unrefrigerated at the grocery store in the Asian food section.

FIRM, EXTRA-FIRM and SUPER-FIRM
These types of tofu tend to be firmer and crispier in texture when cooked. They are best for stir-fry or for baking. They cut well and hold their shape. Extra and super-firm tofu is found in the refrigerated part of the grocery. It is usually packed in water but also can be found in a vacuum sealed package. The water-packed options are better for freshness. Freezing tofu before using makes it chewier.

SPROUTED TOFU
Sprouted tofu is the same as regular tofu as for cooking and uses. Sprouted tofu is made from sprouted soybeans, so the difference is found in its nutrients. Sprouted tofu has a bit more protein and fat and tends to be a little richer in flavor.

Non-Dairy Products

YOGURTS
Wholesoy & Co. and So Delicious plain coconut milk yogurts are good for use in desserts. My grandchildren love most of the flavored yogurts both companies carry.

CREAM CHEESE
Tofutti and Soymage cream cheeses.

NON-DAIRY MILK
Unsweetened ALMOND MILK is my non-dairy milk of choice for its creaminess and taste. My favorite brand of almond milk is 365 Brand® from Whole Foods®. Rice Dream Original rice milk is thinner than almond milk, but works well in some batters, like Okra Cakes (page 128). Avoid sweet or flavored milks which can change the taste of baked goods.

VEGAN BUTTER
There are many choices, but Earth Balance vegan butter has a distinctly creamy flavor and texture.

VEGAN CHEESE
Daiya cheese is low in fat and melts well. It is a little sweet, but good on pizzas or nachos. The secret to using this product is not to pile it on, just use a small sprinkle.

WHIPPED CREAM
Healthy Top by Mimic Creme is a brand I have found which has a creamy texture and taste. Unfortunately, it is often difficult to find in the stores, but it can be ordered online.

Frozen Foods

RICE
Rice Expressions frozen brown rice is perfect when you need rice now. It comes in pre-measured packages of about 2 cups of rice and it takes 3 minutes to cook in the microwave.

NUTS and SEEDS
Nuts and seeds of different kinds are always in my freezer. Use them for snacks, salads or stir-fry. Storing them in the freezer keeps them from going rancid.

VEGGIE BURGERS
I usually try to stick with a burger made with beans or grains and avoid processed soy protein. Make your own in batches and keep in freezer for convenience.

SORBET/FRUIT BARS
Dole makes sorbet in many flavors and Dreyer's whole-fruit bars are good. Look in your freezer section because more choices seem to show up often.

NON-DAIRY ICE CREAM
So Delicious Coconut milk ice cream and Sweet Nothings non-dairy fudge bars are favorites in my house.

FROZEN POTATOES
Frozen hash browns are quick to prepare without oil, so I usually keep plenty on hand.

Chapter One

Salads and Dressings

- ◊ After washing and spinning your lettuce leaves in a salad spinner, lay out a dry dishcloth and spread lettuce out, then roll up the leaves in the cloth and place in refrigerator until ready to use. This creates dry and crisp lettuce that is perfect to dress.
- ◊ For added crunch, substitute finely shredded cabbage for the lettuce in any salad.
- ◊ Keep nuts stored in your freezer in a sealed plastic bag or container to keep them fresh. Just take out amount needed and toss directly into salads.
- ◊ To help lettuce stay crisp longer, chill your salad plates before serving salad.
- ◊ Romaine or iceberg lettuce is a good choice when you are using a thick, heavy dressing that might be too heavy for a lighter lettuce.
- ◊ Try and make your salad dressings with the least amount of oil that is possible. Keep dialing the amount down.
- ◊ To reduce heat in chiles, cut out the membranes and seeds from inside. After handling, wash hands, knives and cutting boards with soap.
- ◊ Don't forget other options for the ingredients for salads:

Dandelion	Parsley	Strawberries
Romaine	Chives	Navel oranges
Baby spinach	Basil	Pears, Asian or red
Kale	Chervil	White mushrooms
Arugula	Tomatoes	Pickled onions
Red or green leaf lettuce	Red onion	Toasted sunflower seeds
Green or red cabbage	Shallots	Red pepper flakes
Butter lettuce	Green onions	Capers
Bibb lettuce	Leeks	Candied nuts
Iceberg lettuce	Cucumbers	Olives, green or black
Red mustard	Carrots	Crisp garlic slices
Watercress	Beets	Fried capers
Baby spring mix	Sweet and hot peppers	Spiced nuts
Radicchio	Avocados	Peanuts
Slivered endive	Mangos	
Thinly sliced fennel bulb	Blueberries	

Now that you are eating a vegan diet, you have a renewed appreciation of fresh vegetables. Their bright colors, crisp textures and sweet juices are meant to be a sensation for the eye and a temptation to the tongue.

When you are not serving a salad, or when you need an appetizer for guests or a snack for the kids, fill bowls and platters with fresh raw vegetables. It seems like a repeat from the 1950's, but carrot and celery sticks with cherry tomatoes arranged around a dip can be a very satisfying first course. To complete a meal, there is often nothing as beautiful as a plate of in-season, ripe tomato slices, slivers of cucumbers and sweet onions, florets of fresh broccoli and cauliflower, juicy jicama sticks, crunchy radishes, or fragrant endive.

Try to shop at the closest farmer's market year-round for what is in season, and seek out organic produce.

Arugula Salad

This nutty flavored green is especially good with crunchy walnuts! You do not need much oil so be careful when you add it to the arugula.

4 cups washed arugula, *small leaves with larger leaves cut in half*
1 tablespoon of walnut or olive oil
1-2 tablespoons of freshly squeezed lemon juice
Salt to taste
Freshly ground pepper, *to taste*
½ cup roasted walnuts, *whole or chopped*

In a large salad bowl, drizzle the oil over the arugula leaves, add 1 tablespoon of lemon juice.

Add a small amount of salt and freshly ground pepper and toss salad in a large bowl. Check flavor and add more lemon juice, salt and freshly ground pepper to taste. Add walnuts on top to finish salad off.

Variations:

- ◊ Add other vegetables, such as tomatoes, onions, boiled new potatoes, steamed chilled asparagus, green beans, or any leftover veggie.
- ◊ Replace oil and lemon juice with Lemon Vinaigrette (page 56). Add ½ cup of roasted cashews instead of walnuts.
- ◊ Add caramelized onions and spicy almonds with Raspberry Vinaigrette dressing instead of the freshly squeezed lemon juice and the walnut or olive oil.
- ◊ Add thinly sliced pears with Balsamic Vinaigrette dressing instead of the freshly squeezed lemon juice and the walnut or olive oil.

Hint:

Arugula is also called rocket. It makes delicious salads but works well sautéed as a side or added to soups.

Arugula with *Roasted Garlic Hummus Dressing*

What makes this salad so good is the combination of pungent, nutty arugula with the creamy, garlicky hummus dressing. You can use any flavor of oil-free hummus. White balsamic vinegar has a lighter taste; regular balsamic vinegar will also work. Not only is the dressing great on salads it can also be a great topping for baked potatoes, steamed greens, like kale, grains or even pasta.

4 cups arugula, *the smaller the leaves the better*
3 tablespoons of Roasted Garlic Hummus Dressing
1-2 roasted beets, *sliced, depending on size (optional)*
½ cup red cabbage, *thinly sliced*
1 carrot, *diced*
½ cucumber, *diced*
½ cup walnuts, *chopped*
Croutons
Salt, *to taste*
Freshly ground pepper

Toss together with 2-3 tablespoons of dressing.

Roasted Garlic Hummus Dressing

½ cup Roasted Garlic Hummus (page 87) or your favorite oil-free hummus
2-3 tablespoons white balsamic vinegar
Freshly ground pepper
¼ teaspoon salt

In small bowl, whisk hummus with just enough vinegar to thin to a creamy texture. Add salt and freshly ground pepper to taste. Store any leftover dressing in the refrigerator.

Baby Spinach & Walnuts with Raspberry Maple Vinaigrette Dressing

This is a mild and fruity flavored salad with contrasting textures and flavors that is perfect for spring or summer lunch or outdoor dinner. The dressing is both sweet and tangy.

6 cups baby spinach, *or any spinach*
½ cup red cabbage, *thinly sliced or radicchio*
½ cucumber, *peeled and thinly sliced or chopped*
1 carrot, *peeled and sliced or diced*
½ red onion, *thinly sliced, separated into rings to taste*
Sliced pears or sliced avocados
½ cup roasted walnuts, *chopped*

Tear lettuce into bite-sized pieces into a large salad bowl. Add 1 to 2 tablespoons of Raspberry Maple Vinaigrette Dressing and toss lettuce with red cabbage, cucumbers, carrots and red onions. Top with pears and walnuts.

Raspberry Maple Vinaigrette Dressing

4 teaspoons raspberry vinegar
2 teaspoons red wine vinegar
1 teaspoon maple syrup
1 shallot, *finely minced*
½ teaspoon salt
Freshly ground pepper, *to taste*
4 tablespoons of canola or olive oil

Whisk together ingredients or use blender. Store any leftover dressing in the refrigerator.

Red Leaf Lettuce & Water Chestnuts with Chili-Spice Vinaigrette Dressing

The water chestnuts add a nice crunch to this salad. The avocado and orange slices are a perfect contrast to the chili-spice vinaigrette.

1 head of red or green leaf lettuce, *washed and drained*
1 small red onion, *thinly sliced*
1 tablespoon of capers, *drained*
½ cup water chestnuts, *sliced*
½ cup canned Mandarin orange slices, *drained, dried with paper towel*
½ avocado, *peeled, pitted and diced*

Tear red leaf lettuce into bite-sized pieces and place in a large salad bowl. Add 1 to 2 tablespoons of dressing and gently toss in remaining ingredients.

Chili-Spice Vinaigrette Dressing

1 clove of garlic, *minced*
3 tablespoons of red wine vinegar
1 tablespoon of orange juice
½ teaspoon salt
1 teaspoon Dijon mustard
½ teaspoon chili powder
4 tablespoons of canola or olive oil
Fresh ground pepper, *to taste*

Mix all ingredients except the oil in a blender or food processor. Slowly drizzle in the oil through the top hole of the blender and continue blending until the mixture slightly thickens. Refrigerate for storage.

Romaine Lettuce with Beets, Cashews & Shallot Vinaigrette Dressing

The contrast of the textures and crunch in the salad with the lively, sharp taste of the shallot dressing is excellent.

1 head of Romaine lettuce, *washed, drained*
½ cup red cabbage, *thinly sliced*
½ cup red onion, *thinly sliced*
4 baby beets, *cooked, sliced*
½ cup roasted cashews, *roughly chopped*

Tear lettuce into bite-sized pieces and place in a large salad bowl. Toss lettuce, cabbage, onions and cashews with 1 to 2 tablespoons of Shallot Vinaigrette Dressing. Add beets last and serve.

Shallot Vinaigrette Dressing

1 large shallot, *peeled and chopped*
2 tablespoons of red wine vinegar
3 teaspoons Dijon mustard
½ teaspoon sugar
4 tablespoons of canola or olive oil
¼ teaspoon salt
Freshly ground pepper, *to taste*

Mix all ingredients except the oil in a blender. Slowly drizzle in the oil through the top hole of the blender and continue to blend until the mixture slightly thickens. Refrigerate for storage.

Romaine & Avocado Salad
with Classic French Dressing

1 head of Romaine lettuce, *washed and drained*
½ red onion, *thinly sliced*
2 ripe tomatoes, *sliced or diced* or
    ½ basket of cherry tomatoes, *halved*
1 avocado, *peeled, pitted and sliced or chopped*
Salt
Freshly ground pepper
Croutons or walnuts

Tear Romaine into bite-sized pieces and place in a large salad bowl with the red onions. Add 1 to 2 tablespoons of Classic French Dressing and lightly toss salad and then gently toss in avocados and tomatoes. Salt and pepper to taste. Add croutons and/or walnuts and serve.

Classic French Dressing

1 clove of garlic, *minced*
2 tablespoons of apple cider vinegar
Juice of 1 medium sized lemon
½ teaspoon sugar
½ teaspoon salt
4 tablespoons of canola oil or virgin olive oil
Freshly ground pepper, *to taste*

Mix all ingredients, except the oil, in a blender or food processor. Slowly drizzle in oil through the top hole of the blender and continue blending until the mixture slightly thickens. Refrigerate for storage.

Variation:

Replace avocado with walnuts and toss with Basic Vinaigrette Dressing.

Hint:

Apple cider vinegar is milder and sweeter than most vinegars. Good cider vinegar is lightly cloudy, like fresh cider and has a fruity, apple flavor.

Romaine & Frisee with Sherry Vinaigrette Dressing

4 cups Romaine
1 cup frisee sprigs
1 shallot, *finely chopped*
1 red pear, *cored and sliced*
½ cup pistachio nuts, *shelled*
Freshly ground pepper
Salt

Tear Romaine and frisee into bite-sized pieces into a large salad bowl and toss with 1-2 tablespoons of Sherry Vinaigrette Dressing. Add salt and freshly ground pepper to taste. Serve salad on plates with pear slices and nuts on top.

Sherry Vinaigrette Dressing

2 tablespoons of sherry vinegar
1 teaspoon Dijon mustard
½ teaspoon agave nectar
1-2 cloves of garlic, *finely minced*
¼ teaspoon salt
Freshly ground pepper
4 tablespoons of canola or of extra virgin olive oil

Mix all ingredients except the olive oil in a blender or food processor. Slowly drizzle in the olive oil through the top hole of the blender and continue blending until the mixture slightly thickens. Refrigerate for storage.

Hints:
- Frisee is a sub variety of endive and has a milder more delicate taste.
- Pears are ripe when they give to gentle pressure.
- Change up the salad by using baby spinach with frisee and add in cashews.

Romaine with Fennel, Carrots & Edamame
with Sherry Vinaigrette Dressing

4 cups romaine
½ cup shaved fennel bulb
½ cup shaved carrots
3 tablespoons of edamame, *shelled, frozen, cooked*
Freshly ground pepper
Salt

Tear bite-sized pieces of lettuce into a large salad bowl. Add fennel, carrots and edamame and toss with 1-2 tablespoons of Sherry Vinaigrette Dressing. Add salt and freshly ground pepper to taste.

Sherry Vinaigrette Dressing

2 tablespoons of sherry vinegar
1 teaspoon Dijon mustard
½ teaspoon agave nectar
1-2 cloves of garlic, *finely minced*
¼ teaspoon salt
Freshly ground pepper
4 tablespoons of canola or of extra virgin olive oil

Mix all ingredients except the olive oil in a blender or food processor. Slowly drizzle in the olive oil through the top hole of the blender and continue blending until the mixture thickens slightly. Refrigerate for storage.

Hints:
◊ If you have a mandoline slicer, use it to cut the fennel and carrots into uniform slices. If not, a wide vegetable peeler works just as well.
◊ Add pesto to simple vinaigrette and serve with a mixed vegetable salad

Romaine Salad & Pine Nuts
with Garlic Vinaigrette Dressing

---

1 head of Romaine, *washed, drained*
½ half cucumber, *peeled, diced or sliced*
3-4 green onions, *sliced*
½ cup cherry tomatoes
½ cup pine nuts
Freshly ground pepper

Roast pine nuts in dry skillet until golden brown. Tear Romaine into bite-sized pieces into a large salad bowl. Add cucumbers, onions and tomatoes and toss with 1 to 2 tablespoons of Garlic Vinaigrette Dressing. Sprinkle on pepper and top with pine nuts.

Garlic Vinaigrette Dressing

2 cloves of garlic, *peeled*
1 cup water
¼ teaspoon salt
1 teaspoon Dijon mustard
2 tablespoons of white wine vinegar
4 tablespoons of virgin olive oil
Fresh ground pepper, *to taste*

In small saucepan, boil garlic in water for 10 minutes, drain. In small bowl, mash garlic with salt to make a paste. Whisk in mustard and vinegar and then drizzle in oil. Whisk until dressing is slightly thickened. Refrigerate for storage.

Variation:

Replace pine nuts with walnuts and toss salad with Spicy Avocado Dressing (page 57)

Hint:

Buy pine nuts that are long and oval in shape; these have a more delicate flavor than the stubby, round nuts which tend to have a sharper flavor.

Spinach Salad with Oranges, Avocados & Red Wine Vinaigrette Dressing

6 cups baby spinach, *stems removed*
2-4 green onions, *finely chopped*
½ cup canned Mandarin oranges, *well drained, dried with paper towel*
1 avocado, *peeled, pitted and sliced or cubed*
½ cup sliced almonds
Freshly ground pepper

Place all ingredients in a salad bowl and toss lightly with 1-2 tablespoons of Red Wine Vinaigrette Dressing. And add freshly ground pepper to taste.

Red Wine Vinaigrette Dressing

¼ cup red wine vinegar
½ teaspoon dry mustard
2 teaspoons vegan Worcestershire sauce
½ teaspoon paprika
2 teaspoons sugar
⅛ teaspoon garlic powder
½ teaspoon salt
¼ teaspoon pepper
4 tablespoons of canola oil or olive oil
½ teaspoon celery seed

Mix all ingredients except the oil and celery seeds in a blender or food processor. Slowly drizzle in oil through the top hole of the blender and continue blending until the mixture slightly thickens. Stir in celery seeds. Refrigerate for storage.

Variations:

- ◊ Spinach, red onion, tomatoes, white mushrooms, walnuts
- ◊ Spinach, toasted sunflower seeds. Parsley, tomatoes, avocado, thinly sliced red cabbage

Hints:

- ◊ Sprinkle flaxseeds on salads for crunch with benefits.
- ◊ Keep canned Mandarin oranges in the refrigerator before using to serve cold on a salad.

Spinach & Romaine Salad
with Balsamic Maple Vinaigrette Dressing

A perfect paring of sweetness and crunch from the apples and pecans added to the complex flavors of the Balsamic Maple Vinaigrette.

6 cups baby spinach, *with stems removed*
2 cups Romaine lettuce, *torn into bite-sized pieces*
1 Granny Smith apple, *cored and thinly sliced*
1 shallot, *finely diced*
½ cup spiced or regular roasted pecans

Toss spinach, romaine, apple slices, pecans, and shallot lightly with 1 to 2 tablespoons of Balsamic Maple Vinaigrette Dressing. Serve.

Balsamic Maple Vinaigrette Dressing

2 tablespoons of balsamic vinegar
1 teaspoon maple syrup
1 tablespoon of shallots, *minced*
4 tablespoons of extra virgin olive oil or canola
Salt to taste
Freshly ground pepper, *to taste*

Mix all ingredients except the oil in a blender or food processor. Slowly drizzle in oil through top of hole of blender and continue blending until the mixture slightly thickens. Refrigerate for storage.

Hint:

Spinach is an excellent source of vitamins A and C, foliate, calcium and potassium.

Romaine with Champagne Vinaigrette Dressing

6 cups red leaf or Romaine lettuce
1-2 shallots, *finely minced or green onions, chopped*
½ cucumber, *peeled, chopped or sliced*
1 carrot, *peeled, sliced or diced*
½ cup pecans, *spicy or plain*
2 tablespoons of dried currants

Tear lettuce into bite-sized pieces into a large salad bowl. Toss all ingredients together with 1 to 2 tablespoons of Champagne Vinaigrette Dressing.

Champagne Vinaigrette Dressing

3 tablespoons of champagne vinegar
4 tablespoons of canola or olive oil
¼ teaspoon salt
Freshly ground pepper, *to taste*

Mix all ingredients except the oil in a blender or food processor. Slowly drizzle in oil through top of hole of blender and continue blending until the mixture slightly thickens. Refrigerate for storage.

Artichoke, Hearts of Palm & Olive Salad

This can be a side salad, served over brown rice or even tossed with soba noodles.

3 tablespoons red wine vinegar
½ teaspoon Dijon mustard
¼ teaspoon salt
Freshly ground pepper
2 tablespoons olive or canola oil
1 (12 oz) jar of marinated artichoke hearts, *drained and sliced*
1 can hearts of palm, *drained and sliced*
½ red bell pepper, *diced*
10-12 black olives, *pitted and sliced, not canned*
10-12 green olives, *sliced*
1 basket of cherry tomatoes, *halved*

Whisk vinegar, mustard with salt and pepper. Slowly whisk in oil until the dressing slightly thickens.

Combine all of the salad ingredients and toss with dressing. Chill 1 hour before serving.

Hints:
- Cooked fresh artichoke hearts tend to have a richer flavor than canned.
- An artichoke salad looks pretty served in a Boston or Bibb lettuce leaf.

Bxroccoli Salad with Nuts & Raisins

This salad is packed with lots of crunch and a lively salty sweet flavor.

4 cups of broccoli florets, *chopped bite-sized, blanched*
1 cup celery, *chopped*
½ cup raisins
¾ cup salted peanuts or sunflower seeds

Mix salad ingredients together in medium bowl. Toss in the dressing until well coated. Refrigerate until serving.

Dressing

3 tablespoons of white balsamic vinegar
½ cup hummus
½ teaspoon salt
¼ teaspoon pepper

Hints:

◊ Broccoli has a one of the best sources of calcium that you can find in a vegetable.
◊ Blanching or parboiling is a process of removing bitterness in vegetables but helps maintain their color, flavor and crispness. Bring a large pot of water to a boil, with a little salt added if preferred. Drop vegetables into water and cook until tender crisp. Depending on the size of the vegetable, cook time is usually 1-2 minutes. Do not overcook. Scoop out vegetables and put them in a large bowl filled with ice and water to stop the cooking process. Remove vegetables after 2-3 minutes and let drain until ready to use.

Brown Rice Salad

This salad is great for picnics, outdoor dinners or potlucks. You can really change the flavor by adding different vegetables or different seasonings and herbs.

- 2 cups brown rice, *cooked*
- 1 cup corn kernels, *frozen*
- 1 cup English peas, *frozen*
- 1 tomato, *coarsely chopped*
- 1 carrot, *finely diced*
- 1 stalk of celery including leaves, *finely diced*
- ½ cup red bell pepper, *diced*
- 1 jalapeño pepper, *seeded, finely diced*
- ½ cup green onions, *part of the greens included, chopped*
- 1 small can sliced black olives, *drained*
- 1 teaspoon fresh chives or other herb
- 1 tablespoon of Dijon mustard
- 1 teaspoon vegan Worcestershire sauce
- 1 tablespoon of olive or canola oil *(optional)* or water
- 2 tablespoon of rice vinegar *(or any vinegar you have on hand)*
- 2 tablespoons of soy sauce or tamari
- Several dashes of Tabasco® sauce
- ½ teaspoon garlic salt
- Fresh ground pepper
- ½ cup walnuts, *chopped*

Mix brown rice, corn, peas, tomato, carrots, celery, green onion, red bell pepper, jalapeño pepper, and olives with fresh herbs in large bowl.

Mix mustard, vegan Worcestershire sauce, oil or water, vinegar and soy sauce in small bowl until smooth. Add a couple of dashes of Tabasco®, walnuts, salt and pepper to taste. Pour over salad and toss well. This salad is good served at room temperature or chilled.

Cabbage Slaw with Vinaigrette Dressing

An old recipe but still good!

¼ cup slivered almonds
¼ cup sunflower seeds
¼ cup cocktail peanuts, *chopped*
2 tablespoons sesame seeds
6 oz chow mein noodles
½ teaspoon of garlic or seasoning salt
4 cups Napa cabbage, *thinly sliced*
8 green onions, *sliced*

In a dry skillet, sauté almonds, sunflower seeds, peanuts and sesame seeds until lightly toasted. Add chow mein noodles and remove from heat. Add garlic or seasoning salt and toss to coat. Let mixture cool.

Mix cabbage, green onions and sautéed chow mein noodle and nut mixture in large bowl. Toss with 2-3 tablespoons of vinaigrette. Taste and add more if needed. Check for salt and add freshly ground pepper.

Noodles and nuts will not stay crispy for long, so this is best eaten soon after being prepared.

Slaw Vinaigrette

⅛ cup toasted sesame oil
¼ cup white wine vinegar
1 tablespoons agave nectar
3 tablespoons soy sauce
½-1 teaspoon crushed red pepper flakes,
    to taste
1-2 cloves garlic, *minced*

Whisk together vinegar, agave nectar, soy sauce, sesame oil, red pepper and garlic. Then place in the refrigerator until needed.

Hint:
We think of peanuts as a nut, but they are legumes.

Grilled Veggie Salad with Spicy Pepper Dressing

Wonderful summer salad.

4 ears of corn, *remove silks, leave on husks to grill*
1 large red bell pepper, *grill whole*
1 poblano pepper, *grill whole*
1 yellow squash, *cut in half lengthwise*
2 zucchini squash, *cut in half lengthwise*
½ sweet or red onion

Grill veggies (refer to grilled vegetables recipes starting on page 144). Cut kernels off of corn cobs and remove seeds from the center of the peppers. Finely dice all vegetables to be similar in size. Toss with dressing. Taste for seasoning.

Spicy Pepper Dressing

¼ cup parsley or cilantro, *finely chopped*
1 tablespoon of oil
1 teaspoon Deb's Seasoning
½ teaspoon cumin
1 Serrano or jalapeño, *seeded, finely diced*
Juice of one lime
¼ teaspoon salt
Freshly ground pepper, *to taste*

Whisk all ingredients together and toss with grilled diced vegetables. Taste before serving for salt and pepper.

Edamame Salad

Edamame salad is colorful and carries a nutritional punch.

1 bag of frozen edamame, *shelled*
1 cup corn kernels, *fresh or frozen, cooked*
1 bunch of green onions, *sliced*
½ cup red bell pepper, *diced*
1 jalapeño, *seeded, diced*
1 tablespoon of fresh parsley, *chopped*
3 tablespoons of rice vinegar
1 tablespoon of canola oil
¼ teaspoon salt
Freshly ground pepper

Boil edamame in salted water for 5 minutes. Drain and mix with the rest of the ingredients in a bowl. Refrigerate for storage.

Hint:

Roasted edamame makes a tasty snack to serve. Just toss 1 bag of edamame with 2 teaspoons of oil and add sea salt and fresh ground pepper. In a single layer on a baking pan, bake at 375°F (190°C) for 35 minutes and serve.

Summer Fruit Salad

This is a beautiful fruit salad for the summer when all the berries and peaches are sweet and ripe. Children love it.

4 cups peaches, *pitted, peeled, cut into small chunks*
1 cup blueberries
1 cup raspberries
1 cup strawberries, *sliced*
3 kiwis, *peeled and sliced*
3 bananas, *peeled and sliced*
2 cups seedless grapes
1-2 tablespoons sugar or agave nectar, *depending on the natural sweetness of the fruit*

Toss fruits with sugar. Refrigerate until served.

Hints:

- Add frozen grapes to fruit salads. They help keep the salad chilled.
- If your strawberries need to be washed, do it at the last minute. Once the stems are removed they absorb water and can quickly turn mushy.

Garbanzo Bean Salad

You can serve this as a side dish; it is great for potlucks. Or, mix this salad with your favorite lettuce for a heartier salad. Serve with pita toasts (page 272).

3 medium carrots, *peeled, diced*
1 can garbanzo beans (14.5 oz)
2-3 tablespoons red onions, *finely diced*
½ cup green olives, *sliced*
Red pepper flakes, *to taste*
1 tablespoon of fresh parsley, *chopped*
1 tablespoon of canola oil *(optional)*
3 tablespoons white balsamic vinegar
Freshly ground pepper, *to taste*
Garlic salt, *a dash or two*

Steam or boil diced carrots until tender, about 5 minutes, drain and set aside. Rinse garbanzo beans in cold water and drain.

Mix beans, carrots, red onions, green olives, red pepper flakes, and parsley together in a salad bowl.

Mix oil (if using) with vinegar, red pepper flakes, garlic salt and pepper in a separate bowl and then pour over the vegetables and toss. Chill well before serving.

Old Fashioned Macaroni Salad

Remembering moms and grandmothers. This will take you back!

1 pound elbow macaroni, *small or mini*
2 tablespoons of red onion, *diced*
¼ cup red or green bell pepper, *diced*
¼ cup celery, *diced*
1 teaspoon celery salt
1 teaspoon garlic powder
2 tablespoons parsley, *chopped*
3-4 tablespoons vegan mayonnaise
Fresh ground pepper, *to taste*

Cook macaroni al dente, in boiling salted water according to package instructions. Drain and rinse with cold water and then drain again. Set aside to cool.

Toss all vegetables with macaroni. In small bowl, mix celery salt, garlic powder, parsley, freshly ground pepper with the vegan mayonnaise. Gently stir into the vegetables and macaroni. Taste for seasonings. Put in the refrigerator until time to serve.

Peanut Noodle Salad

Refreshing for a summer lunch. You can use the same sauce with many different vegetable combinations. Just use the vegetables you have on hand.

3 cups cooked spaghetti
3 heaping tablespoons of natural peanut butter with no sugar added
2 tablespoons of soy sauce or tamari
2 tablespoons of rice vinegar
2 teaspoons toasted sesame oil
2 tablespoons of orange or apple juice
½ teaspoon salt
Freshly ground pepper
1 cup broccoli florets, *blanched*
½ cup red bell pepper, *diced*
1 jalapeño, *seeded, diced*
½ cup cucumbers, *in half rounds*
½ cup roasted peanuts, *chopped*

Cook spaghetti al dente, according to instructions and drain, rinse and let cool. Adding just a bit of oil to the cooking water will keep it from sticking together.

Make sauce by whisking together the peanut butter, soy sauce, rice vinegar and sesame oil. Then add apple or orange juice with salt and freshly ground pepper and whisk into sauce mix. Taste for seasonings.

Combine spaghetti with broccoli, bell peppers, jalapeño peppers and cucumbers and toss with sauce. Check seasonings. Add the chopped peanuts just before serving.

Hints:

- Almond butter can be used instead of peanut butter. Just add chopped roasted almonds just before serving.
- Add nuts last so they do not soften and lose the crunch.

Penne Pasta with Green Beans & Arugula

For those days when you want to serve a light meal and a salad, this is the answer.

12 ounces penne pasta
2 cups of frozen French cut green beans
2 cups arugula
1 teaspoon fresh thyme
2 teaspoons lemon zest
½ cup pistachios, *roasted, salted*
Lemon Vinaigrette (page 56)

Make Lemon Vinaigrette. Set aside.

Cook pasta in lightly salted boiling water al dente, according to package instructions. Add green beans the last 3 minutes of cooking time. Drain green beans and pasta and rinse with cold water.

In a large bowl, mix pasta, green beans, thyme, and lemon zest and ¼ cup of pistachios together. Add 2 tablespoons of dressing at a time, until pasta is lightly coated. Gently toss in arugula to coat. Check for salt and pepper. Sprinkle top with ¼ cup of pistachios.

Pickled Onions

These are great on sandwiches, tacos, and pizzas or even mixed into salads and pastas. They will keep in refrigerator for about 4-5 days.

1 small red onion, *cut into thin rounds*
¼ teaspoon salt
1 teaspoon sugar
Rice wine vinegar or any that you have on hand

Toss onions with a little salt and the sugar in a bowl. Place in a plastic container with a lid and cover with vinegar for approximately 20 minutes.

Easy Potato Salad

This salad becomes more flavorful the longer it chills. If the onions are finely diced, even finicky eaters will hardly notice them. Make this recipe your own with seasonings. Potato salad is a wonderful side for steamed vegetables.

6 medium potatoes *(Red are best, but can be substituted by Yukon Gold)*
1 teaspoon salt, *for boiling water*
½ cup vegan mayonnaise
3 tablespoons of diced dill pickles *(more if you like)*
2 tablespoons regular yellow mustard
1 tablespoon Dijon mustard
2 tablespoons capers, *rinsed and drained*
2 tablespoon fresh parsley, *chopped*
¼ cup celery, *diced*
1 bunch green onions, *white & light green parts*
¼ cup red onion, *finely diced*
½ teaspoon salt
Fresh ground pepper

Place potatoes in a pot of lightly salted water and boil until tender but still a little firm when pierced with a fork; they shouldn't fall apart when pierced. Drain. When potatoes are cool, peel if you prefer (the salad is more robust with the skins on). Then dice into bite-sized pieces.

In small bowl, mix vegan mayonnaise, dill pickles, yellow mustard, Dijon mustard, capers, and parsley together.

In large bowl, combine celery, green onions and red onions with, potatoes and mix in sauce thoroughly. Salt and add freshly ground pepper to taste. Refrigerate until ready to serve.

Hint:

Red potatoes are low in starch, with firm flesh and they hold together well in cooking.

Warm Potato & Baby Spinach Salad

This colorful, zesty salad is a delicious light meal on its own but can be tucked into halved pita bread and served as a sandwich.

5-6 medium red potatoes
1 teaspoon salt
1 clove of garlic, *peeled*
1 tablespoon lemon juice
2 cups baby spinach, *stems removed*
4 sun-dried tomatoes, *diced*
Freshly ground pepper, *to taste*

Prepare dressing first.

Peel potatoes, cut in half, and place in large saucepan. Cover potatoes in water. Add a little salt, garlic and lemon juice to the water. Cover and bring to boil. Reduce heat to simmer until barely done but tender.

While potatoes are cooking, take a small skillet and add ¼ cup of water and steam-fry the sun-dried tomatoes until tender. Remove from heat.

Drain potatoes and cut into bite-size pieces and then toss with dressing. Stir in baby spinach and tomatoes. Add fresh pepper, taste for seasoning and serve warm.

Dressing

2 tablespoons of canola or olive oil
2 tablespoons of lemon juice
½ teaspoon salt
Freshly ground pepper
2 tablespoons of capers
1 tablespoon of fresh chives, *chopped*
½ teaspoon fresh thyme leaves
2 tablespoons of fresh parsley, *chopped*
½ cup of a small red onion, *diced*

Combine all ingredients. The onions will marinate until ready to serve.

Soba Noodle Salad

These room temperature noodles are an excellent party or potluck dish since they refrigerate well.

12 ounces soba noodles
2 cups broccoli florets
3 tablespoons tamari or soy sauce
2 teaspoons toasted sesame oil
3 tablespoons of seasoned rice vinegar
1 tablespoon of mirin
2 tablespoons fresh lime juice
1 teaspoon chili oil
Red pepper flakes to taste
2 tablespoons of fresh parsley, *chopped*
2 carrots, *peeled and cut into matchsticks*
1 cup green onions, *chopped*
½ red bell pepper, *thinly sliced*
1 jalapeño, *thinly sliced, seeded*
2 tablespoons toasted black sesame seeds or cashews, *chopped*
½ teaspoon salt
Freshly ground pepper, *to taste*

Cook pasta in boiling water until al dente. Two minutes before pasta is ready, add broccoli florets to water. Rinse pasta and florets with cold water and drain well. Transfer to large bowl.

In a small bowl, use a whisk to combine tamari, sesame oil, rice vinegar, mirin, limejuice, chili oil and red pepper flakes with parsley. Pour over noodles and toss until well coated. Add carrots, green onions, jalapeño, and bell pepper. Mix well, salt and pepper.

Refrigerate in a covered bowl to blend all of the flavors. Sprinkle sesame seeds or cashews on top just before serving.

Veggie Pasta Salad *with Pine Nuts*

Easy to prepare and full texture, this colorful salad can use any assortment of vegetables you may have on hand, making it very flexible.

12 ounces bowtie or penne pasta
  (mini pastas work well)
1 cup cherry tomatoes, *cut in half*
1 cup orange, red or yellow pepper, *diced small*
1 cup cucumbers, *diced small, peeled or not*
1 cup carrots, *peeled, diced small*
1 cup artichoke hearts, *drained, coarsely chopped*
½ cup finely diced onion
1 small can black olives, *sliced*
  (green are good too)
1 cup corn kernels, *fresh or frozen*
2 tablespoons of fresh basil, *chopped (optional)*
2 tablespoons of olive oil *(optional)*
2 tablespoons of lemon juice
1 tablespoon of rice vinegar
  (or any flavor of vinegar)
Red pepper flakes
1 teaspoon garlic salt or to taste
Fresh ground pepper, *to taste*
½ cup roasted pine nuts or walnuts

Cook pasta al dente, according to instructions. Drain and set aside.

Combine all veggies, pasta, olives and herbs in a bowl. Neither fresh nor frozen corn need to be cooked prior to mixing with pasta. Frozen corn is parboiled before freezing and thaws quickly once added to other ingredients. Fresh corn kernels can be added raw or parboiled and cooled.

In a small bowl, whisk oil, lemon juice, vinegar and garlic salt together with red pepper flakes. Pour over veggies and toss.

Check for seasonings and adjust to your taste. Refrigerate until serving time. This salad only gets better the longer the flavors blend together. Toss in pine nuts just before serving.

Quinoa & Pinto Bean Salad

Quinoa is often called a super food since it is a good source of plant protein, but its light, nutty taste is very appealing. This is a colorful salad with great contrasting textures. The salad keeps well in the refrigerator for a couple of days but the avocado will begin to fall apart and turn brown after that time.

2 cups quinoa, *cooked*
1 can pinto beans, *drained, rinsed*
½ cup red bell pepper, *diced*
1 jalapeño, *seeded, diced*
1 cup halved cherry tomatoes
½ cup green onions, *sliced*
1 shallot, *finely diced*
1 cup corn kernels, *fresh or frozen*
1 small avocado, *peeled, pitted chopped*
1 tablespoon fresh lime juice
1 tablespoon of olive oil
2 teaspoons Deb's Seasoning (page 269)
½-1 teaspoon garlic or seasoning salt
Freshly ground pepper

Cook the quinoa according to package directions. Pour off any liquid not absorbed during cooking.

In large bowl or plastic container toss all ingredients together. Frozen corn is parboiled before freezing and thaws quickly once added to other ingredients. Fresh corn kernels can be added raw or parboiled and cooled.

Taste and adjust seasonings. Refrigerate until serving.

Check seasonings again right before serving.

Hint:

Quinoa is an excellent source of iron, potassium, magnesium and protein.

Mexican Rice Salad

This is a fresh rice salad that goes well with enchiladas, grilled vegetables or can be served as a side on a bed of lettuce with tortilla chips.

- 1½ cups long-grain rice, *white or brown, cooked*
- ½ cup corn kernels, *fresh or frozen*
- ½ cup black or pinto beans, *rinsed, drained*
- ¼ cup of red onion, *finely chopped*
- 1 avocado, *peeled, cubed*
- 1 cup cherry tomatoes, *halved*

Make dressing first.

Mix rice, beans, red onion and corn together with dressing. Frozen corn is parboiled before freezing and thaws quickly once added to other ingredients. Fresh corn kernels can be added raw or parboiled and cooled.

Gently toss avocado into salad. Add cherry tomatoes to top and serve.

Dressing

- 1 small jalapeño or red chili peppers, *seeded, finely diced*
- 1½ tablespoon of olive oil
- 1½ tablespoons of lime juice
- ½ teaspoon salt
- Freshly ground pepper
- 1 tablespoon of cilantro or parsley, *chopped (optional)*

Mix peppers with lime juice, salt and then whisk in oil. Add pepper and cilantro or parsley, if using. Set aside.

Waldorf Salad

This is an adapted version of a classic favorite.

2-3 tablespoons vegan mayonnaise
2 tablespoons fresh lemon juice
½ teaspoon salt
¼ teaspoon fresh ground pepper
2-3 sweet apples, *cored and chopped*
1 cup celery, *thinly sliced*
1 cup red seedless grapes, *sliced*
¼ cup dried currants
1 cup walnuts, *toasted and chopped*

In a bowl, whisk together the vegan mayonnaise, lemon juice, salt and pepper. Mix in the apple, celery, grapes, currants and walnuts. This can be served on a lettuce leaf for a lovely presentation.

Hint:

Currants are produced from a variety of small grapes; these dried fruits resemble tiny raisins but have a stronger, tarter flavor. If you prefer, raisins work just as well in this salad.

Wild and Brown Rice Pilaf Salad

3 cups of wild and brown rice combined, *cooked (A blend can be purchased or you can combine the two before cooking)*
1 tablespoon of olive oil
½ cup red bell pepper, *finely chopped*
½-1 jalapeño pepper, *finely diced (optional)*
½ carrots, *julienne-cut*
¼ cup of red onion, *finely diced*
½ cup snow peas, *ends removed, cut on the diagonal*
2 tablespoons of radishes, *sliced*
1 tablespoon of lime juice
1 tablespoon of seasoned rice vinegar
½-1 teaspoon salt
Freshly ground pepper
¼ cups of sliced almonds, *roasted*

Heat a skillet to medium-high heat, and add olive oil then bell peppers, jalapeño peppers, carrots, and red onion. Cook 2 minutes until vegetables are tender crisp.

Place cooked wild and brown rice in large bowl and add cooked vegetables, snow peas, radishes, the lime juice, and seasoned rice vinegar. Season mixture with salt and pepper and toss together. Serve at room temperature or chilled. Before serving, toss in sliced almonds.

Hint:

To reduce the sharp taste of a raw onion, put slices in a colander in sink and pour boiling water on top, then pour cold water over top. Slices can be used or covered in a bowl with fresh water and kept in the refrigerator until ready to use.

Basic Vinaigrette Dressing

2 tablespoons of red or white vinegar or lemon juice
1 teaspoon Dijon mustard
½ teaspoon salt or to taste
Freshly ground pepper, *to taste*
4 tablespoons of canola or olive oil

Mix all ingredients except the oil in a blender or food processor. Slowly drizzle in oil through top of hole of blender and continue blending until the mixture slightly thickens. Refrigerate for storage.

Lemon Vinaigrette Dressing

2 tablespoons of lemon juice
1 teaspoon lemon zest
1 shallot, *finely diced*
1 clove of garlic, *minced*
1 teaspoon Dijon mustard
½ teaspoon salt or to taste
Freshly ground pepper, *to taste*
4 tablespoons of canola or olive oil

Mix all ingredients except the oil in a blender or food processor. Slowly drizzle in oil through top of hole of blender and continue blending until the mixture slightly thickens. Refrigerate for storage.

Spicy Avocado Dressing

¼ cup juice of a lime
1 small avocado, *peeled, pitted*
1 clove of garlic, *minced*
1 shallot, *finely diced*
½ jalapeño, *seeded, finely diced*
4 tablespoons of olive oil
½ teaspoon salt or to taste
Freshly ground pepper

Mix all ingredients except the oil in a blender or food processor. Slowly drizzle in oil through top of hole of blender and continue blending until the mixture slightly thickens. Refrigerate for storage.

Chapter Two

Soups

- Making soups is a good place for the beginner vegan cook to get started. Most are easy to put together and do not require a long cooking time. Since soups usually improve with time, making several meals from one pot is also convenient.

- Invest in an immersion blender. It is an extremely convenient appliance for preparing soups, sauces or gravies.

- When making vegetable soups, choose vegetables that are in season and at the peak of flavor and texture.

- To keep herbs, pack an ice cube tray half full with a finely chopped fresh herb, then fill with water and freeze. Then just drop cube directly into soups or sauces when needed.

- Store mushrooms by removing them from plastic and placing them, unwashed, in a single layer on a baking sheet pan with a damp paper towel over the top for up to a week.

- A tablespoon of fresh herbs equals about a teaspoon of dried.

- Tomato paste in a tube is much easier to use than canned. It keeps for 2 weeks after opening, so you can use just as much as you need and store the rest in the refrigerator.

- When using salted vegetable broth always adjust your salt in the recipe accordingly. Many vegetable broths have a lot of added salt. Buy salt-free broths to maintain more control over salt flavor and intake.

- Use a wide soup pot to let your vegetables have space to brown when sautéing. In a tall pan, vegetables tend to pile up, causing them to cook in a way that is more like steaming which destroys their texture and makes them mushy.

- Don't overcook or boil vegetable soups for too long, because overcooking breaks down the texture of the vegetables. Turn off the heat when the vegetables are tender and let flavors blend together on the stove from 30 minutes up to 2 hours. Taste for seasonings and reheat right before serving.

- When browning onions for a soup, the darker the onions are browned, the richer in color, body and taste they will be. If you want a more delicate flavor, cook over lower heat and for less time.

- Always add freshly ground pepper soups last. Pepper can turn bitter if it is added too early.

Black Bean Soup

The rich broth that comes from black beans is delicious. This is a chunky, flavorful vegetable soup.

- 1 tablespoon oil or ¼ cup vegetable broth, *for sautéing*
- 1 cup leeks, *chopped*
- ½ red bell pepper, *finely chopped*
- 2 garlic cloves, *finely minced*
- 2 (15 oz) cans black beans, *drained or you can use homemade*
- 2 (15 oz) cans fire-roasted tomatoes
- 1 cup of corn, *frozen or fresh*
- 3-4 cups vegetable broth or water
- 2 teaspoons Deb's Seasoning (page 269)
- 1 teaspoon of cumin
- ½ teaspoon of red pepper flakes or 1 fresh Serrano chile, *seeded, finely diced*
- 2 tablespoons of vegan Worcestershire sauce
- 1 tablespoon red wine vinegar
- 1 teaspoon salt
- Juice from ½ lime

Heat oil or broth in soup pot over medium heat. Sauté leeks until soft and tender, then add garlic and red bell pepper. Cook for about two minutes.

Stir in Deb's Seasoning, cumin and salt until well combined. Add black beans, tomatoes, corn, vegetable broth, red pepper flakes, red wine vinegar, and Worcestershire sauce. Turn to low heat and cook for about 15 minutes.

Lower heat to simmer. For a thicker soup, pour half of the soup into a blender and pulse a couple of times or blend in the pot with an immersion blender.

Right before serving, season the soup with lime juice to brighten flavors. Salt and freshly ground pepper to taste. Another option is to add a half cup of cooked rice to bottom of bowl before pouring in soup.

Hint:

Leeks can have a lot of sand and dirt in their leaves. To wash leeks, start by cutting off the top roots and then the greens 2 inches below the white part. Halve leeks lengthwise. Soak in a sink or a bowl of water for a few minutes, swishing back and forth a bit. Sand will fall to bottom of sink. Rinse, drain and chop as needed.

Three Bean Chili

A hearty, rich and satisfying chili that is perfect for the whole family.

1 tablespoon oil or ¼ cup vegetable broth, *for sautéing*
1 medium onion, *diced*
½ cup red bell pepper, *diced*
1-2 jalapeño peppers, *seeded and minced*
1 Poblano peppers, *seeded and diced*
1 tablespoon garlic, *minced*
1 teaspoon red pepper flakes
2 teaspoons cumin
½ teaspoon Mexican oregano
2½ tablespoons chili powder
½ teaspoon smoked (or regular) paprika
½ teaspoon Deb's Seasoning (page 269)
1 teaspoon salt *(less for salted vegetable broth or beans)*
1 teaspoon fresh ground pepper
1 (15 oz) can black beans, *drained, rinsed*
1 (15 oz) can pinto beans, *drained, rinsed*
1 (15 oz) can small red beans or kidney beans, *drained, rinsed*
3 cups water
1 (28 oz) can fire-roasted tomatoes
2 tablespoons tomato paste
3 tablespoons masa *(corn tortilla mix)*

In a large soup pot, heat the oil or vegetable broth over medium heat. Add onion, peppers, and garlic. Cook until vegetables are tender and onions are light brown in color.

Stir in red pepper flakes, cumin, Mexican oregano, chili powder, paprika, Deb's Seasoning, salt and ground pepper to the mixture. Cook for 2 more minutes.

Add rinsed black, pinto and red beans and mix well. Stir in water then add tomatoes and tomato paste. Bring to a boil.

Lower heat to a simmer. Add masa mixed with half a cup of water. Simmer for 20 minutes, then it should be ready to serve. If chili becomes thick, add a little water to thin. Turn off heat and keep covered until serving time.

Serve with crispy tortilla strips, sliced avocados, or fresh salsa on top.

Hints:

- To adjust the heat of the chili, use more or fewer jalapeños.
- Fresh jalapeño chiles range from mild to fiery hot. Usually, the larger the chile is in size the milder the flavor.
- To allow flavors to settle in, cover the chili and turn off the heat, and let chili or soups sit until it is time to heat and serve. Taste just before serving to see if adjustments are needed for the salt, pepper or spice.

White Bean & Kale Soup

A savory, creamy broth soup that is simple to make but full of rich flavor. Serve with whole-wheat crusty bread.

- 1 tablespoon oil or ¼ cup vegetable broth, *for sautéing*
- 1 medium onion, *finely diced*
- 1 medium carrot, *peeled, diced*
- 1 teaspoon salt
- ¼ teaspoon ground pepper, *or to taste*
- ¼ teaspoon celery salt or seeds
- 2 garlic cloves, *minced*
- 1 teaspoon fresh thyme or ½ teaspoon dried thyme
- 1 tablespoon vegan Worcestershire
- ¼ - ½ teaspoon red pepper flakes
- 2 (15 oz) can of white beans (cannellini or navy), *drained*
- 6 cups water or vegetable broth
- 1 bay leaf
- 1-2 cups kale, *ribs removed, chopped*

Heat oil (or vegetable broth) in large soup pot. Add onions and carrots. Cook until vegetables are just tender. Add garlic, celery salt or seeds, salt, thyme, Worcestershire and red pepper flakes. Cook for one minute.

Add water or vegetable broth, beans and bay leaf to pot and bring to a boil. Lower heat to simmer, cover and cook for 10 minutes.

Discard bay leaf. Puree soup in a blender or food processor or use an immersion blender in the soup pot. Bring soup back to simmer then add kale and ground pepper. Cook until kale is tender (about 10 minutes). Taste to adjust seasonings.

Add Homemade Croutons (page 270), fried shallot, or fried garlic slivers to the top for a bit of flair.

Hint:

Kale is an excellent source of calcium and vitamins A, C, and K.

Cream of Broccoli Soup

This soup serves only about four people. If you are planning to feed a larger crowd, you will need to double the ingredients.

2 medium potatoes, *peeled and chopped*
4 cups broccoli florets
½ cup onion, *diced*
4 cups vegetable broth
½-1 clove garlic, *minced or dried garlic flakes*
1 tablespoon vegan Worcestershire
⅛ teaspoon red pepper flakes
½ teaspoon salt or garlic salt
Ground pepper, *to taste*
2 tablespoons fresh parsley, *finely chopped (optional)*
Homemade Croutons (page 270) or fried capers (page 268), *for garnish*

Place potatoes, broccoli, onion, garlic and vegetable broth in a large pot. Bring to boil. Reduce to medium heat. Cover and cook for about 15 minutes until vegetables are tender.

Put mixture into food processor and pulse until it is smooth and creamy or use an immersion blender directly in the pot. Add Worcestershire sauce, red pepper flakes, and parsley with salt and freshly ground pepper. Heat and serve.

This soup can be made more quickly and easily using frozen broccoli florets and 2 cups of frozen shredded hash brown potatoes. Both really work well. Just cook the onion in the boiling vegetable broth for 10 minutes until tender, and then add frozen broccoli, frozen hash browns, and garlic. Cook 10 more minutes before continuing with food processor instructions from above.

Hint:

Using vegetable broth, instead of water, in soups adds a depth of flavor to the dish.

Corn Chowder

This soup is perfect when you need something quick and easy to prepare. The best part is that it tastes like you spent hours preparing it.

1 tablespoon oil or ¼ cup vegetable broth, *for sautéing*
1 small onion, *finely diced*
1 clove garlic, *finely diced*
½ red bell pepper, *finely chopped*
1 small potato, *peeled, diced in small pieces*
3 cups water
3 cups frozen corn kernels
1 small can chopped mild or hot green chiles
⅛ teaspoon cayenne pepper *(optional)*
½ teaspoon salt
Fresh ground pepper
½ teaspoon Deb's Seasoning (page 269)
1 cup unsweetened almond or rice milk or ½ cup of cashew cream (page 252)

In a medium size pot over medium heat, sauté onion in oil (or vegetable broth) until tender and light brown. Add garlic, bell pepper and potato and cook for 4 minutes. Add corn, water or broth, chiles and seasonings and bring to a boil.

Lower heat to simmer and add unsweetened almond milk or cashew cream. Heat on low simmer for 15 minutes but do not boil.

Take half of the mixture out and puree in food processor or use a handheld immersion blender directly in the pot. You can make it as thick and creamy or as chunky as you like. Taste for seasonings. Serve in warm bowls.

Cashew cream is optional but it can really make this soup thick like chowder. If you use the cashew cream, add 1½ cup of cooked diced potatoes to the soup after the blending of the corn. Add 1 teaspoon of Deb's Seasoning for a thick, spicy corn chowder.

Country Lentil Soup

This may very well be the best lentil soup of all time. For a variation, use 2 cups cooked rice instead of the pasta.

1 cup pasta, *any (small or mini works well, but break up any long pastas, like spaghetti)*
1 tablespoon oil or ¼ cup vegetable broth, *for sautéing*
1½ cups onion, *diced*
2-3 garlic cloves, *minced*
3 carrots, *peeled and diced*
3 celery stalks, *diced*
2 tablespoons tomato paste
2 tablespoons parsley, *chopped*
1 tablespoon chives, *chopped (or your favorite herb)*
1 cup lentils, *rinsed and sorted*
1 teaspoon salt *(use less if vegetable broth contains salt)*
2 quarts vegetable stock
1 can (14.5 oz) of diced or stewed tomatoes
1-2 tablespoons tamari or soy sauce
1 tablespoons vegan Worcestershire
1 teaspoon Deb's Seasoning (page 269)
1 teaspoon grill seasoning to taste
½ teaspoon red pepper flakes
Ground pepper, *to taste*
1 cup greens, *chopped (any fresh or frozen: collards, chard, spinach or mustard)*
Croutons (page 270), *for garnish*

Cook pasta in lightly salted water according to al dente instructions. Save one cup of pasta water in a cup and set aside. Drain excess water.

In large soup pot, heat oil (or vegetable broth) over medium-high heat and add onions. Cook until lightly browned.

Add garlic, carrots, celery, tomato paste, parsley, and chives and salt. Add lentils and vegetable broth, pasta water and bring to a boil. Lower heat and simmer for 30 minutes, partially covered.

Add tomatoes, tamari, Worcestershire sauce, seasonings and red pepper flakes. Taste to adjust salt and add freshly ground pepper. Add chopped greens and cooked pasta. If soup seems too thick, add a little of the saved pasta water to thin. When heated through, garnish with croutons and serve.

Hints:

- French lentils look prettier in soups than other varieties because they tend to hold their shape better when cooked. French lentils also have a wonderful rich flavor. They are dark green in color and smaller than the brown varieties.
- Lentils do not have to be soaked and take about 25 minutes to cook.

Split Pea Soup

Serve this soothing soup with a good, crusty bread.

2 tablespoons oil or ¼ cup vegetable broth, *for sautéing*
1 small onion, *diced*
1-2 cloves garlic, *finely minced*
½ red bell pepper, *diced*
½-1 jalapeño pepper, *seeded, finely diced*
1-3 stalks celery, *diced*
1 large potato, *peeled and diced*
2 carrots, *peeled, diced*
2 cups of split peas, *rinsed*
1¼ teaspoon of Spanish sweet paprika *(for smoky flavor)*
½ teaspoon of Deb's Seasoning (page 269)
½ teaspoon grill seasoning
1 teaspoon garlic salt
1½ quarts of vegetable broth, *unsalted*
½ cup fresh parsley, *chopped (optional)*
Freshly ground pepper
Croutons (page 270), *for garnish*

Heat oil or vegetable broth in soup pot over medium-high heat and sauté onion until soft. Add garlic, peppers, and celery, potatoes, carrots and then sauté 5 more minutes.

Add peas, paprika, Deb's Seasoning, grill seasoning, garlic salt and vegetable broth. Bring to a boil, then turn heat down to low and partially cover pan. Let stew for about an hour or until peas are soft.

Stir in fresh parsley, if desired, and ground pepper. Taste for salt and seasonings. If soup is too thick thin with water.

To let flavors really blend together, turn off heat after cooking and let the soup rest, and reheat right before serving. Garnish with croutons.

Hint:

Keep a bag of tri-colored bell peppers in the freezer for times when you do not have fresh produce. They tend to be softer in texture, but they will get you by in a pinch.

Mexican Red Posole Soup

This soup is infused with the soothing scent of cumin. Serve with a salad and Masa Dumplings (page 271).

1 tablespoon oil or ¼ cup vegetable broth, *for sautéing*
1 onion, *diced*
1 small red bell pepper, *diced*
1 stalk of celery, *diced*
1 carrot, *peeled, diced*
2 cloves of garlic, *minced*
1-2 jalapeño pepper, *seeded and finely chopped*
1 tablespoon of New Mexico red chili powder
½ teaspoon of red pepper flakes
1 teaspoons of cumin
½ teaspoon of coriander
1 teaspoon of Deb's Seasoning (page 269)
1 teaspoon of salt
1 large can of hominy or two smaller cans, *drained and rinsed*
1 cans of pinto beans, *drained and rinsed*
1 can (28 oz) of diced fire-roasted tomatoes, *with juices*
3 cups of vegetable broth or water
3 tablespoons of masa mixed into ½ cup of water

In a large soup pot, warm ¼ cup of vegetable broth or 1 tablespoon of oil over medium heat. Add onion, bell pepper, celery, carrot, jalapeño and garlic. Sauté until onions are tender about 5 minutes.

Stir in chili powder, red pepper flakes, cumin, coriander, Deb's seasoning and salt.

Add hominy, pinto beans, diced tomatoes and pour in 3 cups of broth or water. At this point, if soup is too thick add water to thin. Turn up heat and bring to a boil.

Reduce heat and add masa mixture. Simmer for 30 minutes until soup has reduced to desired thickness.

Potato Corn Soup

Creamy pureed potatoes give this light, wholesome soup extra body.

1 tablespoon oil or ½ cup vegetable broth, *for sautéing*
8 cups vegetable broth
1 medium onion, *diced*
1 leek or shallot, *chopped*
2 celery stalks, *diced*
1 teaspoon garlic, *minced (optional or to taste)*
6 cups potatoes, *chopped*
1 cup frozen corn
½ cup of red bell pepper, *diced* or 1 jar of pimientos, *drained*
1 tablespoon fresh parsley, *chopped*
2 teaspoons chives, *chopped*
1 mild Pablano pepper, *finely diced* or ½ teaspoon red pepper flakes
¼ teaspoon white pepper
1 teaspoon salt
Garlic or herbed croutons (page 270), *for garnish*

In soup pot, sauté onion, leek, celery and garlic in ½ cup of vegetable broth or oil until tender. Add potatoes, corn, red bell pepper and salt and cook for 5 minutes more.

Pour in vegetable broth and bring to boil. Cook until potatoes are tender when they can be pierced easily with a fork. If the mixture is too thick, add more vegetable broth or water. For a thicker soup, either blend half of the soup in a food processor and pulse a couple of times, or use an immersion blender directly in pot until the desired consistency is achieved.

Add the fresh parsley, chives, diced pepper (or red pepper flakes), and white pepper to the soup. Taste and adjust salt.

Simmer until ready to serve. Garnish with garlic or herbed croutons.

Hint:

If using salted vegetable broth in a recipe, always adjust the amount of added salt that is called for.

Creamy Potato Leek Soup

This wholesome potato soup, with its delicate sweetness from the leeks, gets its smooth, richness from the cashew cream.

¼ cups raw cashews, *soaked and blended*
1 tablespoon oil or ¼ cup vegetable broth, *for sautéing*
1 clove garlic, *minced*
1 cup celery, *diced*
4 cups russet potatoes (about 2 large) *peeled and chopped*
1½ cups leeks, *finely chopped white and light green parts only, or scallions*
6 cups water or vegetable broth, *unsalted*
1 teaspoon salt
White pepper, *to taste*
1 teaspoon of Deb's Seasoning (page 269)

Begin with soaking raw cashews in ½ cup of water for 30 minutes.

While cashews are soaking, heat a large soup pot over medium heat. Add one tablespoon of canola oil or ¼ cup vegetable broth to warm pan and sauté leeks until they begin to lightly brown. Add garlic, celery and potatoes. Cook until the vegetables begin to soften.

Pour 6 cups of water or broth into the pot and bring to a boil. Immediately reduce to simmer and add salt, white pepper and Deb's Seasoning.

In a blender, puree cashews and the water in which they were soaking until graininess is gone and mixture is smooth. Stir cashew paste into soup.

For a creamy, smooth soup, blend half or all of the soup mixture in a food processor, or use an immersion blender in the pot until the ingredients reach the desired consistency. For a chunkier soup, just mash a few of the potatoes with a fork and stir.

Taste to adjust seasonings. Simmer on low until ready to serve, but do not let the soup come to a boil. If it becomes too thick, thin with water or vegetable broth.

Hint:

Russet potatoes are great in soups or mashed. They make a thick, starchy broth when cooked.

New Potato, Tomato & Kale Soup

This is a hearty, vegetable soup that can be the centerpiece of a meal and excellent for cold nights. A slice of cornbread is the perfect companion.

1 tablespoon oil or ¼ cup vegetable broth, *for sautéing*
1 onion, *diced*
1-2 cloves garlic, *minced*
1 jalapeño, *finely diced*
2 carrots, *peeled, diced*
1 stalk celery heart, *chopped*
3-4 cups new potatoes, *scrubbed (not peeled), halved or quartered into bite-size pieces*
1 quart water or vegetable broth
1 teaspoon Deb's seasoning (page 269)
½ teaspoon grill seasonings
1 tablespoon vegan Worcestershire sauce
Freshly ground pepper
1 (15 oz) can of fire-roasted diced tomatoes
1 cup corn, *fresh or frozen*
2 cups kale, *chopped*
1 basket cherry tomatoes, *halved*
1 teaspoon salt *(use less if vegetable broth contains salt)*

In large soup pot, sauté onion in oil (or ¼ cup of vegetable broth) until lightly browned. Add garlic, jalapeño pepper, carrots, celery, and potatoes. Pour in vegetable broth and add seasonings, Worcestershire sauce, and pepper. Cook until vegetables are tender.

Add fire-roasted tomatoes, corn, kale and cherry tomatoes. Use vegetable broth to thin the soup if necessary. Bring liquid to boil, then lower heat to simmer for 15 more minutes.

Taste to adjust salt and pepper. Turn off heat and let flavors blend together. Reheat just before serving.

Hint:

New potatoes are low in starch, have firm flesh and are slightly sweet. They hold together well in cooking for soups.

Creamy Tomato Soup

This is perfect for a simple lunch or dinner. The cashew cream adds rich flavor and a creamy texture. Hot, crusty whole grain bread makes for a perfect meal.

- 1 tablespoon of oil or ¼ cup of vegetable broth, *for sautéing*
- 1 cup of leeks, *washed well, chopped*
- 1 medium carrot, *peeled, diced*
- 1 celery stalk, *diced*
- 2 cloves garlic, *minced*
- 2 tablespoons flour
- 1 teaspoon salt
- Freshly ground pepper, *to taste*
- 6 cups of vegetable broth
- 10-12 fresh Roma tomatoes or 1 (28 oz) can of whole diced fire-roasted tomatoes with juice
- 1 tablespoon tomato paste
- 1 bay leaf
- 1 teaspoon Deb's Seasoning (page 269)
- 1 tablespoon fresh parsley, *diced*
- ½ cup cashew cream
- A couple of dashes of Tabasco® for heat *(optional)*

Begin by making cashew cream (recipe below).

Heat soup pot over medium heat. Add oil or ¼ cup of vegetable broth then leeks, carrot, celery and garlic. Cook for 10 minutes or until vegetables are tender.

Stir flour, salt and pepper around in the soup pot and cook for a couple of minutes. Add 6 cups of vegetable broth, tomatoes, tomato paste, bay leaf, Deb's Seasoning and parsley. Reduce heat to simmer and cook for 15 minutes.

Add cashew cream and simmer for 10 minutes, but do not let soup boil. Remove bay leaf. Either puree soup in food processor or use an immersion blender directly in the pot. Check for seasonings and adjust for taste. Garlic croutons added to the top is a nice garnish.

Cashew Cream

- ¼ cup raw cashews
- ½ cup water

Let cashews soak in water for an hour or longer. Put cashews with water in a blender. Blend until all graininess is gone and mixture is smooth. Add to recipe when needed.

Hint:

Cashew cream can be refrigerated for 2-3 days and frozen up to 6 months.

Hearty Tomato Soup

A fresh tomato soup to warm you up on cold nights, this recipe can either be made thin and smooth or chunky and thick. Try it with a pan of Simple Bread (page 283) and a crisp Romaine Salad (page 34).

6 sun-dried tomatoes, *not oil packed*
2 cups of boiling water or broth
1 tablespoon olive oil or ¼ cup vegetable stock, *for sautéing*
1 small onion, *diced*
1-2 cloves garlic, *finely minced*
1 stalk celery, *diced*
10-12 fresh Roma tomatoes or 1 (28 oz) can of whole fire-roasted tomatoes with juice
2 tablespoons of tomato paste
1 cup corn kernels, *frozen*
1 tablespoon vegan Worcestershire sauce
½ teaspoon smoky sweet paprika
1 teaspoon Deb's Seasoning (page 269)
½ teaspoon of red pepper flakes
1 cup unsweetened almond or rice milk
Salt and pepper, *to taste*
2 tablespoons fresh parsley, *chopped*
Homemade Croutons (page 270), *for garnish*

Begin by pouring 2 cups of boiling water over the sun-dried tomatoes. Let soak for at least 15 minutes before removing tomatoes from water and chopping them into small pieces. Return to soaking water. Set aside.

Over medium-high heat, sauté onion, celery and garlic in a soup pot using oil or vegetable stock until the onion is soft and beginning to brown.

Add tomatoes and tomato paste, cook until the mixture begins to boil. Then add sun-dried tomatoes (with soaking water), corn, Worcestershire sauce, paprika, seasoning, and red pepper flakes. Reduce to simmer, cover and cook for 30 minutes.

Stir in almond milk, parsley and taste for salt and pepper. At this point, if you want a smoother soup, use an immersion blender or food processor to reach desired texture. Use almond or rice milk to thin the soup as necessary. Turn off the heat to let the soup flavors blend together. Heat just before serving.

Tomato Rice Soup with Greens

This is a good and simple soup to put together. You can use any greens that you have on hand. Serve with pita toasts (page 272).

1 tablespoon oil or ¼ cup vegetable broth, *for sautéing*
1 small onion, *diced*
1-2 cloves of garlic, *minced*
1 stalk of celery, *finely diced*
1 carrot, peeled, *finely diced*
2 tablespoons of parsley, *chopped*
1 jalapeño pepper, *seeded, finely diced*
½ cup of long grain rice
2 tablespoons of tomato paste
4 cups of vegetable broth (unsalted) or water
10-12 fresh Roma tomatoes, *chopped* or 4 cups of canned fire-roasted tomatoes
1 teaspoon Deb's Seasoning (page 269)
A couple of dashes of Tabasco®
1 cup of greens, *chopped (collards, chard, kale, bok choy, any that you have on hand)*
Splash of red wine vinegar
½-1 teaspoon red pepper flakes
1-1½ teaspoon salt
Fresh ground pepper, *to taste*

Heat soup pot to medium heat and add oil or vegetable broth. Toss in onions, garlic, carrots, celery, jalapeño and parsley. When onions become tender, add rice and cook, stirring frequently, until fragrant.

Stir in tomato paste until well blended. Add vegetable broth or water, Deb's seasoning, and tomatoes and bring to a boil. Simmer with cover, until rice is almost tender (about 25 minutes for white rice and about 45 minutes for brown rice).

Drop greens into soup pot. Pour in red wine vinegar and add Tabasco®, red pepper flakes and salt. Cook until greens are tender (about 10 minutes). Taste for seasonings and add freshly ground pepper. Serve.

Hint:

Roma tomatoes are less sweet and have a full-bodied tomato flavor. They work well for soups and sauces.

Roasted Tortilla Soup

This is a delicious soup worth all of the steps. The tomato stock gives this brothy soup a great depth of flavor. Nice with Romaine and Avocado Salad (page 31) with fresh hot tortillas.

2 tablespoons oil
1 medium onion, *1" slices*
3-4 cloves garlic, *unpeeled*
10-12 Roma tomatoes
6 cups of tomato stock (page 79)
1 teaspoon pureed chipotle chile
1 poblano pepper
1-2 jalapeño chiles
1 teaspoon salt
Freshly ground pepper, *to taste*
Juice from ½ lime

Begin by making tomato stock. While the stock is cooking you can prepare the soup.

Preheat broiler in oven.

In a large bowl, lightly oil the onions, garlic, jalapeños, poblano pepper and tomatoes. Place in oven on a baking sheet 3"–4" from broiler. As the vegetables begin to brown and their skins blister, use tongs to turn them over to their other sides. When the garlic and onions are golden brown remove from the oven. The tomatoes, poblano and jalapeños are ready to remove when their skins are lightly blistered.

Peel the garlic cloves. Peppers can be cut open to remove seeds for a milder soup, or leave them whole for a spicier flavor. Place all vegetables in food processor and puree until smooth, or place vegetables in large soup pot and use an immersion blender.

In a large soup pot, cook pureed mixture over medium heat for approximately 10 minutes. Add stock, lower heat to simmer, cover and cook for about 30 minutes.

Stir in chipotle chile and taste for salt and pepper. Stir in lime juice. When serving add chopped avocados and fried or baked tortilla strips (see hints below) for garnish.

Hints:

◊ You can buy chipotle chiles in a small can. Since just 1 teaspoon is needed, just mince.
◊ To make baked tortilla strips, stack 8-10 corn tortillas and cut in strips or wedges. Brush strips with oil or use cooking spray. Bake in oven at 425°F (220°C), on baking sheet until crisp. Using a spatula, flip tortilla strips a couple of times during cooking. Remove from oven and lightly salt.

Deb's Vegetable Soup

The fresh taste of the vegetables is what makes this soup so appealing. A very flexible soup since you can use nearly any vegetables you have on hand.

- 2 cups vegetable broth
- 1 chopped onion or combine with leeks, *finely diced*
- 2 cloves garlic, *minced*
- 3 large Russet potatoes, *peeled and cut into bite-sized pieces*
- 1-2 teaspoons Deb's Seasoning (page 269)
- 1 stalk celery, *finely diced*
- 1 carrot, *peeled, diced*
- 1 bag frozen mixed vegetables
- 1 (28 oz) can whole peeled tomatoes
- 1 jalapeño pepper, *seeded, diced*
- 1 cup mushrooms, *sliced*
- 1 cup kale, *chopped*
- Any other vegetables can be added
- 1 tablespoon chili powder
- 1-2 tablespoons vegan Worcestershire sauce
- ¼ teaspoon celery seed
- A couple dashes Tabasco® sauce
- ½-1 teaspoons red pepper flakes, *to taste*
- 1 teaspoon salt *(use less if vegetable broth contains salt)*
- Freshly ground pepper, *to taste*

Start with 1 cup of vegetable broth in soup pot over medium heat. Add chopped onion and sauté until soft. Add minced garlic and chopped potatoes and mix in with the tender onions. Lightly sprinkle on Deb's Seasoning and cover pot. Let potatoes cook for a few minutes.

Remove cover and add celery, carrots and frozen veggies. Stir for a couple of minutes to let the vegetables heat up. Add tomatoes, jalapeño pepper, mushrooms, and kale and vegetable broth. Bring all to a boil. Add enough water to keep vegetables submerged.

Reduce heat to low and add chili powder, Worcestershire sauce, celery seed, Tabasco®, red pepper flakes, salt and freshly ground pepper. Partially cover and simmer until potatoes are tender. Taste for seasonings. Turn off heat and let flavors blend together from 30 minutes to 2 hours. Heat before serving.

Hint:

To always have garlic available try this tip. Peel and then mince 10-12 cloves of garlic in a food processor. On wax paper or plastic wrap, shape garlic into a log and wrap up tightly. Cover wrapped log in foil and place in the freezer. When you need a bit, cut off a slice of the log and return the rest to the freezer.

Simple Vegetable & Rice Soup

A brothy, low-calorie vegetable soup that is fast, simple to put together, and very filling. Especially good when you feel like a having a light, but soothing, meal. The vegetable selection can vary according to what you have on hand.

2 teaspoons canola oil or ¼ cup vegetable broth, *for sautéing*
½ cup onion, *diced*
2 leeks, *white and light green parts only, sliced*
½ jalapeño pepper, *diced*
½ cup bell pepper, *diced*
2 cloves garlic, *finely chopped*
1 medium carrot, *peeled, diced*
½ cup English peas, *fresh or frozen*
1 yellow squash, *cut into bite-sized pieces*
1 zucchini, *cut into bite-sized pieces*
1½ cups mushrooms, *chopped*
8 cups vegetable broth
1 tablespoon of vegan Worcestershire
2 cups cooked rice
1 teaspoon salt
Freshly ground pepper
Croutons and green onions, *for garnish*

In medium skillet, add oil or vegetable broth to sauté vegetables. Add onion, leeks, jalapeño, bell pepper and sauté until tender. Add garlic, carrots, peas, yellow squash, zucchini and mushrooms. Cook until vegetables tender crisp, about 2 minutes.

Place vegetable broth in soup pot and add sautéed vegetables with vegan Worcestershire. Bring to boil. Add rice and turn to simmer for 20 minutes. Taste for salt and pepper. Garnish with croutons, sliced green onions or red pepper threads and serve.

Hint:

Red pepper threads are long, thin strings of dried red chiles. They are not only pretty to use as a garnish but add a mild bite to the dish.

Basic Stock

There is a time and place for home-made stock, particularly if you cannot find a prepared stock with a blend of vegetables that suits your tastes and needs. Making stocks is not difficult, but you must plan ahead to be successful. Save leftover vegetable trimmings from cooking. They can be frozen until needed. Only save and use trimmings that are fresh and edible.

Since there isn't always time to make a stock for a single recipe, and stocks can be safely frozen without losing their flavor, storing a supply of prepared stocks in the freezer can keep you ahead of the game. Here is a very basic recipe that can be modified easily by omitting salt or adding a favorite vegetable or herb.

1 tablespoon canola oil
1 large onion, *sliced*, or 2 cups sliced leeks
2 carrots, *diced*
2 celery stalks with leaves, *chopped*
3-4 mushrooms
2-4 cloves garlic, *peeled, chopped*
½ cup fresh parsley
2 thyme sprigs *(optional)*
1 bay leaf
½ teaspoon peppercorns
2 quarts water
1 teaspoon salt, *to taste*

Heat large soup pot to medium-high and add oil. Toss onion or leeks, carrots, celery, mushrooms, herbs, peppercorns, and any trimmings you have in hot oil for a few minutes. Add salt and water. Bring to boil then lower heat to simmer. Cook uncovered for 35-45 minutes. Strain out vegetables and then let stock cool or use right away.

Tomato Stock

Great for using in soups or sauces.

1 tablespoon oil or ½ cup of vegetable broth
1 onion, *peeled, roughly chopped*
2 celery stalks, *roughly chopped*
2 carrots, *peeled, roughly chopped*
4-6 mushrooms, *cremini or white*
1 jalapeño, *halved, seeds removed*
1 bunch scallions, *all parts, chopped*
4 cloves garlic, *peeled, smashed*
2 tablespoons tomato paste
½ teaspoon of Mexican oregano
½ teaspoon of dried thyme
½ cup of fresh parsley, *chopped*
1 teaspoons of salt
½ teaspoons of peppercorns
2 quarts of water

Heat oil in large soup pot over medium-high heat. Add oil or vegetable broth then add onions, celery, carrots, mushrooms and jalapeño. Cook until onions are golden brown, about 6 minutes. Then add scallions, garlic, tomato paste and remaining ingredients with the water. Bring to boil. Reduce heat and simmer, partially covered for 1 hour. Strain out vegetables.

Set aside for later use or refrigerate or freeze for another time.

Chapter Three

Burgers and Sandwiches

Kitchen Tips

- ◊ Sometimes the best SANDWICH ingredients are in your pantry but you just can't think of what combination would be good. Here are a few suggestions that might get you started:

    Cashew butter with sliced bananas
    Arugula sprigs, cucumber and vegan mayonnaise
    Vegan cheese with spicy mustard or vegan mayonnaise
    Tomato and pesto on rustic
    Vegan cream cheese topped with sliced cucumbers
    Almond butter and apple butter
    Bean spread or hummus with a thin slice of red onion
    A salad sandwich with last night's leftover salad

- ◊ You can wrap a lot of good stuff up in a TORTILLA:

    Chili
    Fresh vegetables
    Beans
    Leftover vegetables or potatoes
    Guacamole
    Sloppy Joe mixes
    Pickled onions
    Cabbage slaw
    Crumbled tofu
    Grilled vegetables or tofu (See Grilled Tofu on page 230)

- ◊ These items are great on PITA BREAD:

    Salads
    Hummus
    Chili
    Frozen veggie burger
    Spreads
    Hash browns
    Pico de Gallo
    Beans
    Guacamole
    Spicy Mayo
    Baked tofu
    Pesto

Artichoke & Hummus Open-Faced Sandwich

The warm, creamy taste of hummus is complemented by the little tang of artichokes. This sandwich is tasty and satisfying. Try it on a fresh sourdough baguette with a side salad.

1 jar marinated baby artichoke hearts in oil, *drained*
4 slices thick bread
1 cup oil-free hummus (pages 87-88)
¼ cup sliced pepperoncini peppers, *drained*
¼ cup sun-dried tomatoes, *finely diced*
Salt and Ground pepper
Tomato slices *(optional)*

Preheat oven to 400°F (205°C).

Put artichoke hearts on a baking sheet and place in oven on center rack. Bake for 15 minutes until golden brown.

Spread 3 tablespoons of hummus on each side of bread. Layer sliced artichokes, pepperoncini peppers and sun-dried tomatoes over hummus. Add salt and pepper.

Arrange on baking sheet and bake until warmed through, about 3-5 minutes. Try topping with fresh tomato slices.

Black Bean Tostadas

Everyone loves a tostada, so this recipe is a crowd pleaser! Makes a particularly great lunch or dinner for a large group where guests can choose ingredients to suit their tastes. Just be sure to double up on ingredients.

- 3 teaspoons oil or ¼ cup vegetable broth or water
- ½ cup onion, *finely diced*
- 1 clove garlic, *finely minced*
- 1 jalapeño, *seeded, finely diced*
- 1 can black beans (15 oz) or fresh if you have them
- 8 corn tortillas
- Oil or cooking spray
- Salt

Toppings

Use any or all of the following.

- 2 tomatoes, *diced*
- ½ red onion, *finely diced*
- 2 jalapeño peppers, *seeded and finely diced or pickled jalapeños*
- 2 avocados, *peeled and sliced or made into guacamole (page 258)*
- Pico de Gallo (page 258)
- Corn salsa (page 257)
- Ranchero salsa (page 255)
- Lettuce or cabbage, *shredded*
- Lime wedges
- Non-dairy cheese

Heat oil or broth in a small skillet over medium-low heat. Add onions and cook until they begin to brown. Add garlic and jalapeño. Cook for another minute.

Turn up the heat a little and add half of the black beans with their juices. Mash the beans while stirring until the mixture begins to bubble around the edges. Add remaining beans and continue to mash and stir. Turn off the heat when the bean mixture is hot all the way through; it will thicken as it cools.

Heat a large skillet or a griddle to medium-high. Spray corn tortillas with cooking spray or brush with oil and griddle until lightly brown on both sides.

Spread the bean mixture on each tortilla and then let each person create a favorite combination of toppings.

Hint:

You can also cook tortillas in a 425°F (220°C) oven on a baking sheet until crispy. Lightly spray both sides with canola oil or cooking spray and place on baking sheet. Place in oven and cook for 5 minutes. Flip each tortilla and cook for 5 minutes more until crispy and golden in color.

White Bean Spread

This easily modified spread is amazing on a piece of warm or toasted focaccia bread. Add capers or pickles for extra zing. Finish it off with a variety of vegetables: avocados, tomatoes, arugula, onions, or peppers.

- 1 can white beans, *drained, rinsed or homemade*
- 3-5 green onions, *finely chopped, greens included*
- 1 garlic clove, *minced or ½ teaspoon garlic powder if you do not like raw garlic*
- ½ cup chopped walnuts or roasted cashews
- 1 tablespoon nutritional yeast *(optional)*
- 2 tablespoons fresh lemon juice
- 4-5 green olives, *chopped*
- 1 tablespoon fresh parsley, *chopped*
- A pinch red pepper flakes
- Salt and pepper, *to taste*

Place beans, onions, garlic, ¼ cup chopped nuts, nutritional yeast and lemon juice in a food processor and pulse until smooth.

Stir in olives, parsley and the remaining ¼ cup nuts, but do not use blender. Add salt and pepper to taste. Refrigerate for storage.

Hint:

Any bean can be used in this spread, but the white bean is best for the appearance. White bean spread is creamy in color where pinto or red beans look pinkish when blended and black bean spread is more of a gray color.

Chickpea Sandwich Spread

Makes a delicious sandwich on fresh pita bread and topped with fresh tomatoes or a tangy spread for crackers or pita chips.

- 1 can chickpeas, *drained, rinsed or 2 cups fresh, cooked*
- ¼ cup vegan mayonnaise
- 1 tablespoon Dijon mustard
- 1 celery stalk, *finely diced, with leaves*
- 2-3 tablespoons onion, *finely diced*
- ¼ cup green olives, *chopped*
- 3 teaspoons capers, *drained*
- ¼ cup walnuts, *chopped*
- Pinch cayenne pepper, *to taste*
- Salt and pepper, *to taste*

Put chickpeas in food processor and pulse until they are small, flaky pieces. Place in a bowl with all ingredients and mix together. Salt and pepper to taste.

Hint:

Did you know that *nonpareil* means "without equal" in French? The small pickled capers from Provence, France, are called nonpareil capers because they are considered the very best.

Red Bell Pepper Hummus

Red bell peppers always add a sweet brightness to recipes, particularly this hummus spread. It's particularly good on fresh multigrain bread and topped with cucumbers, crisp romaine lettuce and diced jalapeño chiles.

1 (15 oz) can garbanzo beans, *save liquid*
2-3 ounces roasted red bell peppers, *drained*
¼ cup tahini
4 tablespoons lemon juice
⅓ cup water, *use liquid from garbanzo beans*
Sprinkle garlic powder or fresh garlic clove, *minced*
½ teaspoon Deb's Seasoning (page 269)
Salt, *to taste*

Drain garbanzo beans and save the liquid for thinning the hummus later.

Place all ingredients and ⅓ cup fluid drained from garbanzo beans in a blender or food processor. Blend until smooth. If necessary, thin the mixture by adding more of the liquid from the beans. Taste and adjust seasonings. Store in refrigerator.

Hint:
If you buy your hummus, always try to find the brands that are oil-free.

Roasted Garlic Hummus

Use this garlicky and smooth hummus as a sandwich or cracker spread, a dip, or for salad dressing (page 27).

1 (15 oz) can garbanzo beans, *save one cup of liquid to thin hummus*
2-4 cloves roasted garlic (page 118)
¼ cup tahini
4 tablespoons lemon juice
⅓ cup water, *use liquid from garbanzo beans*
¼ teaspoon ground red pepper
Salt, *to taste*

Drain garbanzo beans and save the liquid for thinning the hummus later.

Place all ingredients in a blender or food processor and blend until smooth. If necessary, thin the mixture by adding more of the liquid from the beans. Taste and adjust seasonings. Store in refrigerator.

Chipotle Hummus

This zesty hummus makes an excellent dip, cracker spread, or sandwich dressing. Try it spread thinly over fresh pita bread halves topped with sprigs of arugula and diced avocado for a spicy treat.

1 (15 oz) can garbanzo beans, *save one cup of liquid to thin hummus*
¼ cup tahini
4 tablespoons lemon juice
⅓ cup water, *use liquid from garbanzo beans*
½-1 teaspoons chipotle powder
Sprinkle garlic powder
Salt, *to taste*

Drain garbanzo beans and save the liquid for thinning the hummus later.

Place all ingredients in a blender or food process or until smooth. If necessary, thin the mixture by adding more of the liquid from the beans. Taste and adjust seasonings. Store in refrigerator.

Hummus Quesadillas

The versatility of the quesadilla is almost unlimited. Kids love them (so do big people)! Great fast lunch or cut them up for a party dish with more salsa and guacamole for dipping.

Hummus, your favorite or homemade (pages 87-88)
Pico de Gallo (page 258) or salsa (pages 254-257)
Fresh flour or whole-wheat tortillas

Heat non-stick griddle or skillet to medium-high, using no oil. Spread hummus on tortilla and top with a couple of tablespoons of salsa. Try not to get sauce too close to edge of the tortilla where it will leak out and make a mess on your grill. Fold tortilla in half and place on grill or pan. When tortilla is golden brown, flip and brown the other side. Serve while warm.

Spinach Quesadillas

When served with a Romaine Salad with Lemon Vinaigrette on the side, these quesadillas make a fast lunch or dinner.

1 tablespoon oil or ¼ cup vegetable broth
½ cup onion, *finely diced*
1 jalapeño, *seeded, finely diced*
4-5 chopped mushrooms *(optional)*
1 clove garlic, *minced*
A pinch dried Mexican oregano
8 cups fresh spinach, *stems removed*
½ teaspoon salt
Ground pepper, *to taste*
4 extra-large (12") flour tortillas
1½ cups hummus (pages 87-88)
Pico de Gallo (page 258) or a salsa (pages 254-258)

In medium skillet, sauté onion, jalapeño, pepper, mushrooms and garlic in oil or vegetable broth until tender. Add oregano, salt, pepper and spinach. Toss ingredients then remove from heat. Spinach should not be entirely wilted. Set pan aside.

Heat a large non-stick skillet or griddle over medium-high heat.

Spread a thin layer of hummus over a tortilla. Cover the tortilla evenly over the surface except near the edge where excess hummus can spill out and make a mess. Top hummus with 2-3 tablespoons of Pico de Gallo or salsa and ¼-½ cup of spinach mixture depending on size of tortilla. Fold tortilla in half and place in skillet or on griddle. Cook until tortilla is golden brown on bottom side, and then flip over to other side. When second side is golden, remove the quesadilla to a warm plate.

Quesadillas can be placed in a 150°F (65°C) oven to keep warm while preparing more. Serve with a salad or Black Bean Salsa (page 254).

Grilled Portobello Mushroom Sandwich
with Spicy Mayonnaise

This is a hearty sandwich that is full of rich flavors and textures. Makes 2 sandwiches.

1 cup vegan mayonnaise
1-2 teaspoons chipotle chili powder or adobe powder
1 large Portobello mushroom
Olive oil
Salt and pepper
Sliced tomatoes
Romaine lettuce
Red onion, *thinly sliced*
2 sourdough baguettes, *toasted*

Mix mayonnaise and chili powder together and let chill for a couple of minutes before using. Store in refrigerator for later use.

Remove stem from mushroom, scrape out the gills and wipe down with a damp cloth or paper towel. Brush both sides with olive oil and salt and pepper.

Broil mushroom 3"-4" from heat for about 4 minutes on each side. They can also be grilled or seared in a skillet. Remove mushroom when browned and slice into ½" strips.

Split toasted baguettes down the center, lengthwise. Spread on spicy mayonnaise on both baguette halves. On one half, layer mushrooms, sliced tomatoes, lettuce, onion slices and added salt and pepper. Close sandwich with other half and serve.

Spicy Mayonnaise

1 cup vegan mayonnaise
1-2 teaspoons of chipotle chile powder or adobe powder

Mix together and chill for 10 minutes before serving. Store leftovers in refrigerator.

Fried Green Tomato Sandwich
with Creole Mayonnaise

A great combination of Southern flavors with crunch! This makes 2 sandwiches. Potato salad is the perfect side (page 48).

- 2 large green tomatoes
- 1 cup yellow cornmeal
- Salt and pepper
- ½ teaspoon Deb's Seasoning (page 269)
- 2 teaspoons oil
- Creole mayonnaise (below)
- Sliced tomatoes
- Red onion, *thinly sliced*
- Shredded red cabbage
- Focaccia, *toasted*

Slice green tomatoes in ½" slices. Combine cornmeal with Deb's Seasoning, salt, and freshly ground pepper. Toss tomatoes in mixture until well coated.

Heat large non-stick skillet over medium heat. Add oil then when skillet is hot. Sauté green tomato slices on both sides until tender and golden, but not soft. Remove to a plate covered in paper towels to absorb any excess oil.

Spread Creole Mayonnaise on toasted bread. Add green tomatoes, sliced red tomatoes, onions and cabbage to top. Enjoy.

Creole Mayonnaise

- 1 cup vegan mayonnaise
- ¼ teaspoon paprika
- ¼ teaspoon garlic powder
- ¼ teaspoon cayenne pepper
- ¼ teaspoon ground black pepper

Stir ingredients together and let chill for 15 minutes. Store in the refrigerator.

Potato Sandwich

A staple in Southern homes, potato sandwiches were favored by mothers like my own. You can use any leftover potatoes, hash browns or make Baked Red Potato Slices (page 168).

Hash browns or any leftover potatoes
1 tomato, *sliced*
1 red onion, *sliced*
Dill pickles, *sliced*
Mustard or flavored mayonnaise
2 slices fresh bread

Coat one side of bread slices with mustard or mayonnaise. Layer ingredients and serve.

Hint:

Choose the best quality, vegan bread you can find; the bread is important to create a wonderful sandwich. Ask your baker if the bread contains dairy or egg products, as many do.

Sloppy Joes

Children always seem to love Sloppy Joes. To experience the recipe with a vegan twist, try this combination adapted from the standard old recipe. The best and least processed way to add texture to this recipe is to use Crumbled Tofu.

1½ cup Crumbled Tofu (page 233)
1 cup ketchup
3 teaspoons mustard, *prepared, regular or spicy*
2 teaspoons rice vinegar
4 tablespoons BBQ sauce
½ cup onion, *finely diced*
1-2 tablespoons vegan Worcestershire sauce
4 fresh hamburger buns, *warmed in oven*

Place all ingredients except the Crumbled Tofu in a nonstick skillet. Simmer on low heat for around 15 minutes or until the onions become tender. Add a little water if mixture becomes too thick.

Just before serving, add tofu to mixture. Scoop a mound on a hamburger bun and serve. If tofu is added to the sauce too soon it becomes soft and loses its texture.

Grilled Tofu Sandwich

There are many ways to change the flavor of this grilled tofu. You can choose a variety of sauces as marinades: BBQ sauce, salsa, flavored mustards, soy sauce with chili sauce mixed in. Marinating can be skipped altogether and plain tofu can be seasoned with salt, pepper and red pepper flakes sprinkled on right before grilling.

1 package tofu (firm), *press excess water out*
Sliced tomatoes
Sliced red onions
Sliced sweet or hot peppers
Sliced avocados
Lettuce
Flavored vegan mayonnaise
4 fresh hamburger buns

Take drained tofu and cut into ½" slabs. Place in flat dish and cover tofu with the marinade or seasoning you are using.

Let marinate anywhere from an hour to overnight, the longer the better.

When ready to cook, scrape off most of the sauce from the tofu, but save the excess. Too much sauce on the tofu will burn on the grill. Plain tofu can now be seasoned with salt, pepper and red pepper flakes.

Place the tofu slabs on a flat grill and slowly heat until grill marks are on both sides. Pan searing on a stovetop will also serve for this purpose. Heat tofu through, but do not dry the tofu out by overcooking.

When building your sandwich, the extra marinade can be used as a sauce for more flavor. Serve with Mexican Rice Salad (page 53) or Cabbage Slaw (page 41) as a side.

Tomato, Avocado & Red Onion Sandwich

This is an amazingly simple sandwich that is crisp and juicy all at once. The family will love it, especially when summer tomatoes are at their peak! Makes two sandwiches.

4 slices fresh country-style bread
1 large fresh tomato, *sliced*
½ avocado, *peeled, pitted, sliced*
½ small red onion, *thinly sliced*
Crisp red leaf lettuce
Mustard or vegan mayonnaise
¼ cup sprouts *(optional)*
Salt and Pepper, *to taste*

Spread mustard or mayonnaise on each slice of bread. Add salt and freshly ground pepper. Then add onion, avocado, tomatoes, lettuce and top with sprouts. Corn Salsa (page 257) makes a good side.

Hint:

To minimize the sharp taste of a raw onion, put slices in a colander in the sink and pour boiling water on top, then pour cold water over top. Slices can be used or covered in a bowl with fresh water and kept in the refrigerator until ready to use.

Grilled Vegetable Sandwich

These are great sandwiches for backyard cookouts on a charcoal or gas grill. For indoor gatherings, use a grilling pan in your kitchen. Much of the flavor comes from the spread or topping you use so try different spicy or flavored mustards or make your own spicy mayonnaise using vegan mayonnaise with roasted garlic, horseradish or chipotle chili powder. How about potato salad on the side?

Canola oil or cooking spray
Use soft long rolls or large flour tortillas to wrap

Top with;
Red onion, *thinly sliced*
Tomatoes, *sliced*
Sliced avocados
Lettuce leaves
1-2 jalapeños, *seeded, diced to sprinkle on sandwich*
Flavored mustards or vegan mayonnaise
Salt and pepper, *to taste*

Use 1 or 2 or all of the vegetables below:
1 large bell pepper, *seeded and halved*
2 zucchini, *cut lengthwise into slices*
Baked potato slices, *precooked, with a sprinkle garlic salt*
1 large red onion, *cut into slices*
4 large mushrooms, *on skewers, sliced after cooking*
2 Anaheim peppers, *sliced in half, seeded*

Brush the vegetables lightly with canola oil or cooking spray. Slowly grill until vegetables are tender and have grill marks on both sides. Remove and season with salt and pepper.

Just do this step if you want warm bread. Wrap bread or tortillas in foil and put on grill for only a couple of minutes to heat them up. Keep an eye on them, because tortillas can overcook fast!

Make sandwiches with grilled vegetables, mayonnaise, mustards, tomatoes, avocados, onions, and diced jalapeño peppers. Serve.

Hint:
Anaheim chiles are usually quite mild. They always taste better roasted.

Spicy Black Bean Burger

A great spicy sandwich that everyone enjoys. Top with Pico de Gallo (page 258) for an extra burst of flavor.

- 1 (15 oz) can black beans, *drained and rinsed*
- ½ cup cooked rice, *chilled*
- ¼ cup fat-free barbecue sauce
- ¼ cup quick cooking oats
- 2 tablespoons cooked beets, *fresh or canned*
- 3 tablespoons onion, *minced*
- 1 jalapeño, *seeded, finely minced*
- 2 teaspoons vegan Worcestershire
- 1 teaspoon garlic, *minced*
- 1 teaspoon chili powder
- ¼ teaspoon ground cumin
- ¼ teaspoon freshly ground pepper
- ⅛ teaspoon cayenne pepper
- Salt, *to taste*
- Glaze *(optional, recipe below)*
- Buns
- Pico de Gallo, *optional*

Place beans in large bowl and mash with a fork or potato masher. Leave chunky to create texture. Shred the cooked beets with a grater. Add remaining ingredients and mix well. Let flavors marry together for about 10-15 minutes.

Form mixture into patties (makes about 6 burgers). Patties can be placed on a dish, covered and refrigerated until ready to cook, or wrapped and frozen.

Heat non-stick grill to medium-high heat. Place burgers on grill and cook until browned on bottom side, then flip. If using glaze, brush on each side of burger while grilling. Continue to cook until both sides are browned. Cooked burgers can be kept in a warm oven on a baking sheet until ready to serve. Top with pico de gallo, any of your favorite vegetables or condiments on a warm bun.

Glaze

- 2 tablespoons soy sauce
- ¼ cup spicy BBQ sauce

Mix together ingredients with a spoon and set aside until needed.

Hint:

Spread soy sauce glaze on the bun for added flavor.

Mushroom & Nut Burger

Nutty, crunchy, spicy, wholesome and not dry or boring. Serve on toasted buns with tomato, lettuce, onions and your favorite condiment.

1 tablespoon oil
1¼ cup mushrooms, *finely chopped*
½ cup carrots, *finely chopped*
¾ cup shallots, *finely diced*
1 jalapeño pepper, *seeded, finely diced*
1-2 tablespoons garlic, *minced*
1 cup chickpeas, *drained*
¾ cup walnuts
½ cup sunflower seeds
¼ cup sesame seeds, *toasted*
¼ cup quick cooking oats
½ cup cooked rice
3 tablespoons tahini
3 tablespoons lemon juice
1 tablespoon vegan Worcestershire
⅛ teaspoon cayenne *(optional)*
½ teaspoon salt
½ teaspoon pepper
¾ teaspoon cumin
Buns
Lettuce, tomato, and onions, *sliced (optional)*

Heat oil in skillet over medium heat. Sauté mushrooms, carrots, shallots, jalapeño, and garlic, until golden brown, about 10 minutes. Set aside and cool.

In food processor, pulse walnuts and sunflower seeds for 3 seconds. Place nut mixture in large bowl and add sesame seeds, oats, and rice.

Blend sautéed vegetables in food processor with remaining ingredients until just blended, not a smooth paste. Then add to the bowl with the nuts, seeds, oats and rice then mix together with a fork or use your hands. When ingredients are well combined, cover bowl and place in refrigerator to chill for at least 20 minutes or until mixture is firm and holds together when pressed with fingertips.

Make small 4" patties. Patties can be refrigerated again at this point until ready to use or wrapped well and frozen.

In askillet, over medium-low heat, lightly spray with cooking oil and sauté burgers for 4 minutes on each side. Be careful when you flip to the other side, so they will not fall apart. If using glaze, brush on each side of burger while cooking. The cooked burgers can be kept in a warm oven on a baking sheet until ready to serve on buns with your favorite vegetables and condiments.

Chipotle Glaze

2 tablespoons soy sauce
¼ cup spicy BBQ sauce
2 teaspoons chipotle hot sauce

Mix together ingredients with a spoon and set aside until needed.

Hint:
Spread chipotle glaze on the bun for added flavor.

Veggie Wraps

You can do anything with this wrap. Use whatever you have on hand and be creative!

4 flour tortillas, *regular or whole wheat*
1 cup hummus, *homemade or store bought*
2 carrots, *peeled and grated*
2 roasted red peppers *(from a jar or homemade)*, *sliced, dried off with paper towels*
½ cucumber, *sliced*
1 avocado, *peeled and sliced*
1 cup lettuce
Alfalfa sprouts
¼ cup green olives, *chopped*
Leftover potatoes or tofu
Walnuts, *chopped*
Salt and pepper, *to taste*

Tortillas can be warmed on a dry griddle for just a minute to soften, but this step is not necessary.

Spread 3 tablespoons of hummus on each tortilla. Arrange veggies on the hummus down the center part of the tortilla. Season with salt and pepper and add nuts. Roll up tortilla. The tortilla rolls can be tightly wrapped in plastic wrap to pack for a lunch or a picnic.

Chapter Four

Fresh Vegetables

- ◊ To ensure you always have garlic on hand, try this tip. Peel and then finely mince 10-12 cloves of garlic in a food processor. Shape garlic into a log. Wrap with wax paper or plastic wrap, then foil. Put in freezer. When you need a bit, cut off a piece of the log and then place garlic back in freezer.

- ◊ Keep a frozen bag of tricolored bell peppers for those times when fresh bell pepper is not on hand. They are not perfect, but they will work in a pinch.

- ◊ Mushrooms are porous and will toughen when washed in water. It is best to wipe with a damp cloth or paper towel to remove dirt.

- ◊ If using salted vegetable broth in a recipe, always adjust the amount of added salt that is called for.

- ◊ Blanching or parboiling is a process of removing bitterness in vegetables but helps maintain their color, flavor and crispness. Bring a large pot of water to a boil, with a little salt added if preferred. Drop vegetables into water and cook until tender crisp. Depending on the size of the vegetable, cook time is usually 1-2 minutes. Do not overcook. Scoop out vegetables and put them in a large bowl filled with ice and water to stop the cooking process. Remove vegetables after 2-3 minutes and let drain until ready to use.

Asparagus, Spinach & Leeks

Especially good in the spring, this recipe is best when the vegetables are sweet and fresh. It can be made anytime now that asparagus can be found year-round. Tasty when served over rice or quinoa.

- ¼ cup vegetable broth or 1 tablespoon oil
- 2 leeks, *white and light green parts only, cut into rounds*
- 1-2 garlic cloves, *finely minced*
- Splash white wine or white wine vinegar
- 1 bundle asparagus, *washed and trimmed to about 5" from the top*
- 3-4 handfuls fresh baby spinach
- Salt, *to taste*
- Fresh ground pepper, *to taste*

Heat vegetable broth or oil in skillet, over medium-low heat, and add leeks and garlic. After a couple of minutes add ½ cup of water and the wine or vinegar. Add asparagus and another ½ cup of water.

Simmer for about 5 minutes until asparagus is tender and the pan juices have cooked down to about ½ cup.

Turn up heat to medium-high. Add spinach and toss around to mix with leeks until spinach is almost wilted. Remove from heat and add salt and pepper to taste.

Hint:

It is always good to soak asparagus and leeks in water for a couple of minutes before using to make sure all of the sand has been removed. Drain for a couple of minutes and then they are ready to go.

Roasted Asparagus

This is a great way to give asparagus a very robust, roasted flavor.

15-20 stalks asparagus, *washed and trimmed*
1 tablespoon oil
Salt, *to taste*
Freshly ground pepper
Arugula leaves *(optional)*
Lemon slices *(optional)*

Preheat oven to 425°F (220°C).

Toss asparagus in oil and lightly salt and pepper. Place on baking sheet pan and add a couple of tablespoons of water and cover with foil. Bake for 10 minutes.

Uncover and continue to bake for another 5-10 minutes until tender crisp and a little brown. Serve on a plate of arugula leaves with lemon slices.

Variation:

After roasting, drizzle with a little roasted sesame oil and sprinkle with black sesame seeds.

Hint:

Twenty stalks of asparagus weighs approximately one pound.

Simple! Fresh like spring! The best way to eat asparagus! It can be served warm, room temperature or cold. Serve with fresh lemon juice squeezed over top and a sprinkle of fresh chives.

15-20 stalks asparagus, *washed and trimmed*
2 tablespoons shallots, *finely diced*
Water or vegetable broth
Salt, *to taste*
Freshly ground pepper
2 tablespoons vegan butter or fresh lemon juice
Fresh parsley, chives or basil, *chopped*

In a large skillet, add asparagus and shallots and add water or vegetable broth to barely cover. Bring to a boil.

Simmer, uncovered for 8-10 minutes, depending on the size of the asparagus. You do not want to overcook! Pierce the asparagus with a knife or fork to make sure asparagus is tender but not limp.

Place asparagus on paper towels to drain and then transfer to a plate. Squeeze fresh lemon juice lightly (or vegan butter) over top then finish with salt, fresh ground pepper and a sprinkle of fresh parsley, chives or basil.

Hint:

When preparing asparagus, trim off the tough part of the stalk. Usually, you can see a color change in the stalk. Cut there. If asparagus is fresh, you can bend gently and let it snap where the tender and tough parts meet.

Basic Baked Beets

Beets can be used as a side dish or on salads cooked or raw. Fresh beets are so much better than canned. You may feel that you don't like beets. Try a sweet, earthy, fresh one; you'll be surprised at the difference. You can mix the colors of the beets for a more interesting looking dish.

4 medium to large beets *(red, yellow, or orange)*
Salt, *to taste*
Freshly ground pepper

Preheat oven to 400°F (205°C).

Wash beets but do not peel. Wrap each one in foil and place on a baking sheet pan. Bake for 45 minutes to 1 hour or until the beets are tender when pierced with a fork or paring knife.

When beets are cool enough to handle without burning your fingers, remove the skin using a small paring knife. Slice and lightly season with salt and freshly ground pepper to taste. Serve warm or store in the refrigerator to use for salads.

Cooking Technique For Small Beets:

This method of cooking works best when using small beets.

1. Preheat oven to 400°F (205°C).
2. Wash beets but do not peel. Place in a baking pan with ½"-1" of water. Cover and bake until beets are tender when pierced with a fork, about 30 minutes.
3. Remove beets from the oven. When they are cool enough to handle without burning your fingers, remove the skin using a small paring knife. Slice in halves, quarters, or cubes. Toss lightly with salt and pepper. Serve warm or refrigerate to use with salads.

Tossed Roasted Beets

Tangy and sweet!

12 small to medium beets
1 tablespoon oil
1 teaspoon salt
½ teaspoon freshly ground pepper
½ teaspoon fresh parsley, *finely minced*
2 tablespoons red wine vinegar
Juice of one large orange
1-2 tablespoons orange zest
1 teaspoon agave nectar

Preheat oven to 375°F (190°C).

Thoroughly wash beets; remove tops. Using a vegetable peeler, peel each one. Cut small beets in half or medium into quarters. Place beets on cooking sheet pan, toss with oil, salt, pepper and parsley and loosely cover with foil. Roast for 30 minutes. Toss with spatula and remove foil. Cook 15 minutes more until tender when pierced with a fork.

Remove from oven. Toss with vinegar, orange juice, agave and orange zest. Taste for salt and pepper. Serve warm or room temperature.

Hints:
- One pound of trimmed beets will serve four people.
- Yellow or gold beets tend to be milder in flavor than most red beets and do not bleed like red beets do.

Steamed Beets with Dressing

The dressing is optional, since the beets are delicious without it, but it does add a tangy zest to this simple dish.

- 6-8 small beets *(depending on size of steamer basket)*
- 2 teaspoons olive oil
- Juice of one lime
- ¼ teaspoon cumin
- Salt, *to taste*
- Freshly Ground Pepper, *to taste*

Bring water under steamer to a boil. Place washed, unpeeled beets in steamer basket. Cover and steam until tender when pierced with a paring knife, about 20 minutes.

If you choose to use the dressing, mix it while beets are steaming. The dressing is made by whisking oil, lime juice, cumin together, then adding salt with pepper to taste. Set aside.

Let beets cool. Peel off skins and cut in half. Toss with dressing mix until coated. Taste for seasoning. Serve warm or refrigerate and use for salads.

Hint:
Wash but do not peel beets before cooking so the juices will not leach out during cooking.

Steamed Bok Choy with Dressing

- 6 baby bok choy, *trim off ¼" at base, use whole or cut in half*
- 1 tablespoon canola oil
- 1 teaspoon roasted sesame oil
- ¼ cup mirin or dry sherry
- 2 teaspoons soy sauce or tamari
- Hot sauce, *to taste*
- 3 tablespoons rice vinegar

Steam bok choy until tender, crisp, about 5-8 minutes depending on the size. You can check tenderness by piercing the base of one of the bok choy with a fork or knife. Do not overcook. When done, drain.

While bok choy is cooking, mix the canola oil, sesame oil, mirin, soy sauce, hot sauce, and rice vinegar together in a small bowl. Strain bok choy, toss with oil and mirin dressing, and serve.

Broccolini or Broccoli Rabé with Lemon

The pleasant but bitter flavor of broccolini or broccoli rabé (also known as rapini) blends well with other strong flavors like garlic, lemon or pepper. This simple dish can be served as a side or cooled to room temperature and used as a salad.

1 pound broccolini, *trim off ends, remove tough stems and wilted leaves*
3 teaspoons olive oil or vegetable broth
Pinch red pepper flakes
½ lemon, *zest and juice*
½ teaspoon salt

Bring large pot of lightly salted water to boil. Cook broccolini until tender, about 3-4 minutes. Do not overcook; you want it to be crisp. Drain and add to ice bath and drain again. Place on paper towels until needed.

Heat oil or broth over medium-high heat in a large skillet. Add lemon zest and cook for about 30 seconds. Add broccoli or broccoli rabé and cook until hot. Add lemon juice and salt. Serve.

Hint:
The key to zesting is not to push into the bitter white part between the skin and flesh. Just get the surface color of the fruit.

Steamed Broccoli

You will lose the bright green color of broccoli if it is overcooked. Steamed broccoli should be a vibrant color and tender-crisp for serving.

Broccoli, *florets or stems with florets*
Salt and ground pepper
Fresh lemon juice or 1 tablespoon vegan butter

Place broccoli into steamer basket, cover and steam for 5 minutes. Use a paring knife to pierce stem to test for tenderness. If using just florets, remember they take less time to cook, approximately 4-6 minutes. Remove to plate and salt and pepper to taste. Squeeze fresh lemon juice or melt vegan butter over top.

Variation:

- ◊ Broccoli with Garlic & Red Pepper Flakes—Heat garlic in skillet with oil and add ¼ teaspoon red pepper flakes, salt and pepper to taste. When the garlic is lightly browned, add steamed broccoli and toss.
- ◊ Broccoli & Salsa—Take steamed broccoli and toss with a fresh salsa of your choice.
- ◊ Broccoli with Mustard & Capers—Mix Dijon mustard with capers and toss steamed broccoli around to coat.
- ◊ Broccoli with Vinaigrette—Toss steamed broccoli with your favorite salad dressing and add to a salad.

Red Pepper Broccoli

This is a delicious Asian style broccoli dish that is perfect as a side or served over rice or soba noodles.

1 tablespoon canola oil or ¼ cup vegetable broth
1 large red bell pepper, *cut into ½" strips*
4 cups broccoli florets, *cut into bite-sized pieces*
½ onion, *thinly sliced*
2 cloves garlic, *minced*
½ teaspoon ginger root, *finely grated (optional)*
¼ teaspoon ground cayenne pepper
2 tablespoons soy sauce or tamari
¼ cup pine nuts, *toasted*
Pine nuts, *for garnish*
Red pepper threads, *for garnish*

Heat wok or skillet over medium-high heat. When hot, add oil or vegetable broth. Toss in bell pepper, broccoli, and onion. Let vegetables warm in pan before stirring in ginger and garlic. Cook and stir all ingredients for about 3 minutes or until tender crisp.

Mix cayenne with soy sauce and pour over broccoli and cook about one more minute. Sprinkle with pine nuts and serve. Red pepper threads look pretty on this dish as a garnish.

Hint:
Red pepper threads are long, thin strings of dried red chiles. They are not only pretty to use as a garnish but add a mild bite to the dish.

Roasted Broccoli

6 cups broccoli florets
1 tablespoon olive oil
1 clove garlic, *minced*
1 teaspoon roasted sesame oil
½ teaspoon salt
Freshly ground pepper

Preheat oven to 425°F (220°C).

Mix broccoli, olive oil and garlic together. Place on baking sheet and roast until edges are golden brown and crispy. This takes about 15-20 minutes. Put in bowl and toss with sesame oil. Add salt and pepper to taste.

Boiled Brussels Sprouts

- 1 pound (4 cups) Brussels sprouts
- 1 tablespoon vegan butter *(optional)*
- 1 tablespoon apple cider vinegar or lemon juice
- ¼ teaspoon salt
- Freshly ground pepper, *to taste*

Wash Brussels sprouts. Remove wilted leaves and cut an X into the bottom of each sprout. Bring 1" water to a boil in a wide skillet. Add salt and Brussels sprouts. Cover and steam until bright green and tender when pierced with a paring knife (about 6-8 minutes).

When done, drain, move to a serving bowl and toss with butter, apple cider vinegar or lemon juice. Season with salt and pepper to taste.

Sautéed Brussels Sprouts

Perfect for a holiday meal.

- 1½ pound Brussels sprouts, *trimmed, cut in half*
- 1 tablespoon olive oil
- 2 dashes of salt
- Pepper
- 2 cups vegetable broth
- ½ cup golden raisins
- 1 cup roasted walnuts, *chopped*

Heat medium skillet to medium heat, then add oil, Brussels sprouts with salt and pepper. Cook about 5-10 minutes until golden brown. Add broth and raisins and lower heat.

Cook uncovered for 5 more minutes until tender when pierced with a paring knife. Broth will boil away during process. If it becomes too dry, add a little more broth or water.

Taste for seasoning and toss with walnuts and serve.

Hint:
There are approximately 4 cups of Brussels sprouts in one pound.

Steamed Brussels Sprouts

2-4 cups of Brussels sprouts

Wash and remove wilted outside leaves from Brussels sprouts. Cut an X in the bottom of each one. When steamer is ready, add sprouts and cook for 8-10 minutes, depending on the size of the sprouts. Pierce the center with a paring knife to test for tenderness. Remove when they are tender but still crisp, not mushy. Add salt, pepper, a sprinkle of fresh lemon juice or a teaspoon of vegan butter depending on taste and toss. Serve.

Hint:
Choose small Brussels sprouts that are fresh and tender. Fresh is much better than frozen.

Roasted Brussels Sprouts

1½ pounds (6 cups) Brussels sprouts, *washed and cut a x into bottom each one or cut in half*
Dash white balsamic vinegar
1-2 cloves garlic, *finely minced*
2 dashes salt and ground pepper
½ cup walnuts or pistachios, *chopped*
Croutons *(optional)*

Preheat oven to 425°F (220°C).

Place Brussels sprouts in bowl and toss with vinegar, garlic, salt and pepper. Place in a baking pan and add 4 tablespoons of water or vegetable broth and cover. Cook for 10 minutes and uncover.

Continue to cook for 20-30 more minutes or until they begin to brown and are tender. Add more water or vegetable broth if sprouts begin to get too brown before they are done.

When tender, remove from oven and toss with walnuts and croutons. A little olive oil can be added to the toss, but is hardly necessary.

Steamed Cabbage

Steaming keeps cabbage sweet, tender, and wonderful.

1 small green cabbage (1½ pound)
½ teaspoon salt
Freshly ground pepper
Dash apple cider vinegar

Cut cabbage in quarters, remove outer leaves and remove center core. Steam for 5-10 minutes, until tender but not soft. Remove cabbage and toss with salt, pepper and vinegar.

Hint:
This works well for red, green, Napa or Savoy cabbage, although red takes a little longer to cook than green.

Braised Red Cabbage

1 red cabbage, *halved, cored and thinly sliced*
½ onion, *cut in half lengthwise and thinly sliced*
1½ cups water or vegetable broth
¼ cup white, red wine or white wine vinegar
½ teaspoon salt
Freshly ground pepper

Add cabbage and onions to skillet or Dutch oven with water or broth and bring to boil. Cook for 10 minutes on medium heat. Add vinegar and salt. Turn heat to low and cover. Cook about 15-20 minutes until just tender crisp, not soft and limp.

Remove from heat and season with fresh ground pepper. Vegan butter can also be used at the end for extra flavor if desired. Cabbage has a natural buttery, sweet flavor that is wonderful.

Skillet Cabbage with Veggies

2 tablespoons oil or ½ cup vegetable broth
4 cups shredded cabbage
1 small bell pepper, *thinly sliced*
1 cup onion, *thinly sliced*
1 cup celery, *diced*
2 tomatoes, *diced*
1 jalapeño pepper, *finely diced*
1 teaspoon Deb's Seasoning (page 269)
½ teaspoon salt
Freshly ground pepper
Pepper sauce, *Tabasco*®

Heat a large skillet to medium and add oil or vegetable broth. Then add cabbage, onions, bell pepper, celery and tomatoes, jalapeño pepper and add seasonings. Cover.

Cook for about 15 minutes until the vegetables are crisp and tender, not mushy. Check for salt and pepper and add pepper sauce. Serve.

Hint:

Keep a frozen bag of tri-colored bell peppers in your freezer for those times when fresh bell pepper is not on hand. They are not perfect but they will be adequate.

Grated Carrots

6 medium carrots, *peeled and grated*
½ cup green onions, *cut diagonally*
1 tablespoon vegan butter or ¼ cup vegetable broth or water
1 clove garlic, *minced*
½ teaspoon salt
⅛ teaspoon pepper
2 tablespoons fresh parsley, *chopped*
1 teaspoon Dijon mustard *(optional)*

Place carrots in medium-sized pan with vegan butter, vegetable broth or water, garlic, salt and pepper.

Cook covered with tight-fitting lid over medium-high heat, stirring occasionally, 10-15 minutes or until tender.

Remove from heat and toss with parsley and mustard.

Hints:

◊ One pound of carrots (6-8 medium or 4 large) is equal to 3½ cups of peeled and sliced.
◊ The flat leaf (Italian) parsley has more flavor than the curly type. When parsley is dried it tastes grassy so try to use fresh.

Sautéed Carrots

Just simple carrots, perfectly cooked! Carrots with the tops still attached seem to be sweeter.

- 3-3½ cups carrots, *peeled and sliced*
- ½ cup water
- 1 teaspoon salt
- ¼ teaspoon ground pepper
- 1 tablespoons vegan butter or lemon juice
- 2 tablespoons fresh parsley, *chopped*

Peel carrots and cut them diagonally into ¼" slices. In a large sauté pan, over medium-high heat, put carrots, with ½ of cup water, salt and pepper and bring to boil. Cover and lower heat to medium-low heat and cook for 7-8 minutes, until the carrots are tender.

Add vegan butter or lemon juice and cook until water is cooked off. Remove from heat and toss with parsley, salt and pepper. Serve.

Hint:
To store carrots the day before use, peel and cut them, then cover them in water in a liquid-tight container or plastic bag. Keep refrigerated and drain well before using.

Steamed Carrots

- 3-3½ cups carrots, *peeled and sliced*
- Salt and freshly ground pepper, *to taste*
- 1 tablespoon fresh parsley, *minced*
- ½ teaspoon fresh thyme *(optional)*

Cut carrots into rounds or sticks, making sure all are about the same size. Steam until tender when a knife is inserted into the center, about 5-10 minutes. Put in a bowl and toss with salt, pepper and parsley or thyme.

Mashed Cauliflower with Caramelized Onions

Mashed cauliflower is great alone without anything else. Just cook like you would cook mashed potatoes. With caramelized onions, it creates a more unique dish that is different from routine. This is a great dish to make around the holiday season.

1 medium or large head cauliflower
Vegan butter, *to taste*
Unsweetened almond milk
½ cup of cooking water
Salt, *to taste*
Ground pepper, *to taste*

Cut out the center the cauliflower and then chop the rest into medium pieces.

Steam or boil cauliflower pieces until tender and mash like you would potatoes in a mixer. Add a little almond milk and butter to add creaminess. Use part of the ½ cup of cooking water to thin if necessary. Salt and pepper to taste.

Caramelized Onions

1 tablespoon canola oil
1 small onion, *thinly sliced*

Place oil in a small skillet, over medium-low heat and then add onions. Stir occasionally, but do not over stir. Cook until golden brown, which takes about 30 minutes, allow the onions time to bring out the sugar and caramelize. The longer they cook, the better they are. Stir into mashed cauliflower by hand or drizzle on top.

Roasted Cauliflower

Cauliflower, *cut into 1½" florets or sliced into slabs*
1-2 teaspoons olive oil
Salt
Ground pepper
Fresh lemon juice from ½ lemon
Smoked or regular paprika, *lightly sprinkled (optional)*

Preheat oven to 450°F (230°C).

Toss cauliflower with oil and season with salt and pepper to taste. Spread into a single layer on a baking sheet and roast until browned (about 25 minutes), stirring occasionally. If desired, after removing from the oven, cover lightly with lemon juice and/or paprika.

Steamed Cauliflower

1 cauliflower, *cut off florets to steam or cut whole head into slabs*
Salt, *to taste (optional)*
Freshly ground pepper, *to taste*
2 tablespoons fresh parsley, *chopped*

Steam cauliflower until tender when pierced with a knife, about 5-8 minutes. Toss with salt, pepper and parsley.

Cauliflower with Curry Butter & Rice

1 steamed cauliflower
2 tablespoons oil or vegan butter
1 teaspoon curry powder
Juice of one lime
2 tablespoons fresh chives, *chopped*
2 tablespoons fresh cilantro or parsley, *chopped*
1 cup cashews, *roasted, chopped*

In large skillet mix all ingredients together, except cauliflower and cashews, over medium heat. Add in steamed cauliflower and toss until well coated. Transfer to a serving bowl and top with cashews. Serve over brown rice.

Whole Roasted Garlic

A garlic-lover's treat. The roasting brings out the sweetness of the garlic and is wonderful squeezed on a thick slice of hot bread or a baked potato. Whole roasted garlic can also add a deeper flavor to vegetable or pasta dishes.

1 head garlic, *per person*

Preheat oven to 375°F (190°C).

Begin by removing all but the last layer of skins on the garlic. Set garlic upright in baking pan and add 4 tablespoons of water. Cover tightly with foil and bake 25-30 minutes. Then remove foil and bake 30 minutes more until garlic is soft inside. Test by squeezing one of the cloves for softness.

Remove garlic from the oven. Serve one whole head per person with a slice of hot bread.

Hint:
Buy heads of garlic that are firm and not soft or shriveled.

Simple Green Beans

2 pounds (6 cups) fresh green beans, *whole or broken in half with tips removed*
4 cups vegetable broth
½ cup onion, *finely chopped*
Salt and pepper, *to taste*

Place beans in large pot with vegetable broth, water and onions. Bring to a hard boil for about 5 minutes and then lower heat. Add salt and pepper to taste. When beans are close to having the crispness you prefer, cover and turn off heat. Heat back up right before serving. Serves 4 to 6.

Hint:
Everyone has a different preference on how they like their green beans so you have to decide if you want to cook them more or less than the recipe. Just don't overcook because you will lose all of the flavor and crunch of a fresh bean.

Garlic Green Beans with Almonds & Mushrooms

- 2 pounds (6 cups) fresh green beans, *whole or broken in half with tips removed*
- 4 cups vegetable stock
- 1 tablespoon oil or ¼ cup vegetable broth
- 2 shallots, *finely minced*
- 1 cup mushrooms, *sliced*
- 1½ garlic cloves, *minced*
- ½ teaspoon salt
- Freshly ground pepper
- Almonds, *sliced or chopped and toasted*
- 1 tablespoon fresh parsley, *chopped*

Place beans in large pot with vegetable broth. Bring to boil and cook for 5 minutes or until almost cooked. Drain.

Heat up oil or vegetable broth in skillet over medium-high heat. Add shallots, mushrooms and garlic and cook until translucent and beginning to brown. Add green beans with salt and pepper. Cook until you have reached the level of tenderness you prefer. Stir in almonds with parsley and serve.

Hint: One pound of trimmed green beans is approximately equivalent to 3 cups of raw or 2 cups of cooked.

Green Beans with Balsamic Brown Butter

- 1½ pounds (4½ cups) fresh green beans, *whole or broken in half with tips removed*
- ½ cup onion, *finely diced*
- 4 cups vegetable broth
- 2 tablespoons vegan butter
- 1 tablespoon balsamic vinegar
- 1 tablespoon capers
- Salt, *to taste*
- Freshly ground pepper, *to taste*

Over medium-high heat, cook beans and onion in vegetable broth for 5-7 minutes then drain.

Melt butter in small saucepan over medium heat, stirring until golden brown. Remove from heat and stir in vinegar, capers and salt and pepper. Pour over beans and serve.

Green Beans with Easy Caper Sauce

1½ (4½ cups) pounds fresh green beans, *whole or broken in half with tips removed*
4 cups vegetable broth or water
½ cup vegan mayonnaise
1 tablespoon capers
2 tablespoons parsley, *chopped*
1 garlic clove, *finely minced*
½ teaspoon salt
⅛ teaspoon ground pepper

Cook green beans over medium-high heat in vegetable broth for 5-7 minutes. Drain.

Mix vegan mayonnaise, capers, parsley, garlic, salt and pepper together. Taste for seasonings. Toss with green beans and serve.

Sautéed Greens

This is an easy, quick way to cook greens of any kind. Mix collard, chard, spinach, kale, turnip greens, broccoli, bok choy, or zucchini together for a colorful side dish or serve over rice for a full dinner.

½ cup vegetable broth
1 small onion, *diced*
1 jalapeño pepper, *seeded, finely diced*
1-2 cloves garlic, *finely minced*
6 cups greens, *chopped to be about the same size*
2 tablespoons red wine vinegar
2 tablespoons soy sauce
Pinch red pepper flakes
½ teaspoon Deb's Seasoning (page 269)
1 teaspoon salt
Freshly ground pepper

Heat a large nonstick skillet to medium-high. Add vegetable broth with onions, peppers and garlic and cook until tender.

Add greens with red wine vinegar, soy sauce, red pepper flakes, salt, Deb's Seasoning and cook until liquid from the greens is beginning to brown. Taste for salt and add freshly ground pepper. Serve.

Hint:
When buying greens look for brightly colored leaves with stiff stems without brown spots or wilting.

Skillet Chard Greens

The bright red stalks and dark green leaves make chard one of the most beautiful greens. This recipe can also be used to cook any greens or a mix of different ones like collards, kale, dandelion, mustard or turnip.

- 1 or 2 bunches chard, *red or green*
- ½ cup vegetable broth
- ½ cup onion, *finely diced*
- 1-2 garlic cloves, *minced, depending on amount chard used*
- Red pepper flakes, *to taste*
- Salt, *to taste*
- Freshly ground pepper, *to taste*
- Pinch cayenne pepper *(optional)*

Wash greens in a sink filled with fresh water to ensure all sand and dirt is removed. Drain and cut out the lower, thick tough stems off of leaves. Coarsely chop leaves and drop them into a pot of lightly salted boiling water. Cook for 5 minutes for young, tender leaves, 3 minutes longer if using coarse, outer leaves. Strain boiled greens in a colander and squeeze out the excess moisture.

Heat ½ cup vegetable broth with onion and garlic in skillet. Cook for 2 minutes and then add drained chard.

Add red pepper flakes, salt and pepper to taste. For a little more kick, add a dash or two of cayenne pepper.

Hint:
Stems can be saved to use in making a vegetable broth.

Collard Greens

The best green around—full of nutrients! Perfect for soups or pastas.

2 bunches (2 pounds) collard greens
1 onion, *medium, finely chopped*
2 cups vegetable broth
1 teaspoon salt *(or less if desired)*
Freshly ground pepper
1 jalapeño, *finely chopped, or ½ teaspoon red pepper flakes*
2 tablespoons apple cider vinegar
1-2 cloves garlic, *minced (optional)*
Pepper sauce, *(optional)*

Wash greens in a sink filled with fresh water to ensure all sand and dirt is removed. Drain and cut large ribs (larger than ¼") out of the leaves. Roll-up a few leaves at a time and thinly slice creating long ribbons. Then cut each ribbon roll into 2 or 3 lengths.

Place greens in large pot and fill with water about half way up the greens. Bring to boil. Add salt, onions, vegetable broth and jalapeño or pepper flakes. Boil until greens begin to wilt and become tender, about 15 minutes.

Add vinegar, garlic and more salt, if needed. Simmer until desired tenderness is reach. Be sure not to overcook! Add your favorite pepper sauce, such as Tabasco, to taste for more spice.

Sautéed Kale

- 1 bunch kale, *dinosaur is lighter in flavor and tender*
- ½ cup onion, *finely diced*
- 1 teaspoon olive oil or vegetable broth
- 2 cloves garlic, *minced*
- 2 teaspoons apple cider vinegar
- ½ teaspoon salt
- Freshly ground pepper, *to taste*
- ½ teaspoon cumin *(optional)*
- ¼ teaspoon paprika *(optional)*

Wash kale in a sink filled with fresh water to ensure all sand and dirt is removed. Drain and cut out large ribs from leaves. Roll a few leaves together in a long roll and slice into 1" ribbon-like rolls. Then roughly cut ribbon rolls in half.

Heat large skillet to medium heat and add oil or vegetable broth. Add onion and garlic and sauté until light brown and tender. Add kale and cover until tender crisp and still bright green.

Remove cover and add apple cider vinegar, salt, pepper, cumin, and paprika. Toss together and taste for seasonings. Serve.

Steamed Kale

- 1 large bunch of kale, *with large spines removed*
- Juice from one lemon
- 1 teaspoon olive oil *(optional)*
- ½ teaspoon salt
- Freshly ground pepper, *to taste*

Wash kale in a sink filled with fresh water to ensure all sand and dirt is removed. Drain.

Steam kale for 5-10 minutes. Remove and toss with lemon juice or 1 teaspoon of olive oil, salt and pepper to taste.

Top the steamed kale with Walnut or Cashew Dressing (page 252).

Hint:

Kale is an excellent source of Vitamin A, and C and foliate, calcium and potassium.

Kale with Peanut Dressing

1 large bunch kale, *large spines removed*
2 carrots, *peeled, julienned*
3 tablespoons natural peanut butter, *creamy or crunchy*
¼ cup warm water
2 tablespoons soy sauce or tamari
1 tablespoon chili sauce or ketchup
½ teaspoon red pepper flakes
1 teaspoon agave nectar or sugar
2-4 cups brown rice, *cooked*
½ cup green onions, *slivered and chopped for topping*

Wash kale in a sink filled with fresh water to ensure all sand and dirt is removed. Drain. Remove large spines.

Steam kale and carrots for 5 minutes.

While the kale and carrots are cooking, mix peanut butter, water, soy sauce, chili sauce, red pepper flakes, and agave nectar together in small bowl.

Place kale and carrots in a bowl. Pour sauce over and toss. Serve over brown rice and top with green onions.

Hints:

◊ Buy natural peanut butter without added sugar and salt.
◊ Julienne means simply cutting vegetables into matchstick like shapes.

Kale, Zucchini & Tomatoes

1 tablespoon oil or ¼ cup vegetable broth, *for sautéing*
4 cups kale, *washed, chopped*
1 cup shallots or leeks, *chopped*
1 jalapeño, *seeded, diced*
2 large tomatoes, *roughly chopped*
2 small zucchini, *sliced*
½ teaspoon salt
Freshly ground pepper, *to taste*
Pepper sauce, *to taste*

In large skillet, sauté kale, shallots, and jalapeño over medium heat with oil or vegetable broth for about 3 minutes or until tender. Add tomatoes, cover and lower heat and simmer for 8 minutes.

Add zucchini, salt and pepper and cook uncovered about 5 more minutes.

Taste for salt and pepper and add a couple of dashes of pepper sauce if using.

Sautéed Mushrooms

- 1 pound (20-25 medium-sized) mushrooms, *wiped clean with wet paper towel (do not wash in water)*
- 1 tablespoon olive oil or ¼ cup vegetable broth
- 1 large garlic clove, *minced*
- ½ teaspoon salt
- Freshly ground pepper, *to taste*
- ½ lemon juice
- 2 tablespoons fresh parsley, *chopped*

Cut mushrooms into halves, quarters or slices. Add broth or olive oil to a wide skillet over medium heat. Add mushrooms and stir thoroughly so they can pick up the liquid. Keep sautéing even though the pan seems dry.

Once the mushrooms begin to release their juices they will begin to brown. When golden in color, add garlic, and season with salt and pepper. Cook 3 more minutes then remove skillet from heat and add a squeeze of lemon, and chopped parsley. Serve.

Hints:

- ◊ Mushrooms are porous and will toughen when washed in water. It is best to wipe with a damp cloth or paper towel to remove dirt.
- ◊ Do not salt mushrooms until they have cooked if you want them golden brown. Salting the mushrooms before they are cooked causes them to release their juices which will prevent browning.

Mushroom Stir-Fry

A quick and savory mushroom dish. Try over rice or pasta.

2 teaspoons canola oil
½ pound mushrooms, *sliced (Shitake are good but any will do)*
1 jalapeño or Serrano pepper, *seeded, diced*
2 cloves garlic, *minced*
1 tablespoon soy sauce or tamari
Salt and freshly ground pepper, *to taste*
Sesame seeds, *toasted*

Heat skillet over medium-high heat. When hot, add oil then mushrooms and stir-fry for one minute. Add jalapeño, garlic and soy sauce. Cook for 2 more minutes. Check for seasonings and sprinkle with sesame seeds. Serve warm or at room temperature.

Stuffed Portobello Mushrooms

Portobello mushrooms have a meaty, rich, earthy flavor which can carry a meal on its own.

1 tablespoon oil or ½ cup vegetable broth
2 shallots, *diced*
1 leek, *chopped*
2-3 cloves garlic, *minced*
3-4 medium zucchini, *cubed*
½ teaspoon thyme
2 tablespoons fresh parsley, *chopped*
1 tablespoon oil
½ teaspoon salt
Freshly ground pepper
6 Portobello mushrooms
½ cup breadcrumbs
1 tablespoon vegan butter, *melted*

Preheat oven to broil.

In nonstick skillet, heat broth or oil and cook shallots, leeks and garlic until tender about 3 minutes. Mix in zucchini, thyme, and parsley and cook another 4 minutes. Add salt and pepper and remove from heat.

Cut off stems from mushrooms, scrape out the gills and wipe down with a cloth or paper towel. Brush mushrooms with oil and sprinkle a little salt inside the mushroom top. Broil mushrooms 3-4 inches from heat for 4 minutes each side. Remove and fill with zucchini mixture.

Toss breadcrumbs with 1 tablespoon of melted vegan butter and sprinkle on top of mushrooms. Broil mushrooms 2 minutes more to brown the topping.

Hints:
- To remove the gills from portobello mushrooms, hold mushroom cap in your palm and use a spoon to scrape away the gills from the underside.
- Couscous makes a great stuffing for Portobello mushrooms because it is so moist.

Okra Cakes

This is a great way to have fried okra without all the oil. This makes a thin crispy, cornmeal cake. Your family won't be able to get enough of these!

- 1 tablespoon canola oil or cooking spray
- 1½ cups all-purpose cornmeal
- ½ cup medium or coarse ground cornmeal
- 1½-2 cups unsweetened almond or rice milk
- 1 teaspoon Deb's Seasoning (page 269)
- ½ teaspoon salt
- ¼ teaspoon pepper
- 1 cup okra, *thinly sliced into rounds. Okra needs to be sliced thin so it will cook quickly.*
- ½ teaspoon sea salt

Preheat oven to 250°F (120°C) to warm okra cakes.

Heat non-stick griddle to medium-high heat. Mix together regular and coarse cornmeal, milk, seasoning, salt and pepper. Let batter sit for a few minutes. The batter should not be too thick, so add more milk or water if needed. Stir in okra.

Reduce heat to medium and add a little oil or cooking spray to griddle. Using a tablespoon, spoon batter onto griddle. Do not flip until batter begins to form bubbles and you feel that they are golden brown. Flip to other side.

When cakes are golden brown on both sides, remove and place on a sheet pan. Place in warm oven, until you have finished cooking all of the batter. Sprinkle with sea salt.

Variation:

Other seasonings can be added: finely minced jalapeños, pepper sauce, and finely chopped onion. Be creative.

Hint:

When buying okra look for small pods 2-3 inches long; they are more tender than the large ones. Avoid dull, dry or wilted looking pods; they should snap when broken in half.

Roasted Red Bell Pepper

4 red bell peppers

Preheat broiler

Cut peppers into quarter wedges and place on a broiler pan with shiny side up. Place pan 3"–4" under broiler for about 8 minutes or until the skin of the peppers is blistered and black in places. Remove pan from oven.

Cover peppers with foil until they are cool enough to handle without burning your fingers, approximately 10-15 minutes. Peel off skins and remove stems and seeds. Cut each pepper quarter into small lengthwise strips.

Roasted red bell peppers can be stored in the refrigerator for several days for use in stir-fry dishes, on wraps, in Red Pepper Hummus (page 87), over pastas and in sauces. Chop them up for use in salads.

Stuffed Red Bell Peppers

When you have leftover rice or grains from recipes like Spinach Rice or Easy Spanish Rice, they can work great to create another dish for the next meal.

1-2 bell peppers cut in half, *seeds and membranes removed*
Leftover Spinach Rice (page 181) or Easy Spanish Rice (page 180)
Salsa, *jarred*
Breadcrumbs
1 tablespoon nutritional yeast
1 tablespoon fresh parsley, *chopped*

Preheat oven to 400°F (205°C). Lightly oil the baking pan that will be used.

Place peppers in pan. Fill each halve with 2-3 tablespoons of your favorite salsa. Then fill with the leftover rice mixture. Mix breadcrumbs with nutritional yeast and parsley and cover the tops of the peppers. Loosely cover pan with foil and cook for 30 minutes. Uncover and continue cooking for 10-15 more minutes or until top is golden brown. Remove and let rest for 10 minutes and then serve.

Sautéed Peppers

This is a great dish to serve with rice, baked potatoes or any grains. It is also good used on sandwiches or tacos.

1 tablespoon olive oil or ¼ cup vegetable broth
1-2 bell peppers, *any color, thinly sliced*
1-2 jalapeño or Serrano peppers
1 onion, *thinly sliced*
1-2 cloves garlic, *minced*
1 cup mushrooms, *sliced*
½ teaspoon salt
Freshly ground pepper, *to taste*

In large skillet, heat oil or vegetable broth on medium-high heat. Add pepper, onion, and garlic and toss until tender and beginning to brown. Then add mushrooms, salt and pepper. Remove from heat and serve.

Hint:

Serrano chiles are usually much hotter than jalapeños. Jalapeños are now bred to be milder in flavor.

Sautéed Spinach

This is an easy way to serve spinach. Please note that it should be the last step before you serve your meal. Plan on having all the ingredients together so it just takes 5 minutes.

1½ pounds fresh, baby spinach leaves
    (or 9 cups of leaves)
1 tablespoons olive oil
1 clove garlic, *minced, more if you like lots of garlic flavor*
1 shallot, *finely minced*
½ teaspoon salt
½ teaspoon ground black pepper
Squeeze of fresh lemon juice or a splash of red wine vinegar
Pinch of red pepper flakes

Rinse off spinach and place in a salad spinner, removing most of the water on leaves.

In a large saucepan that has a cover, heat olive oil and sauté shallot with garlic for about 1-2 minutes. Add spinach, salt, and pepper and cover for 2 minutes. Remove cover and cook until most spinach leaves have wilted. You want spinach to be tender crisp so do not overcook.

Remove with a slotted spoon to a serving bowl and mix with lemon juice or vinegar, red pepper flakes, and taste for salt and pepper. Serve.

Hint:

Remember that fresh spinach cooks down so plan on more if you have more people to serve. 1½ pounds cooks down to approximately 4 cups.

Baked Acorn or Butternut Squash *with Kale*

2 small acorn squash or 1 butternut squash, *halved, seeded*
1 bunch kale, *coarsely chopped*
Dressing
2 tablespoons olive oil
2 tablespoons white wine vinegar
1 shallot, *finely minced*
⅛ teaspoon salt
Freshly ground pepper, *to taste*

Preheat oven to 425°F (220°C). Prepare baking pan with cooking spray.

Cut squashes in half lengthwise and remove seeds and membrane. Sprinkle inside cavity with salt then place on a baking pan cut side down. Bake until tender, about 20-30 minutes. Test tenderness by piercing middle with a fork or paring knife.

Remove from oven and add kale to pan with squash and bake for 10-15 more minutes.

Make dressing in a blender by mixing olive oil, vinegar, shallot with salt and pepper until creamy. Remove squash and kale from oven. Cut squash into small chunks and peel. Then toss squash and kale with 2 tablespoons of dressing until lightly coated. Serve.

Hint:
The heavier squashes for their size tend to have more edible flesh inside.

Stuffed Acorn Squash

Great for the holidays! Small squashes make individual servings, but larger ones can be sliced smaller right before serving. This recipe is for stuffing four halves.

- 2 acorn squash, *halved lengthwise, seeds and membrane removed*
- 3-4 cups brown rice, *cooked*
- ½ cup onion, *finely diced*
- 6 green onions, *chopped*
- ¼ cup pecans or walnuts, *chopped*
- ¼ cup dried currants
- ¼ cup red bell pepper, *finely diced*
- ½ cup Arugula or kale
- 1 tablespoon vegan Worcestershire sauce
- Red pepper flakes
- 2 tablespoons fresh parsley, *chopped*
- ½ teaspoon salt
- ¼ teaspoon ground pepper
- Vegetable broth or water to moisten the mixture, *if needed*
- Breadcrumbs for top *(optional)*
- 1 tablespoon vegan butter *(optional)*

Preheat oven to 375°F (190°C).

Place squash halves, cut side down on a baking pan (it might take two pans). Bake for 30 minutes or until tender when pierced with a paring knife.

Remove from oven. Using a tablespoon gently scrape out part of the inside flesh of the squash, leaving enough so the squash will hold its shape. Add a light sprinkle of salt and pepper to the inside of the squash shell. Chop excess flesh for use in the stuffing.

Mix rice with onions, green onions, nuts, currants, bell pepper, arugula, chopped flesh from squash. Stir Worcestershire sauce, red pepper flakes, parsley, salt and ground pepper into the mixture. Use vegetable broth or water to keep the stuffing moist, if needed. Take rice mixture and press into halves of squashes, mounding it up on top.

At this point you can add breadcrumbs to the top with a little vegan butter mixed in for extra richness; however, you may prefer to save those calories for some pie!

Cover pans with foil and bake until squash flesh is tender. This takes about 30 minutes, depending on the size of your squashes. You can take off the foil at the end to brown the top. Remove from oven and let rest before serving.

Leftover rice can be used the next day as a side.

Hint:

Before halving squash, slice a small, thin sliver of a piece off of each side. This creates a flat surface for the squash to sit on the baking pan. Be careful not to cut too thick a slice or your squash will fall apart.

Baked Butternut Squash

Surprisingly simple and tasty! Baking brings out the depth of flavor in the squash.

1 butternut squash, *halved lengthwise and seeded*
2 tablespoons vegan butter
1 teaspoon salt
2 fresh sprigs thyme

Preheat oven to 350°F (175°C). Oil or use cooking spray on baking pan.

Cut butternut squash in half and clean out the seeds and membrane. Place squash cut side up, in pan. Spread 1 tablespoon of vegan butter over each squash half. Sprinkle with salt and top with thyme sprigs. Bake 30-45 minutes or until tender.

Remove from oven and let cool slightly. Slice squash into individual servings or scoop out flesh into bowl. Discard skin and thyme sprigs. Serve.

Hint:
Try to cook your recipes with the least amount of oil or vegan butter that is possible.

Stuffed Yellow Squash

2 large yellow squash or zucchini
2 teaspoons canola oil or vegetable broth
½ cup red bell pepper, *finely chopped*
¼ cup onions, *finely chopped*
1 garlic clove, *minced*
⅓ cup corn, *fresh or frozen*
¼ cup breadcrumbs
2 teaspoons fresh parsley or 1 teaspoon dried
¼ teaspoon dill, *dried (optional)*
½ teaspoon salt
Freshly ground pepper, *to taste*
4 tablespoons of breadcrumbs *(for topping)*
1-2 tablespoons of vegan butter *(for topping)*

Preheat oven to 350°F (175°C).

Cut squash in half lengthwise and scoop out the center, leaving shells ½" thick. Finely chop center flesh.

In skillet, heat oil or broth over medium-high heat. Add chopped squash, bell peppers, onions, and garlic; cook until softened about 3 minutes. Stir in corn, breadcrumbs, parsley, dill (if using), salt and pepper.

Fill each half of squash with filling. Place on baking sheet and cover with foil. Bake 20 minutes until squash shells are tender. At this point squash can be served but if you would like more of a browned top, you can uncover and mix a little vegan butter with breadcrumbs and sprinkle on top. Place under broiler until golden brown. Watch closely so they don't burn!

Hint:

The flat-leaf parsley has more flavor than the curly variety. When parsley is dried it tastes grassy so try to use fresh as much as possible. Herbs are easy to grow in your kitchen or in an outside pot or flower bed.

Squash Casserole

¼ teaspoon garlic powder or fresh garlic, *minced*
½ teaspoon black pepper
A sprinkle Deb's Seasoning (page 269)
½ teaspoon salt
1 container plain soy yogurt
6 cups chopped yellow squash, zucchini or a mix
½ cup shallots, *diced*
½ cup chopped green onions
1 cup breadcrumbs or cracker crumbs
1 tablespoon fresh parsley or chives

Preheat oven to 375°F (190°C). Lightly spray casserole dish.

Combine garlic powder, black pepper, seasoning and salt with yogurt. In large bowl toss yogurt mixture with squash, shallots and green onions. Pour into casserole dish and top with breadcrumbs mixed with parsley or chives.

Bake uncovered for 30-45 minutes or until golden brown on top and bubbling.

Hint:

To make fresh breadcrumbs, cut away crusts of coarse textured bread. Crumble the bread into a food processor and pulse to the desired consistency. For dried crumbs, dry fresh crumbs in an oven set on 200°F (95°C) for about 30-45 minutes.

Boiled Yellow Squash

This is how my mom always loved to fix summer squash. Simple and fast!

4-5 yellow squash
½ cup onion, *diced*
1 tablespoons vegan butter
1 tablespoon parsley or fresh chives, *chopped*
½ teaspoon salt
Freshly ground pepper, *to taste*

Cut squash into rounds. Put rounds and onions in saucepan and fill up halfway up the squash with water. Add a sprinkle of salt. Bring to a boil for 3-5 minutes. Add butter and cover. Lower the heat to simmer for 8-10 minutes. Turn off heat and add parsley or chives, taste for salt and pepper. Let flavors blend together for at least 10 minutes. Serve.

Sautéed Yellow Squash with Onions

This can be made with zucchini or a mix of the two squashes.

4-5 medium yellow squash
1 tablespoon vegan butter or olive oil
10 green onions, *chopped, white and green parts*
½ teaspoon Deb's Seasoning (page 269)
Chopped parsley, *for color*
½ teaspoon salt
Freshly ground pepper, *to taste*

Halve the squash lengthwise or cut into rounds. Heat oil in skillet; add squash, and sauté over medium-high heat until lightly colored around the edges, about 3-4 minutes.

Add green onions and a couple of spoonfuls of water. Lower heat and cover. Cook until squash is tender, about 6 minutes. Add parsley and salt and pepper to taste.

Steamed Summer Squash

4-5 medium yellow squash, *washed*
Salt, *to taste*
Freshly ground pepper
2 tablespoons fresh chives, *finely chopped*

Slice squash into chunks or rounds. Steam until tender, 5-8 minutes, depending on size and amount. Toss with optional salt, pepper and fresh chives.

> **Hint:**
> Yellow squash is very delicate and tender and needs very little cooking.

Garden Bake

You can experiment with an endless variety of vegetables for this dish.

2 tablespoons oil or ½ cup vegetable broth
1 medium onion, *diced*
1 bell pepper, *any color, diced*
1-2 tablespoons jalapeño, *finely diced*
1 clove garlic, *minced*
2 cups yellow squash, *thinly sliced*
2 cups fresh or frozen corn
2 tomatoes, *diced or cherry tomatoes, halved*
Handful collards, spinach, kale, *chopped*
1 tablespoons vegan Worcestershire sauce
1 teaspoon Deb's Seasoning (page 269)
1 tablespoon ground flaxseeds *(optional)*
1 teaspoon salt
Freshly ground pepper
2 tablespoons fresh parsley, *chopped*
⅓ cup water or vegetable broth
½-1 cup breadcrumbs
⅓ cup nutritional yeast
2 tablespoons vegan butter
1 tablespoon parsley, *finely chopped*

Preheat oven to 375°F (190°C).

In large skillet, add oil or vegetable broth and sauté diced onion, bell pepper, jalapeño, and garlic. Add squash, corn, tomatoes, collard greens, Worcestershire sauce and seasoning. Add flaxseed, salt and pepper to taste and parsley. Mix together with water or vegetable broth and pour into a casserole dish.

Bake covered for 20 minutes. In a separate bowl, mix breadcrumbs, nutritional yeast, butter and parsley. Remove the cover and add the breadcrumb topping to the casserole dish. Return dish to oven and bake for 20 minutes or until top is golden brown. Remove from oven and let flavors blend together for 10 minutes before serving.

Steamed Julienne Vegetable Medley

So easy and colorful! At the very least, easy after the vegetables are julienned. Serve over rice or quinoa or as aside.

- 4 medium zucchini, *unpeeled, cut in ¼" julienne strips*
- 4 medium carrots, *peeled and cut into ¼" julienne strips*
- 2 medium yellow squash, *cut into ¼" julienne strips*
- ¼ cup onion, *finely diced*
- 1 tablespoon vegan butter, *room temperature (optional)*
- Salt and pepper, *to taste*
- ½ teaspoon Deb's Seasoning (page 269)

Steam vegetables until tender crisp about 5 minutes. Toss with seasoning and vegan butter, if using. Easy.

Hint:

Julienne strips are simply cutting vegetables into matchstick like shapes. It does take time to do but practice helps you develop a faster technique.

Steamed Vegetables with Spicy Soy Sauce

This is a great way to spice up steamed vegetables. You can do any vegetable combination you like.

- 1 pound broccoli, *florets*
- 1 red bell pepper, *seeded, chopped into bite-sized pieces*
- 2 zucchini, *sliced*

Steam vegetables for 5 minutes. If you have too many for your steamer just cook in two batches. Use spicy soy sauce as a dip or lightly drizzle over steamed vegetables. Serve.

Spicy Soy Sauce

- ½ cup soy sauce or Tamari
- 1 clove garlic, *minced*
- 1-2 teaspoons chili paste, *depending on heat wanted*
- 1 teaspoon rice vinegar

Mix sauce ingredients together.

Roasted Vegetables

When planning a meal for a group, don't forget the ease of roasting vegetables. They make a savory centerpiece for a simple supper or to a holiday meal. Add an Arugula Salad (page 26), beans, Caramelized Onion Gravy (page 251) or Mushroom Gravy (page 253) to top it off.

3 large red potatoes, *not peeled*
2 large carrots, *peeled*
10 medium white mushrooms, *halved*
3 cups broccoli florets
1 medium onion, *½" sliced*
6 cloves garlic, *whole unpeeled*
1 red bell pepper, *seeded and sliced*
2 jalapeños, *seeded and chopped*
2 tablespoons olive oil
2 teaspoons Deb's Seasoning (page 269)
1 teaspoon salt
Freshly ground pepper, *to taste*
Fresh herbs like parsley, chives or thyme, *finely chopped*

Preheat oven to 400.

Cut vegetables in 2-3" pieces for even cooking. In a large bowl, toss all vegetables with olive oil, seasoning, salt and pepper to taste. Place on a baking sheet pan in a single layer. The pan can be covered with parchment paper for an easy clean-up. Use two pans if vegetables are crowded.

Cook uncovered for 30-45 minutes. Turn vegetables a couple of times with a spatula while cooking until thicker vegetables, like the potatoes and carrots, are tender. If other vegetables seem to be done beforehand, just remove those and set aside.

Remove from oven when done. Remove the cloves of garlic and snip off the end and squeeze the roasted garlic on top of the vegetables. Sprinkle in the fresh herbs, if using. Lightly toss vegetables. Then check for seasoning before serving.

Hint:

Avoid turning vegetables that are roasting too often, or they will collapse and lose their shape and become saucy.

Variation: Roasted Root Vegetables

Follow the same recipe for the Roasted Vegetables except use root vegetables, and add a ½ teaspoon of chili powder when the chives and parsley are added.

Parsnips, *peel*
Turnips, *peel*
Potatoes, *peel*
Carrots, *peel*
Beets, *peel*
4 whole garlic cloves, *peel after cooked*

Variation: Roasted Vegetables with Chickpeas

A colorful mix of vegetables with a sweet and spicy flavor combination.

Carrots, *peel*
Sweet potatoes, *peel*
Red or russet potatoes, *peel*
2 tablespoons oil or vegetable broth
4 cloves garlic, *minced*
Salt and pepper, *to taste*
1 (16 oz) can chickpeas, *drained*
½ teaspoon red pepper flakes, *for spice*

Cut carrots, sweet potatoes and red potatoes into bite-sized pieces for even roasting. Toss with oil or vegetable broth, garlic and salt and pepper. Place vegetables in a single layer on a baking sheet pan. Bake for 30-40 minutes until tender. Do not overcook. During the last 15 minutes of cooking, toss chickpeas and red pepper flakes into vegetable mixture.

Remove and add salt and pepper if desired. Serve over rice or toss in with pasta.

Zucchini Cakes

Serve these with a side of pasta and marinara sauce. Zucchini cakes may also be served with a salad for a lighter meal. This recipe contains capers and pine nuts but can easily be altered for Southwestern flavors by adding ¼ cup of corn, ¼ teaspoon of chili powder and one seeded and diced jalapeño.

- 5 cups zucchini, *coarsely grated (about 4 zucchini)*
- ½ cup tofu, *silken*
- 1 clove garlic, *minced*
- 1 jalapeño, *seeded, finely diced*
- 3 tablespoons parsley, *chopped*
- 3 tablespoons chives, *chopped*
- ½ teaspoon marjoram or your favorite seasoning
- Zest 1 lemon
- 1 cup breadcrumbs
- ¼ cup capers, *drained*
- ½ cup pine nuts, *toasted in a dry skillet, chopped*
- ½ teaspoon salt
- Fresh ground pepper, *to taste*
- Oil or cooking spray, *for cooking*

Preheat oven for warming to 250°F (120°C).

After grating, squeeze excess moisture out of the grated zucchini. Toss zucchini with tofu, garlic, jalapeño, parsley, chives, marjoram and lemon zest. Add breadcrumbs, capers, pine nuts, salt and pepper to form a batter.

Heat a non-stick griddle or non-stick skillet to medium heat and add a very thin coat of oil or cooking spray. When hot, add a large tablespoon of the zucchini batter. Cook mixture on each side about 4 minutes or until golden brown. Keep warm in oven until all are cooked and you are ready to serve.

Zucchini Stir-Fry

Fast, fresh and delicious. Serve over rice or as a side.

2 teaspoons canola oil
2 small zucchini, *thinly sliced*
1 bunch green onions, *chopped*
½ red bell pepper, *cut into strips*
1 clove garlic, *minced*
1 tablespoon soy sauce or Tamari
1 teaspoon black sesame seeds, *toasted*

Heat wok or skillet over medium-high heat. When hot, add oil. Drop slices of zucchini, onions, red bell pepper into hot oil and stir-fry one minute. Add garlic, soy and sesame seeds and cook for one more minute. Do not overcook. Serve hot or room temperature.

Grilled Vegetables

Grilled vegetables are wonderful. You can eat them at room temperature or hot, with a sauce or plain, on a sandwich, pasta, salad, you can save leftovers to add to soups, the choices are endless. So don't forget the pleasure of being outside in the warmer months and cooking dinner out of the kitchen. It's a nice break!'

Serving Suggestions

- Salad (pages 23-58)
- Guacamole (page 258)
- Any of the vinaigrette dressings (pages 56-57)
- Chili Marinade (page 230)
- Tamari Sauce (page 259)
- Hummus Dressing (pages 27)
- Cashew Cream (page 252)
- Nutty Miso Dressing (page 262)
- Ranchero Salsa (page 255)
- Pico de Gallo (page 258)
- Quick Peanut Sauce (page 254)
- Verde Sauce (page 261)
- Spicy Mayo (page 90)
- Fresh lime juice

Hints:

- Use a vegetable grill rack that is a pan with small holes cut out to allow the flames and smoke to touch food. The grill rack helps tender vegetables, veggie burgers and tofu slices hold their shape.
- Grilled vegetables retain their texture if you serve quickly after grilling.
- Leave grill lid up while grilling vegetables for a crisp texture.

Grilled Veggie Kabobs

Children seem to enjoy kabobs, especially these. Change them up with anything you have on hand, such as over brown rice or couscous with a green salad.

Try to cut vegetables all about the same size for even cooking. The number of skewers you will be making will determine the amount of vegetables you will need. One vegetable will usually get you about eight pieces.

Onions or small boiling onions
Zucchini or yellow squash
Mushrooms
Any color bell peppers
Hot peppers can be added for flavor *(optional)*
Cherry tomatoes
Corn on the cob, *cut into 2" pieces*
Fennel bulb
Small red potatoes, *precooked*

Dressing for Kabobs:
Olive oil
White balsamic vinegar or your choice
1 clove garlic, *minced*
Salt and pepper, *to taste*
Grill seasoning *(optional)*
Red pepper flakes *(optional)*

Place cut vegetables on skewers. Mix olive oil, vinegar, garlic salt, pepper, grill seasoning or red flakes together. Brush on vegetable skewers. Cook on grill until tender crisp. Remove from skewers and serve.

Grilled Asparagus

Asparagus with thicker stalks work best, tough ends removed and stalks peeled. Brush with olive oil and salt. Cook slowly, turning often until stalks can be pierced with a knife to check for tenderness.

Grilled Corn

There are two ways to prepare the corn for cooking. It depends on your time. Both are great but the first one is slightly better.

Corn on the cob
1 teaspoon vegan butter or olive oil
Salt and pepper

First way to prepare: Pull back the husks of the corn, leaving the husks attached, and remove the silks. Then soak in water for 20 minutes. Drain. Pull husks back over kernels, twisting them around to stay closed. Grill for 15-20 minutes, pulling back the husks the last few minutes so the corn can lightly brown. Serve with vegan butter or just lime juice plus salt and freshly ground pepper to taste.

Second way to prepare: Remove husks and silks. Brush with melted vegan butter and add salt and pepper to taste. Wrap in foil. Grill 15 minutes, turning often. Remove from grill and remove the foil. Add grill seasoning or a sprinkle of chili powder or squeeze on juice of a lime or eat as is.

Hint:

It is best to buy corn in the husks. Look for green husks with plump corn kernels. When you peel back the husks the silks should look green and a little sticky.

Variations:

- ◊ A seasoning grill mix and slices of lime.
- ◊ Mix pesto with vegan butter and spread on grilled corn on the cob.

Grilled Eggplant

To make sure the eggplant will not taste bitter, slice into rounds and salt and let it sit out for at least 30 minutes before cooking to draw out the juices. Then dry off with paper towels and brush with oil. Grill until you have nice grill marks on each side.

Grilled Garlic

Remove all outside skins except the one closet to cloves. If you like, drizzle with a little olive oil and add salt and pepper. Then wrap in foil. Grill about 30 minutes, turning garlic often. Cloves should be very soft inside when fully cooked. To serve, squeeze a clove on a nice, hearty, hot piece or bread or potatoes. Yummy!

Grilled Leeks

Trim the green top of the leeks down to the light green part and then cut the roots off. Cut the leeks in half lengthwise. Swish back and forth in large bowl of water or sink and then let soak for about 15 minutes to dislodge dirt and sand. Drain and dry with paper towels. Brush with olive oil and salt. Grill on both sides until light grill marks appear.

Grilled Portobello Mushrooms

These are great to make a burger out of or eat them plain. Add different vegetables to the center and have a complete dish.

2 Portobello mushrooms, *stems removed, wiped clean with a wet cloth or paper towel*
2 tablespoons olive oil
2 cloves garlic, *minced*
Fresh parsley, *chopped*
½-1 teaspoon Mexican oregano *(optional)*

Combine olive oil, garlic, parsley and Mexican oregano. Brush over mushrooms. Grill for about 8-10 minutes per side until they are soft to the touch. Slice, add salt and pepper and pour remaining olive oil over.

Grilled Mushrooms on Skewers

Baby Portobello or White Button mushrooms
Olive oil
Lemon juice
Salt

Toss mushrooms in a light coating of olive oil and lemon juice with a little salt. Let flavors marry for 15 minutes. Place on skewers and grill. Add freshly ground pepper when finished.

Grilled Red Bell Peppers

While grilling anyway, it is a great time to roast peppers for future use. Place red bell peppers on grill and char on all sides. Then place peppers in a paper bag or covered bowl. Let steam for at least 10 minutes and cool. Remove charred skin, slice and remove seeds from inside. You can toss with a little olive oil, salt and pepper and store in refrigerator for 2 weeks.

Grilled Okra

When you want a great okra flavor without the fried heaviness, try it grilled.

Wash and remove all the little stickers on the sides of the okra. Pierce 4-5 okra pods with 2 grilling skewers, making a ladder or place in a grilling basket. Brush with oil and sprinkle with salt. Grill on both sides until lightly marked. Sprinkle with your favorite grill seasoning or lemon juice.

Grilled Onions

Peel a large onion and then slice into ½" rounds. Toothpicks can be used to keep the rounds from falling apart. Brush with olive oil and salt and pepper. Grill on both sides until dark grill marks have formed and onion slices are tender, about 8 minutes. Add vegan butter or a splash of your favorite vinegar when you remove from grill.

Grilled Potatoes

Red potatoes work well here since they tend not to fall apart when tender. Steam or boil whole potatoes unpeeled until tender.

Cut steamed or boiled potatoes in half if small or into slices if large. Do not overcook first step. You want the potatoes to be tender but firm and not falling apart. Drain and dry off with paper towels. Brush with canola or olive oil and salt. Grill, both sides, until well marked. Add pepper or add any other favorite seasoning.

Grilled Sweet Potatoes

Cut sweet potatoes in half or in thirds and steam or boil until tender.

Cut steamed or boiled sweet potatoes in ½" slices. Brush with canola or olive oil. Grill for about 8 minutes until marked on both or just one side. Add salt and pepper to taste. Try a pesto served on the side.

Grilled Squash

Slice zucchini or yellow summer squash, lengthwise. Brush each side with olive oil and season with salt. Grill on both sides until browned, turning just once. Do not overcook; you want squash to be tender crisp. Serve with a dab of vegan butter or a mixture of lemon juice and fresh chopped parsley.

Grilled Vegetables with Sesame Marinade

Vegetables marinated in Sesame Soy Seasoning adds a different twist to a outdoor party. Delicious!

Sesame Grilling Marinade
3 cups Red potatoes, *halved or quartered depending on size, parboiled*
1½ cups pearl onions, *peeled*
1 yellow squash, *cut into bite-sized pieces*
2 cups small button mushrooms
1 red bell pepper, *cut into bite-sized pieces*
1 pound firm tofu, *drained, pressed and cut into cubes (optional)*
Bamboo skewers

Begin by creating marinade.

Place potatoes in a saucepan of water and bring to a boil for 2-3 minutes until they are beginning to become tender but not fully cooked. Drain and set aside.

Place all vegetables and tofu in bag with marinade. Refrigerate for one hour.

Soak bamboo skewers in water so they will not burn on the grill.

Thread vegetables and tofu on bamboo skewers. Save leftover marinade. Grill, inside or out, turning often until brown. Serve over rice. Leftover marinade can be used to lightly drizzle across top of plate if needed.

Sesame Grilling Marinade

1 cup soy sauce or Tamari
2 tablespoons agave nectar
1 tablespoon rice vinegar
1 teaspoon garlic powder
1 teaspoon sesame oil
½ teaspoon cayenne pepper

Mix ingredients in a large plastic bag or container.

Vegetable Packets for the Grill

Vegetables grilled together with a little butter, olive oil or dry white wine, topped with fresh herbs and allowed to steam in their own juices taste wonderful. Just cut the vegetables into similarly sized pieces and wrap in heavy duty foil lined with parchment paper. Easy and no clean up! You can make a large combination packet or individual packets. Open up the foil packet and lay vegetables over rice, pasta or any favorite grain and you have a delicious meal. Be creative in building your combinations.

To make a packet just take a piece of foil large enough to hold the vegetables with their juices. Place a piece of parchment paper on top of heavy-duty foil or 2 pieces of regular foil. Add the vegetables to the center with the seasonings. Fold long edges up 3-4 times over the vegetables, then fold up the short ends 3-4 times to seal. It should end up being a sealed packet so the vegetables can steam and cook in a short time. Grill for 20 minutes on a closed grill. The packets will hold heat for 20 minutes after removed from the grill. Serve hot.

Spring Combo Packet

- 3 cups diced red potatoes, *pre-boiled for 5 minutes and drained*
- ½ onion, *chopped*
- 3 thin slices of fennel bulb
- 8 white mushrooms, *halved*
- 1 small carrot, *diced*
- 1 sprig of thyme or parsley
- Dabs of vegan butter *(optional)*
- ½ teaspoon salt
- Freshly ground pepper, *to taste*

To add a depth of flavor, when pre-boiling the potatoes, add a ½ teaspoon of salt to the cooking water. This is an optional step for all who are watching their salt intake.

Summer Combo Packet

2 cups green beans, *whole or sliced*
8 small red potatoes, *halved, pre-boiled for 5 minutes and drained*
6 mini size carrots, *whole or sliced*
4 pearl onions, *peeled and whole*
Slices of sweet or hot peppers
1 clove garlic, *minced*
1 tablespoon fresh chives, *chopped*
½ teaspoon salt
Freshly ground pepper
Splash of dry white wine *(optional)*

Green Combo Packet

This just takes 10-15 to cook.

10 white mushrooms, *halved or quartered*
8 cups fresh baby spinach
1 clove garlic, *minced*
1 bunch green onions, *chopped*
½ teaspoon red pepper flakes
½ teaspoon salt
Freshly ground pepper
A couple drops of olive oil or toasted sesame oil *(optional)*

Chapter Five

Corn, Potatoes, Rice and Grains

- To always have garlic available try this tip. Peel and then mince 10-12 cloves of garlic in a food processor. Then shape garlic into a log. Wrap with wax paper or plastic wrap, then foil. Put in freezer. When you need a bit, cut off a piece of the log and then put garlic back in freezer.

- Store potatoes in a dark place in your kitchen. When stored in light, they will turn bitter and green in color.

- Red potatoes are low-starch, firm fleshed and slightly sweet. They hold together well and keep their shape.

- To keep herbs, pack an ice cube tray half full with a finely chopped fresh herb, then fill with water and freeze. Then just drop cube directly into soups or sauces when needed.

Corn Cakes

These may disappear before you can get them to the table. Makes a great little appetizer, a side for any vegetable or to top a salad. I like to serve them with black beans, guacamole and a hot salsa.

½ cup cornmeal
½ cup all-purpose flour
½ teaspoon salt
1 teaspoon baking powder
½ cup silken tofu
½ cup water
1 tablespoon chili sauce or chipotle sauce
2 cups corn, *fresh or frozen*
2 tablespoons parsley or cilantro, *finely chopped*
½ red bell pepper, *finely diced*
¼ cup onion, *finely diced*
1 jalapeño pepper, *finely diced*
1 tablespoon canola oil, *for cooking*
Salsa *(optional)*

Preheat oven to 250°F (120°C).

Place cornmeal, flour, salt and baking powder in food processor and pulse until well mixed. Add tofu, water and chili sauce and pulse until just mixed. Then add corn and parsley or cilantro and pulse a couple of times until the corn kernels are partly chopped. It is okay to have some kernels left whole. You do not want a smooth creamy batter but one with texture.

In a bowl, combine batter with peppers and onions.

Heat a non-stick griddle or non-stick skillet to medium heat and add a little oil. When hot, spoon a large tablespoon of batter onto pan. Cook each side 3-4 minutes until golden and crisp.

Remove from skillet and place on paper towels to remove all excess oil. Lightly salt and place in warm oven until you are ready to serve. Serve with your favorite salsa.

Mom's Creamed Corn

My Mom was famous for this recipe in our family. She would buy a bushel basket of sweet, white corn from a local farmer and spend all day putting it up in 2-cup bags to freeze. What a job! One skillet is work enough. Mom never used milk, only water, because she felt it took away from the corn's sweetness.

- 8-10 ears white corn or yellow, *shucked and cleaned*
- 1-2 tablespoons vegan butter
- ½ cup water
- ½-1 teaspoon salt
- Fresh ground pepper, *to taste*

In a large bowl, place a smaller bowl, turned upside down in the center. Hold a corn cob upright on the smaller bowl. Use a sharp paring knife to shave the tops off of the corn kernels by cutting in a downward motion and letting the kernels fall into the bowl. Using the blade of the paring knife, go over the cob scraping out the milk of the corn. Go around the cob several times to make sure all the milk is out. Pour corn with its milk to a clean bowl, making sure you get all the pulp and milk out of the large bowl. Once the cobs are shaved and milked, you should have about 6 cups of creamed corn.

Heat up a large non-stick skillet to medium-low and add vegan butter. When it is hot, add the creamed corn and water. Stirring often, you want to bring this to an easy boil for about 15 minutes. You want to cook down the sugar in the corn and let it thicken up.

If it begins to thicken too fast just add more water. Taste for salt and pepper.

Mixed Cream Corn

This is marvelous when made with corn cut off the cob, but only a little of the corn flavor is lost when this dish is made with frozen.

- 6-8 ears white or yellow fresh corn, *or 3 cups frozen*
- 1 tablespoons canola oil
- 1 cup onion, *diced*
- ½ cup red bell pepper, *diced*
- 1-2 cloves garlic, *minced*
- ½ cup fresh parsley, *chopped*
- 1 cup dry white wine or water
- ½ teaspoon Deb's Seasoning (page 269)
- Splash or two Tabasco® sauce
- 1 large tomato, *diced*
- ½ teaspoon salt
- Freshly ground pepper, *to taste*

Remove corn from cob, scraping out all of the milk. Set aside.

Heat oil in large skillet. Add onions, pepper, garlic and parsley and cook until tender, 3-4 minutes. Add corn, wine or water, and seasonings. Lower heat and simmer, stirring occasionally, for about 30 minutes.

Add chopped tomato and taste for salt, pepper and seasonings. Serve.

Roasted Corn on the Cob

This can be cooked in the oven or on a grill.

- 8 ears corn, *with husks and silks remove*
- ¼ cup vegan butter *(optional)*
- 2 teaspoons chives, *chopped*
- 2 tablespoons parsley, *chopped*
- Salt
- Pepper

Preheat oven to 400°F (205°C).

Melt vegan butter and mix with chives and parsley. Brush corn with butter mixture and sprinkle with salt and pepper. Another option is to just use the salt, pepper and herbs without the butter. Wrap in foil and cook 30 minutes in the oven or on the grill, turning frequently.

Hint:

Mix pesto with vegan butter as a spread for corn on the cob.

Succotash

You really want to use fresh corn on the cob with this dish to get the corn milk. Frozen just doesn't do the trick.

2 cups frozen baby lima beans
6 ears corn
½ cup onion, *finely diced*
2 tablespoons vegan butter or canola oil
½ teaspoon salt
Freshly ground pepper, *to taste*
Paprika

Cook lima beans in saucepan with water until done. Drain beans but save water.

Remove corn from cob, scraping out and keeping all of the milk. Add corn kernels and corn milk to the saucepan with the vegan butter or oil and ½ teaspoon salt. Cover with the cooking water from the lima beans and cook on low until most of the water is cooked off. This will take 5-10 minutes, however stir occasionally to make sure corn does not stick to bottom of pan.

Add lima beans back and salt and pepper to taste and a sprinkle of paprika.

Baked Stuffed Potatoes

Remember stuffed baked potatoes. They are a great way to use leftovers for toppings. Use steamed or sautéed vegetable mix, beans, collard greens, spinach, salsa (fresh or bottled), salad, sauces or just a mix of fresh herbs. Skip the butter or oil and save the calories. The choices are endless and so easy!

Russet potatoes, *scrubbed*

Preheat oven to 500°F (260°C).

Potatoes can be wrapped in foil or baked without foil. Place potatoes in hot oven and bake until tender when squeezed. This usually takes 40-60 minutes to cook, depending on the size and number of potatoes you are using. Remove from oven and cut in half. Either scoop out part of the potato flesh to be mixed with toppings of choice and your favorite seasonings or just place toppings on top.

Hints:
- Potatoes are also delicious topped with Mushroom Gravy (page 253) or Caramelized Onion Gravy (page 251).
- Mix pesto with vegan butter and spread on top of baked potato.

Rusty's Mashed Potatoes

My husband makes the best-mashed potatoes ever! Mashed potatoes are a comfort food that brings back memories of holiday meals, Sunday lunches, and dinners with the family. Try them with Mushroom Gravy (page 253), Caramelized Onion Gravy (page 251), or add horseradish, sold in jars, for zesty mashed potatoes.

10-12 Yukon Gold or Russet potatoes, *medium-sized*
4 tablespoons vegan butter
1 cup unsweetened almond milk
1 teaspoon salt
½ teaspoon pepper
½-1 cup potato water

Peel potatoes, cut into large chunks all about the same size for even cooking and place in large pot. Add water to cover potatoes and boil until potatoes can be easily pierced with a fork.

Using lid to partially block the top of the pot, slowly pour off most of the thin top water but retain a couple of cups of the thick potato water at the bottom of the pot. Using a mixer, add butter, potatoes, salt and pepper into the large mixer bowl.

Turn on the mixer on a slow speed and gradually add the thick potato water (½-1 cup) from the bottom of the potato pot. Gradually increase mixer speed until potatoes and water are a smooth but thick consistency. Then add almond milk and continue to mix until the potatoes are smooth and creamy. Add more salt or pepper to taste if desired.

Smashed Potatoes

These are inviting for appetizers or dinner. Nice and crispy and best eaten with fingers. Serve with Pico de Gallo (page 258) or any flavor of pesto.

12-16 red potatoes, *small or medium*
2 tablespoons olive oil
1 tablespoon fresh chives, *chopped*
Sea salt, *to taste*
Freshly ground pepper

Preheat oven to 425°F (220°C). Lightly oil a baking sheet pan.

In a large saucepan, over medium heat, boil potatoes for 20 minutes until tender. Drain.

Place on a baking sheet and mash each one with a fork a couple of times. Drizzle each one with a couple of drops of olive oil; add salt, pepper and a sprinkle of chives. Bake for about 25 minutes until golden brown and crisp.

Mushrooms & English Peas Over Mashed Potatoes

This is wonderful served with a salad or it also makes a great side dish. Use Yukon Gold potatoes in this dish. Yukons exhibit a buttery, flaky texture, and they do not require peeling.

4-5 Yukon Gold potatoes
2 cups vegetable broth
1 tablespoon oil or ¼ cup vegetable broth
1½ cups onions, *chopped*
1 garlic clove, *minced*
3 cups mushroom caps and stems, *diced* (any type)
1 cup cooked English peas *(fresh or frozen)*
½ teaspoon salt
Freshly ground pepper
Fresh parsley, *minced*

Leave skins on potatoes and cut up into similar-sized pieces. Place in pot with vegetable broth and added water to cover potatoes and bring to boil. Cook until tender. Pour off 1 cup of the water into a separate bowl to save for later use and drain. Place in a warm bowl, salt to taste and cover until mushroom mixture is done.

In skillet, heat vegetable broth or oil to medium-high heat. Add onions; cook, stirring until they begin to brown, about 5 minutes. During the last couple of minutes add garlic. Add mushrooms and peas; cook about 4 minutes, stirring until softened. If mixture begins to dry out before vegetables are done, add a little of the saved potato water. Salt and pepper to taste. Sprinkle with parsley.

Roughly mash potatoes in pan to desired consistency. Check for seasoning. Place on plate or pasta bowl and pour mushrooms and peas over top. Enjoy.

Hint:
Any leftover potato water can be refrigerated to use in upcoming dishes or soups.

Oven Fries

These crisps, golden potatoes are simple to prepare and work for an appetizer or a side.

- 2 medium baking potatoes, *unpeeled and scrubbed*
- 2 teaspoons canola oil
- Sea salt *(optional)*

Preheat oven to 425°F (220°C).

Cut potatoes into ¼" thick rounds or sticks. Place in a bowl and mix potatoes with oil and salt until completely covered. Place on baking sheet in single layer. Bake 20 minutes or until golden on top. Flip and bake another 10 minutes. Sprinkle with extra sea salt if desired.

Variation:

Add minced garlic, parsley, chives, diced jalapeño peppers or any herbs or seasoning you prefer to the mix.

Cajun Sweet Potato Fries

Cajun spices add a spark to these simple sweet potatoes.

- 1-2 sweet potatoes, *unpeeled but scrubbed, cut into ¼" thick fries*
- 1 tablespoon canola oil
- 2 teaspoons Deb's Seasoning (page 269)
- 1 teaspoon of arrowroot
- Salt, *to taste*

Preheat oven to 425°F (220°C).

Toss sweet potatoes with oil, salt, arrowroot and seasonings. Spread on a baking sheet in a single layer. Bake for 20 minutes then flip to other side and cook 10 minutes more or until fries are browned and crisp. More salt can be added when fries are remove from the oven.

Spicy Potato Casserole

A zesty potato casserole is a great addition to almost any meal. This recipe features a topping that gets perfectly crispy around the edges.

6-8 medium red potatoes, *peeled and sliced into ½ slices*
½ teaspoon salt
⅛ teaspoon pepper
1½ cup corn, *fresh or frozen (if fresh be sure to use the corn milk)*
2 tablespoons onions, *finely minced*
1 can green chiles (4 oz) mild or medium
3 tablespoons chives, *minced*
Vegan butter *(optional)*
2 cups vegetable broth
½ teaspoon Deb's Seasoning (page 269)
2 cups cashew cream (page 252)

Preheat oven to 375°F (190°C). Lightly oil a 9"×13" pan or baking dish. Begin by making the cashew cream.

Arrange potato slices in a single layer on bottom of a baking dish or pan. Lightly sprinkle with salt and pepper. Then add half of the corn, 1 tablespoon of onion, and half of the chiles, and 1 tablespoon of chives. You can dab little pieces of vegan butter around if you like. Starting with sliced potatoes, repeat making another layer. If you have any leftover potatoes use them to top the dish. Pour vegetable broth over top of layers.

Add the Deb's Seasoning to cashew cream and mix well. Then pour the cashew cream over the top of the potatoes.

Bake for about 1 hour uncovered. Check with knife to make sure potatoes are tender. If top becomes brown but potatoes are still not tender, cover with foil until done. Remove from oven and let rest for a few minutes before serving.

Baked Red Potatoes with Onions & Balsamic Vinegar

The onions in this recipe become caramelized while the balsamic vinegar adds a nice tartness to the crispy potatoes.

Small red potatoes, *half larger ones*
2 cloves garlic, *sliced*
1 small onion, *quartered*
1 tablespoon olive oil
White balsamic vinegar or any vinegar choice
Salt and pepper

Preheat oven 400°F (205°C).

Place potatoes, garlic and onions on small baking sheet and lightly toss with oil. Drizzle white balsamic vinegar over top and add salt and pepper to taste.

Bake uncovered until potatoes are tender when pierced. Cook for around 30 minutes or less if potatoes are small.

Variation: Crispy Red Potatoes with Sweet Roasted Garlic

6 red potatoes, *cut into chunks or wedges*
6 cloves of garlic, *unpeeled*
2 teaspoons olive oil
1 tablespoon fresh chives, *sniped*
Garlic salt, *to taste*
Fresh ground pepper

Place potatoes and garlic cloves on small baking sheet. Lightly toss with oil, salt and pepper. Bake uncovered until potatoes are tender when pierced and are golden brown in color around 30–45 minute, depending on size of potatoes. Flip potatoes around with spatula a couple of times during cooking.

Remove from oven when done. Take garlic cloves and clip off one end with kitchen scissors. Squeeze roasted garlic out of each clove onto potatoes. Mix and toss until potatoes are partially covered. Add chives and toss again. Check for salt and pepper and serve hot.

Baked Red Potato Slices

These are great as a side dish or snack; baked potato slices complement salads and sandwiches beautifully. Try the two different versions below for variety. Both are delicious!

4 large red potatoes
Spicy mustard
⅓ cup Dijon mustard
1-2 tablespoons Deb's Seasoning (page 269)
½ teaspoon sea salt

Preheat oven to 400°F (205°C).

Slice potatoes into ½" slices but leave the skin on. Toss mustard and seasoning together in a bowl, and add potato slices to coat.

Add a light coat of cooking spray to baking pan and add potatoes. Bake for 35-40 minutes or until tender and lightly brown. Sprinkle on top sea salt after baking.

Creamy Garlic Potato Slices

A garlicky mayonnaise gives a powerful kick to mild flavored potatoes.

4 large red potatoes
⅓ cup of vegan mayonnaise
1 tablespoon of garlic flakes or fresh minced
½ teaspoon sea salt

Preheat oven to 400°F (205°C).

Slice potatoes into ½" slices but leave the skin on. Toss vegan mayonnaise and garlic together in a bowl and toss potato slices to coat. Place potato slices on sheet pan in single layer. Bake for 35-40 minutes until tender and lightly browned. Sprinkle sea salt on top after taking out of oven.

Red New Potatoes

These are delicious and make great leftovers, so you may want to make extra. Peeling the potatoes just around the center also makes a pretty presentation for a special meal.

6 cups red potatoes
1 tablespoon olive oil
½ cup onion, *diced*
1 clove garlic, *finely minced*
½ teaspoon salt, *(depending on salt included in vegetable broth)*
2 cups vegetable broth
1 teaspoon Deb's Seasoning (page 269)
Dash of freshly ground pepper
1 tablespoon fresh chives
1 tablespoon parsley
Water

Wash potatoes, trim off any dark spots and cut in half.

Heat large skillet to medium heat and add oil and onion. Cook until onions are soft and light brown, then add garlic. Add potatoes and lightly sprinkle with salt. Toss until potatoes begin to stick to the pan. Add vegetable broth and seasonings. Pour in enough water that potatoes are almost completely covered.

Bring pot to a boil and cook until potatoes are tender but not falling apart. Add chives and chopped parsley and taste for salt, pepper and seasonings. Cover and remove from heat. Reheat when ready to serve.

Hints:

◊ Red potatoes are low-starch, firm-fleshed and slightly sweet. They hold together well and keep their shape.
◊ Toss drained boiled potatoes with pesto for a different zesty flavored dish.

Baked Sweet Potato Dinner

Although baked sweet potatoes are perfect plain, you can use any of the following to change them up a bit and give them a little something extra:
- Sautéed red onions, red bell peppers and tofu with an added dash of soy sauce.
- Sautéed Brussels sprouts and shallots, with a sprinkle of pecans and dried red currants.
- Sautéed shallots with shredded kale or arugula with a little peanut butter sauce.
- Grilled tofu with a touch of dark sesame oil.
- Steamed broccoli with drizzle of spicy Thai sauce
- Scoop out flesh of sweet potato and blend with a little orange juice, a pinch of cinnamon and a touch of chili powder.
- Swirl pesto on the top.

1 medium sweet potato per person, *washed and individually wrapped*

Preheat oven to 450°F (230°C).

Bake sweet potatoes until tender to the squeeze usually one hour depending on size. Cut in half and fill with any of the detailed above.

Steamed Sweet Potatoes

2 medium sweet potatoes

Peel each potato and cut into similar-sized pieces. Steam for 30-50 minutes, depending on size of pieces. They are ready when easily pierced with a paring knife. Sweet potatoes are so flavorful they require no seasonings, but any of the suggestions for the Baked Sweet Potatoes above would apply here. Serve warm or room temperature.

Sweet Potato Casserole

A modern twist to the popular sweet potato casserole our grandmothers used to make, you can even add vegan marshmallows to top if you like!

- 4-5 cups sweet potatoes, *boiled and mashed*
- ½ teaspoon salt
- ¼ cup brown sugar or ¼ cup maple syrup
- 1 teaspoon cinnamon
- ⅛ teaspoon nutmeg *(optional)*
- 2 tablespoons vegan butter, *melted*
- ¼ cup unsweetened almond milk or soy creamer

Preheat oven to 350°F (175°C). Lightly oil a casserole dish.

Mix sweet potatoes, salt, sugar, cinnamon, nutmeg and vegan butter together and mix well. Adding a small amount of milk at a time to the sweet potato mixture to smooth it out, make sure the potatoes do not get too soupy. Mixture should be a little stiff. Pour into casserole dish.

With a wooden spoon, mix all topping ingredients together and sprinkle over casserole. Bake, uncovered for 25-30 minutes or until golden brown.

Topping

- ½ cup brown sugar
- 2 tablespoons vegan butter, *melted*
- 2 tablespoons all-purpose flour
- 1 cup pecans or walnuts, *chopped*
- Vegan marshmallows for top *(optional)*

Hint: Choose sweet potatoes that are firm and heavy for their size and free of cracks and soft spots.

Candied Yams

This is a colorful and classic recipe that smells divine. The cinnamon sticks and oranges with the sweet potatoes make an appealing dish. You can cut back on the sugar if you want it to be a little less sweet.

- 2-3 sweet potatoes, *peeled and cut into rounds*
- ¼ cup vegan butter
- 5 tablespoons brown sugar or maple syrup
- 2 cinnamon sticks
- ½ teaspoon nutmeg
- ½ teaspoon salt
- 1 orange, *cut into rounds*

Preheat oven to 350°F (175°C). Prepare casserole dish with cooking spray.

In baking dish, place sweet potato slices, overlapping and slightly upright and covering the dish.

In saucepan, place butter, sugar, cinnamon sticks, nutmeg, and salt. Cook until sugar is dissolved and then add oranges. Pour over sweet potatoes. Cover and place in oven and cook for 30 minutes.

Remove cover and cook for about 20 more minutes until sweet potatoes are tender and tops are golden brown. Remove from oven and let rest for a few minutes before serving.

Hint:

Garnet sweet potatoes are often called "yams." They are dark red to purple in color with a deep orange flesh. They are my favorite to use in pies, cakes or breads.

White & Sweet Potato Casserole

This makes an elegant dish that is great for holidays or when you are serving a large group.

2 russet potatoes, *large*
2 sweet potatoes, *large*
1 teaspoon salt
¼ teaspoon pepper
½ onion, *finely diced*
1 teaspoon Deb's Seasoning (page 269)
2 cups vegetable broth
¼ teaspoon fresh thyme
¼ teaspoon fresh parsley

Preheat oven to 350°F (175°C). Lightly spray a 13"×9" baking dish.

Peel and thinly slice potatoes. Line potato slices up around the inside of the dish. Make any design you like, all white and then all sweet or alternate every 6 slices, mainly fill up dish so potatoes are upright to slightly angled, not flat.

Salt and pepper potatoes. Sprinkle onions and Deb's Seasoning around on top and pour vegetable broth over all. Broth should come about halfway up the side of the dish. Sprinkle fresh thyme and parsley on top.

Bake 45 minutes to an hour until potatoes are cooked through and slightly browned on top. Use a knife or fork to check tenderness. Remove, cover and let rest before serving.

Basic Brown Rice

1 cup brown rice
2 cups water
½ teaspoon salt *(optional)*

Rinse rice well in a colander with water and drain. Bring water to boil and add rice. Cover and lower heat to simmer and cook for 40 minutes. Keep rice covered and don't check on it. Turn off heat and let rice rest for 5 minutes. Fluff and add salt if using.

Basic White Rice

1 cup white rice
1½ cups water
½ teaspoon Salt *(optional)*

Bring water to boil and add rice. Cover and lower heat to simmer. Keep rice covered and don't check on it. Let rice simmer for 20 minutes. Turn off heat and let rest for 5 minutes. Fluff and add salt.

Hot Rice with Fresh Vegetables

This dish is like a warm salad. The warm rice over the crunchy fresh vegetables is delectable. If you do not have bean juice to use in this recipe, you can use the tomatoes to add moisture to the dish.

2 cups brown rice
4 cups water
1 cup bean broth, *preferably from white beans**
3-4 tomatoes, *chopped, with their juice*
1 bunch green onions, *finely chopped*
1 jalapeño pepper, *seeded, finely chopped*
3 celery ribs, *finely diced*
1 carrot, *finely diced*
1 zucchini, *cut into small cubes*
2 artichoke hearts, *jarred, finely diced*
1 small bell pepper, *diced*
2 garlic cloves, *minced*
½ cup parsley
½ basil, *chopped*
2 tablespoons celery leaves, *chopped*
½ teaspoon salt *(optional)*
⅛ teaspoon freshly ground pepper
¼ cup fresh lemon juice

Rinse brown rice and drain. In a medium-size saucepan, bring 4 cups of water to a boil and add rice. Cover, lower heat and simmer for 45 minutes or until liquid has been absorbed. Remove from heat and let set for 5 minutes then fluff with a fork. Cover to keep hot.

While rice is cooking, boil bean broth in small pan until reduced to ⅓ cup. Pour broth into bottom of serving bowl large enough to hold rice and vegetables. Set aside and cool to room temperature.

Add all vegetables and herbs to the bowl with the bean broth. Pour rice over the vegetables, while steaming hot. Toss well and season with salt, pepper and lemon juice.

*Bean broth can be drained off homemade Navy or Great Northern beans or used from canned beans as well.

Hint:

To keep herbs, pack an ice cube tray half full with a finely chopped fresh herb, then fill with water and freeze. Then just drop cube directly into soups or sauces when needed.

Green Rice

A colorful and healthy change to regular rice.

2 cups water
1 cup long grain brown rice
½ teaspoon salt *(use less if vegetable broth contains salt)*
1 clove garlic, *minced*
½ cup arugula or spinach, *baby, chopped*
Dash of freshly ground pepper

In a saucepan, bring water to a boil and add rice. Then add salt and minced garlic. Cover and lower heat to simmer for 45 minutes. Turn off heat and let sit for 5 minutes. Mix in spinach or arugula and pepper and serve.

If using white rice reduce amount of liquid to 1½ cups and cook for 25 minutes.

Try this lemon-flavored rice with roasted or grilled asparagus—wonderful and fresh!

1 cup long grain white rice
1½ cups water
½-1 teaspoons salt *(use less if vegetable broth contains salt)*
1 tablespoon lemon juice
3 teaspoons lemon zest
3 tablespoons fresh parsley, *chopped*
Salt and freshly ground pepper, *to taste*

Place rice in saucepan with water and bring to boil. Cover and lower heat to simmer for 25 minutes. Turn off heat and let sit without opening the lid for five minutes. After letting the rice sit for five minutes, add lemon juice and lemon zest and parsley. Salt and pepper to taste.

If using brown rice add 2 cups of liquid and cook for 45 minutes.

Hints:

- If you feel that the lemons you have are not juicy enough, pop them in the microwave for 10 seconds. It helps them release their juices.
- The key to zesting is not to push into the bitter white part between the skin and the flesh. Just zest the color on the surface of the fruit.

Orzo & White Rice with Fresh Salsa

The addition of a colorful, fresh salsa brightens up this dish. You can use your favorite store-bought variety as an alternative, but you might end up with pink rice.

1 tablespoon canola oil
½ cup orzo
1 cup white rice
2 cups water
½ teaspoon salt

Fresh Salsa
1 jalapeño, seeded, *diced*
1 tomato, *diced*
½ cup red onion, *diced*
Juice from ½-1 lime
Salt to taste

In saucepan, over medium heat add oil and orzo and rice and brown for 4 minutes. Add water and bring to boil. Cover and simmer for 25 minutes or until rice mixture is dry. Set aside for 5 minutes. Fluff with fork.

To make salsa, chop jalapeño, tomato and onion. Mix with lime juice and add salt to taste.

When rice mixture is cooked toss with fresh salsa. Serve.

Rice Pilaf

1 tablespoons canola oil
1 cup white rice*
1½ cups water
½ cup onion, *finely minced*
½ teaspoon salt, *to taste*
½ cup raisins, *soaked in cold water for 10 minutes, drained*
½ cup slivered almonds, *toasted*
Freshly ground pepper
2 tablespoons almonds, *toasted and chopped, for topping*

In a saucepan, sauté the rice and onions in oil until golden brown. Add water and bring to a boil. Cover and over low heat, simmer for 25 minutes. Turn off heat and let rest for 10 minutes.

Combine rice mixture with soaked raisins, salt, pepper and almonds. Taste for seasonings. Put in serving bowl and top with additional almonds.

*For brown rice, use 2 cups of water or broth and cook for 45 minutes.

Fresh Salsa Rice

This is an old recipe that a friend from Mexico gave me years ago. You will love it.

1 tablespoon oil
1 cup white rice*
2 tablespoons onions, *diced*
1 garlic clove, *minced (optional)*
1-1½ cups water
1 jalapeño, *seeded, minced*
1 tablespoon parsley, *chopped*
½ teaspoon salt, *to taste*
1 small tomato, *diced*

Heat saucepan to medium heat and add oil to sauté rice, onion and garlic until lightly browned. Add water and bring to a boil. Add jalapeño, parsley, salt, and tomato. Cover tightly and lower heat to simmer for 25 minutes without lifting the lid. Turn off heat and sit for 5 minutes. Fluff with a fork.

*For brown rice, use 2 cups of water or broth and cook for 45 minutes.

Easy Spanish Rice

This is so quick to throw together and the results are splendidly spicy.

1 tablespoon oil or ¼ cup vegetable broth
1 red bell pepper, *finely chopped*
1 jalapeño pepper, *seeded, finely diced*
¼ cup onion, *diced*
¼ cup celery, *diced*
¼ cup carrots, *diced*
1 cup long grain rice
1 (10 oz) can RO*TEL®, *mild or spicy*
1 cup water
Salt and pepper

In saucepan with oil or vegetable broth, sauté bell pepper, jalapeño pepper, onion, celery and carrots until tender. Add rice and cook until rice is golden brown, stirring frequently.

Add RO*TEL® *(diced tomatoes and green chiles)*, water, salt and pepper to taste. Bring to boil. Cover, reduce heat and simmer for 25 minutes. Do not remove cover. Turn off heat and let rice rest for 5 minutes. Fluff with fork.

If using brown rice use 1½ cup of water and cook for 45 minutes.

If using white rice use 1 cup of water and cook for 25 minutes.

Spinach Rice

An easy meal to create with a truly excellent flavor. Kids even like spinach rice if it is not too spicy with red pepper flakes and jalapeño. Serve with beans of any kind. Keeps well in the refrigerator for leftovers, which can be used to make Stuffed Bell Peppers (page 129) the next night.

- 2 cups raw brown rice
- 1 cup red bell pepper, *finely chopped*
- ¼ cup parsley, *chopped*
- 1 cup green onions and tops, *finely chopped*
- ½ -1 jalapeño pepper, *finely chopped* or 1 Poblano pepper, *finely diced*
- 1 cup spinach, *frozen, thawed, squeeze excess liquid out*
- 1½ tablespoon vegan Worcestershire sauce
- 1 teaspoon salt
- ¼ teaspoon red pepper flakes
- Freshly ground pepper, *to taste*
- 4 cups vegetable broth, *unsalted*

Preheat oven to 375°F (190°C). Lightly oil 2 quart baking dish.

Mix all ingredients together. Bake without stirring in a tightly covered casserole dish for 1 hour, or until rice is not too soupy. Turn off heat and let rice rest for 5 minutes. Remove cover and stir to mix the seasonings that are on the top with the rice. Serve.

Wild & Brown Rice with Corn

- ½ cup wild rice
- ½ cup brown rice
- 1-2 tablespoons canola oil or ¼ cup vegetable broth
- ½ cup shallots, *diced*
- 2¼ cups vegetable broth
- 1-2 teaspoons Deb's Seasoning (page 269)
- 1 cup corn, *fresh or frozen*
- Salt to taste *(Use less if your vegetable broth contains salt)*
- ½ cup parsley, *chopped*
- ½ cup almonds, *toasted and slivered*
- Fresh ground pepper

Preheat oven to 350°F (175°C). Lightly spray baking dish or pan with canola cooking spray.

Wash and drain wild and brown rice. In medium saucepan heat oil or broth to medium and add shallots and cook until tender. Add wild and brown rice, Deb's Seasoning, and salt. Cook for 2-3 minutes then add vegetable broth and bring to boil. Cover saucepan, reduce heat to simmer for 30 minutes.

After 30 minutes, transfer rice mixture to a baking dish or pan. Cover and put in oven for 15 minutes. Remove from oven and make sure mixture has enough broth, if not add more. Add corn, parsley, almonds and pepper. Carefully stir into rice. Put back in the oven, uncovered, for 10-15 more minutes. Taste for seasonings. Serve. This is better served shortly after baking.

Hint:

Shallots have a milder than onion taste. Use them in sauces or when you do not want a sharp onion flavor.

Wild & Brown Rice Casserole

This is a hearty-flavored casserole that really works around the holiday season. Fix this for Thanksgiving dinner, as is, or prepare it for Stuffed Acorn Squash (page 133).

4 cups of wild and brown rice, *combined, cooked (A blend can be purchased or you can combine the two before cooking)*
1 tablespoon vegan butter or ¼ cup vegetable broth
½ cup onions, *diced*
1 clove garlic, *minced*
½ cup red bell pepper, *diced*
1 cup mushrooms, *sliced*
1 (14.5 oz) can of stewed tomatoes
½ cup olives, *sliced (optional)*
½ cup of water
1 teaspoon salt
Freshly ground pepper
½ cups of sliced almonds, *roasted*
Zest of 1 lemon

Preheat oven to 350°F (175°C). Lightly oil casserole dish or pan.

Cook brown and wild rice together per instructions on package.

In skillet add vegan butter or vegetable broth to sauté onions, garlic, red bell pepper, and mushrooms until tender crisp. Put mushroom mixture, wild and brown rice, stewed tomatoes, olives, water, salt and pepper together in casserole dish. Taste for seasonings.

Cover and bake for 35 minutes. Remove from oven and stir and add water or broth if too dry. Remove cover and return to oven for 15 more minutes.

Remove when ready and taste for salt and pepper. Sprinkle almonds and lemon zest over top of casserole. Keep covered until time to serve.

Basic Barley

Barley is a fantastic addition to any table and can easily be used as an alternative to rice or quinoa.

3 cups water
1 cup pearl barley, *rinsed well*
½ teaspoon salt *(optional)*
Freshly ground pepper, *to taste*

Bring water to boil in saucepan. Add ½ teaspoon salt and the barley. Cover and lower heat and simmer until tender 30 minutes. Let stand for 5 minutes before uncovering. Add pepper and salt to taste.

Basic Quinoa

For a satisfying alternative to your rice dishes, try quinoa.

1 cup quinoa, *well rinsed*
2 cups water
Salt and pepper, *to taste (optional)*

Bring water with quinoa to a boil. Cover and reduce heat and simmer for 15 minutes. Let stand for 5 minutes. Add salt and pepper if using.

Variation: Toasted Quinoa

Gives quinoa a delicious roasted flavor. Toast quinoa in a dry skillet before cooking. Then cook as directed in the recipe above.

Basic Couscous

Couscous is not a grain; this delicious recipe is actually based on pasta that is made of semolina. It's a nice change in pace from rice on certain dishes.

1 cup couscous
1 cup water
¼ teaspoon salt *(optional)*

In medium saucepan bring water and salt to a boil. Add couscous, stirring quickly. Cover and remove from heat and let stand of 5 minutes. Fluff with fork before serving.

Hint:

Couscous makes a great stuffing for Stuffed Portobello Mushrooms (page 127) or squashes (pages 132-137) because it is moist.

Quinoa Pilaf

This dish is also great when topped off with Mushroom Gravy (page 253), Caramelized Onion Gravy (page 251) or steamed vegetables. To make it a little sweet, just add the currants.

1 cup quinoa, *rinsed and drained*
1¾ cup water
¼ cup onion, *finely minced*
½ teaspoon salt
Ground pepper, *to taste*
1 teaspoon of fresh chives, *sniped*
1 teaspoon of fresh parsley, *chopped*
¼ cup of green onions, *sliced for topping*
¼ cup currants *(optional)*

Heat a medium saucepan over medium-high heat. Add quinoa and stir until lightly toasted. Add water and onions and bring to boil. Cover, reduce heat to simmer and cook for 15 minutes. Remove from heat and let sit for 10 minutes before taking the top off. Add salt and pepper to taste. Stir in fresh chives, parsley and currants. Top with green onions and serve.

Hint:

Pilaf simply refers to a dish of seasoned rice with vegetables or fruits or nuts added.

Quinoa Sauté

This is excellent hot or cold. Lots of color, textures and spices make this a savory main or side dish.

1 cup quinoa, *rinsed*
2 cups water
1 tablespoon oil, or ¼ cup vegetable broth
½ cup onion, *finely diced*
1 clove garlic, *minced*
1 jalapeño, *seeded, finely diced*
½ cup red pepper, *diced*
1 cup corn, *fresh or frozen*
1 cup black or red beans, *drained and rinsed*
1 teaspoon cumin
1 teaspoon chili powder
1 cup baby arugula, *chopped, or any green*
½ teaspoon salt
¼ teaspoon freshly ground pepper

Bring water to boil and add quinoa. Lower heat to simmer, cover, and cook for 15 minutes then remove from heat for 10 minutes without removing lid. Drain if all liquid has not been absorbed. Set aside.

In a non-stick skillet, heat oil or broth to medium heat. Sauté the onions and garlic until tender. Add jalapeño, red pepper, corn, beans, cumin, and chili powder. To the skillet, stir in the prepared quinoa and the arugula. Taste for salt and add pepper. When all ingredients are heated through remove from heat and serve.

Chapter Six

Pastas and Pasta Sauces

Kitchen Tips

- When cooking pasta, al dente means that the texture of the pasta is firm to the tooth or has a little stiffness to the pasta. Instead of relying on your timer, you can taste the pasta near the end of the cooking time to determine its tenderness. There is only a short time frame between rawness and al dente, so be alert!

- Fresh pasta cooks more quickly than dried.

- To keep herbs, pack an ice cube tray half full with a finely chopped fresh herb, then fill with water and freeze. Then just drop cube directly into soups or sauces when needed.

- Store mushrooms by removing them from plastic and placing them, unwashed, in a single layer on a baking sheet pan with a damp paper towel over the top for up to a week.

- A tablespoon of fresh herbs equals about a teaspoon of dried.

- Tomato paste in a tube is much easier to use than canned. It keeps for two weeks after opening, so you can use just as much as you need and store the rest in the refrigerator.

- Those times when you are tired and need a meal quickly, I turn to pasta with a store-bought sauce. My favorite is 365 Brand® Fat-Free pasta sauce. Change it up by adding seasonings such as capers, red pepper flakes, chopped dried tomatoes, mushrooms and even kale or broccoli.

Pasta with Chickpeas & Cherry Tomatoes

This is a fast little wholesome dish. Just add a green salad and slice of French bread.

10 ounces pasta of your choice *(whole wheat pasta shells go well with the chickpeas)*
1 tablespoons olive oil or ¼ cup vegetable broth, *for sautéing*
½ onion, *diced*
1-2 cloves garlic, *minced*
½ teaspoon red pepper flakes
2 cups chickpeas, *liquid reserved*
½ cup fresh parsley, *chopped*
2 cups cherry tomatoes, *halved*
½ teaspoon salt
Freshly ground pepper, *to taste*

Start a large pot of lightly salted water to boil for pasta.

Heat the oil or vegetable broth in a large skillet over medium heat and add onion, garlic and red pepper flakes. Cook until tender and then add the chickpeas, and parsley, with salt and pepper to taste. Add the liquid from the chickpeas and turn heat down to simmer.

Add pasta to water and cook al dente, according to package instructions. Right before it is done, scoop up and set aside one cup of the pasta water to use later.

Add cherry tomatoes to sauce. Drain pasta and toss with the sauce. Add part of the pasta water if sauce is too thick. Check for salt and pepper. Serve in warm bowls.

Edamame Pesto with Soba Noodles

The Edamame Pesto makes this an outstanding but simple dish to prepare.

8 ounces soba noodles
2 cups red cabbage, *thinly sliced*
Edamame pesto *(see below)*

Bring large pot of water to boil. Add soba noodles and cook for 4-5 minutes. When noodles are ready, reserve one cup of the noodle water for thinning pesto, then pour remaining liquid and noodles into colander. Rinse with cold water and drain.

Put pesto in large bowl and add noodles and cabbage. Toss together until well blended. Use noodle water to thin if needed.

Edamame Pesto

½ cup fresh parsley leaves
½-1 teaspoons red pepper flakes
1-2 small cloves garlic
½ cup shelled, *frozen edamame, thawed*
½ cup whole raw almonds
½ teaspoon salt
3 tablespoons lime juice
2 tablespoons olive oil
2 tablespoons water

Put the parsley, garlic, edamame, red pepper flakes, almonds and salt in food processor and pulse for 30 seconds. Add in the lime juice, olive oil, and water and process until smooth. Add more water if mixture is too thick.

Hint:
Pesto can be used to add flavor to pastas, sandwiches, soups or salads.

Farfalle with *Red Beans & Chiles*

Simple! Just make your own tomato sauce or use your favorite bought one. See tomato sauce recipes on page 208.

14 ounces farfalle
3 cups of your favorite tomato sauce or 1 (25 oz) jar of store-bought
1 (15 oz) can of small red beans, *Kidney or small, drained, rinsed*
1-2 jalapeño or Serrano peppers, *seeded, diced or use red pepper flakes*
Salt and freshly ground pepper, *to taste*
2 tablespoons fresh parsley or cilantro

Cook farfalle al dente in a large pot of lightly salted water, according to instructions. Save one cup of pasta water at the end of cooking time to use to thin sauce, if needed.

In large skillet over medium heat, add tomato sauce, beans and jalapeño pepper. Bring to a low boil. Add salt and pepper to taste and lower heat.

When pasta is cooked, drain and toss with sauce mixture. Toss in chopped parsley or cilantro. Serve hot.

Hints:

- ◊ When cooking pasta, al dente means tender but chewy.
- ◊ Serrano peppers tend to be hotter than jalapeños but have a great chili flavor.

Farfalle with Sun-Dried Tomato Pesto & Zucchini

So simple! So good!

- 1 tablespoon oil from sun-dried tomatoes *(see below)*
- 10 ounces farfalle pasta
- 2 small zucchini, *sliced*
- Salt, *to taste*
- Freshly ground pepper
- Sun-Dried Tomato Pesto *(see below)*
- ½ cup sliced almonds, *roasted, chopped*

In a 6 quart pot, bring lightly salted water to a boil. Add pasta and cook according to package instructions, al dente. Begin making pesto as the pesto water is coming to a boil. Just before pasta is drained, remove 1 cup of pasta water. You will add ½ cup to the Sun-Dried Tomato Pesto below.

While pesto is cooking, heat small skillet to medium high and add 1 tablespoon of oil from the sun-dried tomatoes. Sauté the zucchini in the skillet with the oil for three minutes or until the zucchini is just tender crisp. Set aside.

Combine pasta and pesto in a large bowl. If the sauce seems too thick, add a little pasta water to thin. Toss in zucchini. Add salt and add freshly ground pepper as desired. Add chopped almonds to top of bowl. Serve.

Sun-Dried Tomato Pesto

- ½ cup almonds, *roasted*
- ½ cup oil-packed sun-dried tomatoes, *drained, save oil*
- ¼ cup combined fresh parsley
- ¼ cup basil leaves
- 1 clove garlic, *peeled, halved*
- ½ teaspoon red pepper flakes
- ½ teaspoon salt
- ¼ teaspoon pepper
- 2 tablespoons olive oil
- ¼ -½ cup water

Retain oil from sun-dried tomatoes in a separate bowl for use in pasta dish. Combine almonds, tomatoes, basil, parsley, garlic, and red pepper flakes in a food processor or blender. Pulse until finely chopped. Add olive oil and water and blend, but not completely smooth. Salt and pepper to taste. Put pesto in a large pasta bowl.

Hint:

A couple of tablespoons of miso can be added to pesto for a salty, cheesy flavor.

Fettuccine with Broccoli & Lemon Pesto

This is a light and fresh pasta dish that is great for spring and summer.

14 ounces fettuccine
2 cups broccoli florets, *steamed*
Lemon Pesto *(see below)*
¼ teaspoon parsley, *chopped, fresh*
¼ teaspoon lemon juice *(optional)*

Cook fettuccine in 6 quart pot of lightly salted water al dente, according to package instructions. Do not overcook. Before draining pasta, save one cup of pasta water and set aside water in a small bowl or cup. You will use the pasta water to thin pesto if needed. Steam broccoli for 5 minutes or until tender crisp.

Drain pasta and combine with pesto. Add pasta water to pesto, one tablesoon at a time if mixture seems too dry. Lightly toss broccoli as desired. Add salt and add freshly ground pepper into the pasta and pesto mixture. Sprinkle top with chopped parsley. For more lemon flavor, squeeze fresh lemon juice over top.

Lemon Pesto

1 cup basil
1 cup arugula
½ cup pine nuts, *toasted*
2 tablespoons olive oil
2 tablespoons lemon zest
1 clove garlic, *peeled, halved*
½ teaspoon salt
¼ teaspoon freshly ground pepper
Pinch cayenne pepper

Place all ingredients in food processor or blender and turn on high while slowly drizzling in oil through the top hole. If pesto seems too dry add a couple of tablespoons of water to thin. Add salt, pepper and cayenne as desired.

Hint:
Remember when using fresh pasta, it cooks very quickly!

Macaroni & Peanut Butter

While this may sound like an odd pairing, *Macaroni and Peanut Butter* is a favorite among the children and adults in my family. The peanut sauce seems to please all ages. Red pepper flakes can be added for adults who might enjoy a little heat. This is great for picnics or school lunches.

8 ounces macaroni, *small, whole wheat*
1 cup peas and carrots, *frozen or fresh, diced*
7 tablespoons natural peanut butter, *smooth or crunchy*
½ cup hot water, *use hot pasta water*
1 tablespoon rice vinegar
3 teaspoons lemon juice
2-3 tablespoons soy sauce, *start with 2 and taste*
Dash garlic powder
½ cup roasted peanuts, *chopped*

In 6 quart pot of lightly salted boiling water, add macaroni and cook according to package instructions, al dente. Set aside 1 cup of pasta water just before draining. Drain.

Boil peas and carrots until tender and crisp. Drain.

Combine peanut butter, warm pasta water, rice vinegar, lemon juice and soy sauce, mixing until smooth. Taste for seasoning.

Toss pasta in a large bowl with 2 tablespoons of the peanut sauce, adding more sauce until macaroni is lightly coated. Gently stir in peas and carrots. Thin with more pasta water if sauce is too thick. Top each serving with chopped peanuts.

Hint:
Buy natural peanut butter without added sugar and salt.

This is a simple noodle dish that has a spicy, sweet, tangy light sauce. Eat alone, add baked tofu or toss in steamed vegetables.

½ pound spaghetti or soba noodles, *cooked al dente*
2 teaspoons olive oil
1 mild green or red chile pepper, *cut into sticks*
1 bunch green onions, *chopped*
2 cloves garlic, *minced*
3 tablespoons soy sauce or Tamari
1 tablespoon chili paste
1 teaspoons sugar
1 tablespoon apple cider vinegar
1 teaspoon toasted sesame seed oil

Prepare soba noodles as directed on package instructions. Set aside in medium bowl.

Heat a medium-sized skillet to medium-high heat. When hot, add oil and sauté pepper, onions and garlic for one minute. Add soy sauce, chili paste, sugar, vinegar, sesame oil and cook just until hot. Gently toss in noodles. Serve.

Penne Pasta with Broccoli, Capers, Green Olives & Pine Nuts

The caramelized onions combined with the capers, green olives and pine nuts make this a savory dish. The longer the onions are cooked, the better they taste, so start them early.

- 2 tablespoons olive oil or ½ cup vegetable broth
- 2 large onions, *diced*
- 2 garlic cloves, *finely minced*
- 1 cup green olives, *chopped*
- 2 tablespoons capers
- 1 tablespoon vegan Worcestershire sauce
- 1 teaspoon oregano or marjoram
- Red pepper flakes, *to taste*
- 1 teaspoon seasoned salt
- ¼ teaspoon fresh ground pepper
- 3 cups broccoli florets
- 8 ounces whole-wheat penne pasta
- 1 cup pasta cooking water reserved
- ½ cup pine nuts, *toasted*
- 1 tablespoon parsley or basil, *chopped*

Heat large skillet to low to medium heat. Add oil or vegetable broth and then the onions. Let them cook, stirring just a couple of times until they are golden brown in color. Too much stirring slows down the caramelization process and browning. Add garlic the last 5 minutes after onion is brown and starting to caramelize.

Add green olives and capers to the onions. Stir in Worcestershire sauce, oregano or marjoram, red pepper flakes, salt and pepper. Add a little water or broth if mixture is too dry. Simmer over low heat for 10 minutes.

In a separate 6 quart pot, prepare penne pasta according to al dente instructions. Five minutes before pasta is cooked, add broccoli. Cook broccoli with pasta for five minutes. Before draining pasta, reserve ½ cup of pasta water and set aside. Drain.

Mix pasta and broccoli with the caramelized onions. Add pasta water, one tablespoon at a time until sauce consistency is as desired. Serve into warm bowls or plates. Sprinkle parsley or basil on top for garnish with pine nuts.

Hint:
A tablespoon of fresh herbs equal about 1 teaspoon of dried.

Fusilli & English Peas with Pistachio Pesto

Simply toss Pistachio Pesto with fusilli and heat up a loaf of bread and you have dinner! The pesto is also good on a grilled vegetable sandwich.

1 cup English peas, *fresh or frozen*
10 ounces fusilli pasta
Pistachio Pesto *(see below)*
2 tablespoons fresh parsley, *chopped*
½ teaspoon salt
Freshly ground pepper, *to taste*

Boil peas for 7-10 minutes until tender and crisp in lightly salted water. Drain and set aside.

In 6 quart pot filled with lightly salted water, cook fusilli al dente, according to package instructions. Prior to draining pasta, reserve one cup of pasta water to use for sauce.

Drain pasta and toss with pesto. If the pasta becomes too dry, use one tablespoon of pasta water until sauce consistency is as desired. Toss in peas and chopped parsley. Add salt and add freshly ground pepper as desired. Serve.

Pistachio Pesto

3-4 cups arugula
¼ cup parsley or basil or a mix the two
1-2 cloves garlic, *minced*
1-2 tablespoons nutritional yeast
½ cup pistachios, *shelled, roasted, salted*
A good pinch cayenne pepper
2 tablespoons olive oil
½ teaspoon salt
¼ teaspoon pepper

Place all ingredients, except oil, salt and pepper in food processor. Pulse until finely chopped. Add the oil through top hole of your food processor and blend together. Add salt and pepper to taste. Toss pesto with hot penne pasta and 3 tablespoons of pasta water.

Hints:
◊ Swirl pesto into vegan mayonnaise and use it for a dip.
◊ For a great bread to serve with a simple pasta or soup, spread Pistachio Pesto on slices of a French baguette. Bake on a baking sheet at 450°F (230°C) until lightly brown and crisp.

Pasta Primavera Sauce

Fresh and flavorful! This is a quick, fast paced recipe so have all of the vegetables prepared and ready before you begin.

- 10 ounces pasta your choice
- ½ onion, *minced*
- 1 clove garlic, *minced*
- 1 tablespoon oil or ¼ cup vegetable broth
- 1 cup mushrooms, *quartered*
- 1 basket cherry tomatoes, *halved*
- 1 red bell pepper, *julienned*
- 1 zucchini, *sliced*
- 1 yellow squash, *sliced*
- 1 jalapeño, *seeded, finely diced*
- Salt and pepper, *to taste*
- ½ teaspoon red pepper flakes

Begin making sauce right before you start pasta cooking.

Bring salted water to boil in 6 quart pot. Add pasta to boiling water and cook al dente, according to package instructions. Reserve 1 cup of pasta water. Drain pasta.

While pasta is cooking, heat a large nonstick pan over medium-high heat. Sauté onion and garlic in oil or vegetable stock until onions and garlic are tender. Add mushrooms to onions and cook for 3 minutes, until juices begin to run. Add tomatoes, red bell pepper, zucchini, yellow squash, jalapeño and cook for 2-3 minutes to warm all thoroughly. Do not overcook vegetables; remove from heat when they are tender crisp. Add salt and red pepper flakes to taste. Toss pasta with vegetables. Use pasta water, one tablespoon at a time, to thin sauce if too thick. Serve.

Hint:
Al dente means tender but chewy!

Variation:
For a creamier sauce, stir about ½ cup of Cashew Cream (page 252) in right before you add the pasta to the sauce, then salt and pepper to taste.

Spinach, Beans & Bowtie Pasta

1 cup fresh baby spinach
1 can white beans, *drain and rinse*
¼ cup sun-dried tomatoes, *diced*
1 bunch green onions, *chopped*
1-2 cloves garlic, *minced*
1 teaspoon lemon zest
2 tablespoons lemon juice
1 tablespoon olive oil
2 teaspoons fresh thyme, *finely minced*
½ teaspoon red pepper flakes, *for bite*
½ teaspoon salt
½ teaspoon pepper
10 ounces bowtie pasta
½ cup pine nuts, *toasted (page 267)*

In large serving bowl combine spinach, beans, sun-dried tomatoes, onions, garlic, lemon zest, lemon juice, olive oil, thyme, red pepper flakes, salt, and pepper. Cover and let the flavors marry together while you cook the pasta.

In large pot of salted water, cook the pasta al dente. Save one cup of pasta water and drain pasta.

Toss pasta with spinach mixture. If pasta becomes too dry, use one tablespoon of pasta water until consistency is as desired. Toss pine nuts into mixture just before serving. Serve warm or room temperature.

Spinach Linguine *with Zucchini, Peas & Carrots*

Colorful pasta loaded with savory flavors and a variety of colorful vegetables.

14 ounces spinach linguine or spaghetti
2 medium zucchini, *cut into sticks*
2 medium carrots, *peeled, cut into sticks*
1 tablespoon olive oil or ¼ cup vegetable broth
3 shallots, *diced*
2 garlic cloves, *finely minced*
½ cup white wine *(optional)*
2 cups vegetable broth
2 tablespoons vegan Worcestershire sauce
2 cups frozen English peas
Pinch red pepper flakes
½ cup pine nuts, *toasted*
½ teaspoon salt
¼ teaspoon pepper
2 tablespoons of fresh parsley, *chopped*

Bring lightly salted pasta water to boil and add pasta to water, cooking al dente. Bring a medium skillet to medium heat, add oil or ¼ cup of vegetable broth, add garlic and shallots until tender. Add white wine and simmer.

Five minutes before pasta is ready, add zucchini and carrot sticks to pasta water.

While the vegetables are boiling with the pasta, add 2 cups of vegetable broth and Worcestershire sauce to the garlic and shallot mixture. Gently stir in English peas.

Reserve one cup of pasta water then drain pasta, zucchini and carrots together. Gently toss pasta and vegetables into the skillet with English pea mixture. Add salt and pepper to taste, then add red pepper flakes and sprinkle in toasted pine nuts. If sauce seems too dry, add a little pasta water to thin. Top with chopped parsley and serve.

Kid-Friendly Spanish Spaghetti
(Fideo)

A simple yet satisfying meal at any time of year.

2 tablespoons canola oil
2 cloves garlic, *minced*
1 medium white onion, *diced*
1 package vermicelli, *angel hair or capellini pasta*
1 can tomato sauce (8 oz)
1 teaspoon ground cumin
½ teaspoon paprika
½ teaspoon salt
Dash pepper
1 cup vegetable broth
2 cups water
2 zucchini, *diced*

Place oil in large skillet on medium heat until hot. Cook garlic and onion for one minute. Break pasta in half and lay in skillet with onions and garlic to brown for 2-3 minutes. Add tomato sauce and stir. Add cumin, paprika, salt and pepper. Stir in vegetable broth and water. Add zucchini and cover over medium heat for 15-20 minutes. Uncover and add more seasonings as desired. Serve warm.

Hint:
To give this dish kick add in 2-3 chopped chipotle chiles in adobo sauce with zucchini.

Spaghetti *with Chile Pesto*

This dish can be spicy if using the right chili peppers. One or two fresh jalapeños or Serrano peppers can be substituted for the dried red chili. For less heat in the pesto, simply remove the seeds from the fresh peppers before they are finely diced and added to the pesto.

14 ounces spaghetti
Chile Pesto *(see below)*
¼ teaspoon basil, *chopped (optional)*
¼ teaspoon parsley, *chopped (optional)*

Bring large pot of salted water to a boil. Cook spaghetti al dente, according to instructions on package. Save ½ cup of cooking water. Drain.

In large serving bowl, mix pasta with pesto. Use two tablespoons of the pasta water at a time to thin pesto. Chopped basil and parsley can be added to the top for garnish. Serve in warm bowls.

Chile Pesto

1 red bell pepper, *large, roasted (page 129)*
1-2 cloves garlic, *peeled, halved*
¼ cup pine nuts, *toasted*
1 dried small red chili, *stemmed and seeded*
3 tablespoons olive or canola oil
Salt and freshly ground pepper, *to taste*

Place peppers, garlic and pine nuts in a food processor and pulse until paste is smooth, adding oil one tablespoon at a time along the way. If paste seems dry, use a tablespoon or two of water instead of oil. Add salt and pepper to taste. Refrigerate until using.

Hint:
Use leftover pesto on veggie burgers or sandwiches.

Whole-Wheat Penne Pasta
with Miso & Sun-Dried Tomato Pesto

A robust, tomato flavored pesto that holds up well with all whole-wheat pastas. The miso in the pesto adds a salty, cheese-like flavor.

16 ounces of whole-wheat penne
Miso & Sun-Dried Tomato Pesto *(see below)*
½ cup of pine nuts, *toasted*
2 tablespoons of fresh parsley or fresh basil, *thinly cut into ribbons*

Bring large pot of salted water to a boil. Cook penne al dente, according to package instructions. Reserve ½ cup of pasta water and set aside. Drain.

In a large serving bowl, mix the pasta with the pesto, using some of the pasta water to thin the pesto if necessary. Serve warm in bowls and top with pine nuts and chopped parsley or thin ribbons of fresh basil.

Miso & Sun-Dried Tomato Pesto

½ cup almonds, *roasted*
¼ cup oil-packed sun-dried tomatoes, *drained*
½ cup fresh parsley
½ cup fresh basil leaves
1 clove garlic, *peeled, halved*
½ teaspoon red pepper flakes
1-2 tablespoons miso
2 tablespoons olive oil
½ cup water
½ teaspoon salt
¼ teaspoon pepper

In a food processor or blender, combine the almonds, drained tomatoes, basil and parsley, garlic, and red pepper flakes. Pulse until finely chopped. Add miso, olive oil and water and blend until slightly chunky. Add salt and pepper to taste. Place pesto in a large pasta bowl and set aside until pasta is prepared.

Olive Pesto *with a Kick*

This pesto goes well with whole-wheat or regular fusilli served with a Romaine Salad with Pine Nuts and Garlic Vinaigrette Dressing (page 34) and a warm slice of fresh rustic bread. It also makes a great base sauce when making a Vegetable pizza (page 218).

1 jalapeño or Serrano pepper, *stemmed, seeded*
½ cup good black olives, *pitted*
1-2 cloves garlic, *peeled, halved*
¼ cup pine nuts, *toasted*
2 tablespoons olive or canola oil
¼ tablespoon salt
¼ teaspoon freshly ground pepper
Fresh lemon juice from one lemon *(optional)*

Place pepper, olives, garlic, and pine nuts in a food processor. Pulse until smooth, adding oil one tablespoon at a time, until smooth. One or two tablespoons of water can be added if pesto appears too dry. Add salt and pepper to taste. Squeeze lemon juice into mixture and stir. Serve with your choice of pasta.

Hints:
◊ Spread pesto on bread and make pesto bread instead of garlic bread.
◊ Miso added to pesto adds a salty, cheese-like flavor.

Tomatoes, Olives & Capers *with Pasta*

This is a rich, salty flavored dish that is tasty and easy to assemble.

- 2 tablespoons olive oil
- 3 garlic cloves, *2 sliced, 1 minced*
- 5-6 Roma tomatoes, *peeled, seeded and chopped*, or 2 pints cherry tomatoes, *halved*, or 1 (15 oz) can diced tomatoes
- ½ cup Kalamata olives, *pitted, coarsely chopped or Nicoise or green*
- ¼ cup capers, *drained*
- 1 cup roasted red bell peppers, *chopped*
- ½ teaspoon red pepper flakes
- 1 tablespoon of fresh basil or ½ teaspoon of dried basil
- ½ teaspoon salt
- Freshly ground pepper, *to taste*
- 10 ounces of spaghetti or your choice pasta
- ½ cup fresh parsley, *chopped*

To make the sauce, heat oil with garlic slices in large skillet over medium heat. When garlic is golden, discard the garlic slices. Add tomatoes, minced garlic, olives, capers, red bell peppers, red pepper flakes, and basil. Simmer for 10 minutes and season with salt and pepper.

Cook pasta in boiling, lightly salted water al dente. Save ½ cup pasta water to thin sauce if needed. Drain.

Place in a large serving bowl, add sauce to pasta and toss. Top with the parsley.

Hint:

To peel tomatoes, cut an x in the top and drop in boiling water for two to three minutes. Remove when skin begins to split, and peel off skin.

Quick Canned Tomato Sauce

1 tablespoon olive oil or ¼ cup vegetable broth
½ cup onion, *finely diced*
1 clove garlic, *minced*
1 (15 oz) can diced tomatoes
Pinch dried oregano
1 rablespoon tomato paste
Salt and pepper, *to taste*

Heat oil or broth in small skillet over medium-high heat and add onion with garlic. Cook until lightly brown or tender crisp. Add tomatoes, the oregano and tomato paste. Taste for salt and pepper.

Fresh Tomato Sauce

Roma tomatoes are less sweet with full tomato flavor and work well for sauces.

1 tablespoon olive oil or ¼ cup vegetable broth
2 shallots, *finely diced*
2 cloves garlic, *minced*
12-14 fresh Roma tomatoes, *quartered*
2 tablespoons fresh basil, *chopped or ½-1 teaspoon dried basil*
1 jalapeño pepper, *diced (optional)*
2 tablespoons tomato paste
Salt and pepper, *to taste*

Heat oil or broth in saucepan over medium heat and add shallots with garlic. Cook until tender and then add tomatoes, basil, jalapeño and tomato paste. Cover and cook for about 10 minutes. Continue cooking on simmer until desired thickness is reached. If tomato sauce is too chunky, cool and place in food processor to smooth or use an immersion blender in the saucepan. Taste for salt and pepper.

Hint:

Those times when I am tired, out of time and just ready for a fast meal, I turn to pasta with a store-bought sauce. My favorite is 365 Brand® Fat-Free pasta sauce. Change it up by adding seasonings to our taste like capers, red pepper flakes, chopped up dried tomatoes, mushrooms and even kale or broccoli.

Rus & Niki's Fresh Pasta Sauce *with Vegetables*

So simple, so fresh and so flavorful!

Pasta of choice
1-2 tablespoons olive oil or ¼ cup vegetable broth or ¼ cup wine
12-14 fresh Roma tomatoes
1-2 bunches Italian chard, *spinach, or kale, washed and chopped*
5-6 mushrooms, *sliced*
1-2 zucchini, *chopped*
3-4 large shallots
4 garlic cloves, *minced*
½-1 jalapeño pepper, *seeded, finely chopped*
2 tablespoons fresh basil, *chopped*
Salt, *to taste*
Freshly ground pepper, *to taste*

Bring lightly salted water to boil for pasta in a 6 quart pot. Cook al dente per package instructions. Drain. Set aside. In a separate large skillet on medium-high heat, add oil or vegetable broth or wine. Add all vegetables to skillet and cook until all are tender yet crisp. Add salt and pepper to taste and add to pasta. Serve in warm bowls with warm, hearty bread.

Quick Penne & Beans

- 8 ounces penne pasta, *cooked al dente, I like whole wheat*
- 1 tablespoon olive oil or ¼ cup vegetable broth
- ½ cup onion, *finely diced*
- 1-2 cloves garlic, *minced*
- 1 can diced fire-roasted or regular tomatoes (15 oz)
- 1 can Navy or Great Northern beans (15 oz), *drained*
- 1 tablespoon fresh basil, *chopped or ½-1 teaspoon dried*
- ⅛ teaspoon red pepper flakes
- ¼ teaspoon salt, *to taste*
- ⅛ teaspoon freshly ground pepper

Cook pasta al dente in a large pot of salted water, according to package instructions. Save one cup of pasta water before draining pasta.

Separately, in a large skillet over medium heat, add oil or vegetable broth and cook onion and garlic for 2-3 minutes. Add tomatoes, beans, and basil with red pepper flakes. If needed, add some pasta water to thin sauce. Heat sauce until hot and bubbly. Toss with pasta. Add salt and freshly ground pepper, to taste. Serve.

Hint:

As a rule of thumb, use ⅓ to ½ the amount of dried herbs to the fresh herb amount. The older the dried herbs are the less potent they are. Rub the dried herb between your fingers to determine the strength of the aroma; if aroma is weak, use more of the herb.

Chapter Seven

One-Dish Meals

Bean & Chili Pasta Bake

This is an easy pasta casserole. Try serving it with a green salad and a piece of cornbread.

- 8 ounces penne pasta, *or preference*
- ¼ cup vegetable broth or 1 tablespoon canola oil
- 1 small onion, *diced*
- 1-2 cloves garlic, *minced*
- 1 medium red bell pepper, *seeded, diced*
- 1 jalapeño, *seeded, diced*
- 1 (15 oz) can of fire-roasted diced tomatoes
- 1 can beans, *drained, Kidney, pinto or small red*
- ¼ cup sun-dried tomatoes, *diced*
- ½ cup corn, *frozen*
- 2 teaspoon chili powder
- 1 tablespoon of vegan Worcestershire
- 1 teaspoon Deb's Seasoning (page 269)
- 1 teaspoon salt
- ⅛ freshly ground pepper, *to taste*
- Breadcrumbs for top

Preheat oven to 375°F (190°C). Use cooking spray to oil a 9"×13" baking dish or pan.

Cook pasta in lightly salted water until a little under al dente, as according to package instructions. Do not overcook, pasta will finish cooking in the oven. Reserve one cup of pasta water.

In a medium to large skillet, heat broth or oil over medium heat. Add onions, garlic, peppers and jalapeño, cooking until tender. Add fire-roasted and sun-dried tomatoes, beans and corn. Stir in chili powder, vegan Worcestershire, Deb's Seasoning, salt and pepper. Toss mixture over pasta in casserole dish using pasta water to thin mixture if needed.

Top mixture with breadcrumbs. Bake for 30 minutes or until bubbly and top is golden brown.

Tofu & Vegetable Lasagna

A flexible recipe which will work well with any of your favorite vegetables.

1 (16 oz) box lasagna noodles
1 pound firm tofu, *drained, squeezed*
¼ cup nutritional yeast
½ teaspoon garlic powder or 1 finely minced clove of garlic
½ teaspoon oregano or marjoram
1 tablespoon fresh basil
1 teaspoon salt, *to taste*
Freshly ground pepper, *to taste*
⅛ teaspoon cayenne pepper
2 tablespoons fresh parsley, *chopped*
2 tablespoons lemon juice
2 tablespoons capers *(optional)*
2 jars (25 oz) spaghetti sauce *or 6 cups homemade*
2 small zucchini, *thinly sliced*
3 tablespoons sun-dried tomatoes, *finely chopped*
1 cup mushrooms, *thinly sliced*
½ cup red bell pepper, *diced or 1 jar pimentos, drained*
1 small can sliced black olives
10 ounce box frozen spinach *(thawed with juices squeezed out)*
1 cup breadcrumbs
¼ cup vegan butter
1 tablespoon fresh parsley or basil, *chopped*
½ cup pine nuts, *toasted*

Preheat oven to 375°F (190°C). Lightly oil a 9"×12" casserole dish or pan. Cook lasagna noodles in boiling salted water as directed unless using noodles that require no pre cooking. Rinse with cold water and drain.

Mix tofu with nutritional yeast, garlic powder, oregano or marjoram, basil, salt, pepper, cayenne pepper, parsley, and lemon juice in food processor or with potato masher. Stir in capers.

Pour ⅓ of the spaghetti sauce in the bottom of the casserole dish or pan. Place lasagna noodles over sauce, overlapping slightly so that bottom of dish is fully covered. Fold edges of pasta if necessary. Cover lasagna noodles with ½ of the tofu mixture and layers of zucchini, sun-dried tomatoes and mushrooms. Add another layer of noodles and cover in ⅓ of sauce with red bell pepper, olives and spinach. Keep alternating layers of lasagna noodles and vegetables until casserole dish is almost full. End with a layer of noodles last with the remaining sauce on top.

In a separate bowl, mix breadcrumbs, vegan butter, parsley or basil and pine nuts together. Cover top of lasagna dish with mixture. Cover with foil. Place on baking sheet and bake for 45 minutes covered. Remove foil and bake an additional 15–30 minutes more until bubbly and golden brown. Remove lasagna from oven and let rest for 15–45 minutes before serving.

This can be made the evening before and refrigerated. Just leave the breadcrumb mixture off and add just before baking the lasagna the following day.

Hints:

- If you do not have a premixed Italian seasoning just mix one teaspoon thyme, one teaspoon marjoram and ½ teaspoon of sage together.
- Nutritional yeast has a rich, nutty, cheese-like flavor can be used in sauces.

Spinach & Mushroom Enchiladas

Who doesn't love enchiladas? We serve them with tamales for our Christmas dinner. There are so many different variations to the fillings and the sauces. To save time, make your filling and sauce before you begin assembling the tortillas. The process of making enchiladas gets easier with each try.

1 tablespoon oil or ¼ cup vegetable broth, *for sautéing*
1 small onion, *finely diced*
½ a red bell pepper, *finely diced*
1 Poblano pepper, *finely diced*
1-2 jalapeño peppers, *finely diced*
1-2 cloves garlic, *minced*
2 cups mushrooms, *sliced or chopped*
6 cups fresh spinach
1 tomato, *finely diced*
Salt and freshly ground black pepper
2 dozen corn tortillas
Enchilada Filling *(see next page)*
Verde Sauce (page 261), Enchilada Sauce (page 251) or Ranchero Salsa (page 255)

Suggested sides:
Guacamole
Black Bean Salsa
Corn Salsa
Pico de Gallo
Tortilla Strips

Preheat oven to 375°F (190°C). Spray casserole dish with canola cooking spray.

To prepare enchilada filling, heat a large skillet to medium-high heat. Add oil or vegetable broth and cook onions, bell pepper, Poblano pepper and jalapeño pepper until tender or lightly brown. Add garlic and cook one minute more. Add mushrooms and salt, tossing in skillet until juices begin to flow. Add spinach and tomato, mix with other vegetables. Remove from heat. Add salt as desired and black pepper then set aside.

To prepare tortillas for enchiladas, heat a griddle to medium-high heat. Place verde sauce in a pie plate. Using tongs, place one tortilla at a time on heated griddle for about 20 seconds. Then flip to the other side until the tortilla is soft. Leave on the griddle only long enough to soften the tortillas making them easy to roll.

Lightly dip one side of the tortilla in verde sauce and place in a casserole baking dish with coated side down. Add vegetable filling down the center and roll so that seam faces bottom of casserole dish. Continue assembling enchiladas in this manner until dish is full.

When ready to bake, cover casserole dish with foil and bake in oven for 15 minutes. Remove cover and after 15 minutes add ½ cup of the verde sauce to top and continue cooking another 15 minutes or until bubbly and beginning to brown. Remove from heat and serve.

Enchilada Fillings:

- Mashed pinto or black beans mixed with finely diced jalapeños and onions.
- Corn and leftover potatoes with sautéed garlic, jalapeños, diced onion, diced red bell pepper, a touch of cumin and salt and freshly ground pepper.
- Leftover vegetables (carrots, corn, greens, hominy, green beans or any combination you like) mixed with sautéed diced onions, diced peppers of any kind and salt.
- Roasted asparagus with corn and black beans mixed with sautéed diced onions, minced garlic, mushrooms and salt.
- Zucchini sautéed with diced red bell peppers, diced onions, diced jalapeño and corn.
- Country style hash brown potatoes with peppers and onions, with added hot peppers.
- Two bunches of chard, garlic, onions, jalapeño, Mexican oregano, and parsley.
- Cabbage, zucchini, carrots, mushrooms, bell peppers, hot peppers, thinly sliced and sautéed.

Hints:

- For the best results, make fillings and sauces well ahead of time and assemble enchiladas right before serving.
- Poblano chiles are usually not very hot and very tasty. Their flavor improves with roasting.

Macaroni Casserole

This one of those go-to casseroles, when you need something fast but are too tired to think of what that might be. You may easily adjust the spices, reducing the amount of RO*TEL® and hot sauce for less of a kick.

- 8 ounces whole-wheat macaroni or any pasta
- 1 can (15 oz) stewed or fire-roasted tomatoes
- 1 (10 oz) can RO*TEL®, *mild or hot*
- 1 cup black beans, *drained, fresh or canned*
- 1 cup mixed vegetables, *frozen*
- ½ cup onion, *diced*
- ½ cup celery, *diced*
- 1 tablespoon nutritional yeast
- 1 cup pasta water or vegetable broth
- ½ teaspoon garlic powder or fresh garlic, *minced*
- ½ teaspoon Deb's seasoning (page 269)
- 1 tablespoon vegan Worcestershire sauce
- 2 tablespoons capers
- 1 small jar pimientos, *drained*
- 2 tablespoons fresh parsley, *chopped*
- ½ teaspoon chili powder
- Hot sauce to taste *(optional)*
- 1 cup breadcrumbs
- 1 teaspoon garlic salt
- 1 teaspoon dried parsley

Preheat oven to 375°F (190°C). Lightly oil a 10"×13" casserole dish or pan.

Cook macaroni according to package instructions, al dente. Be careful to not overcook pasta because it will be baked. Reserve 1 cup of the pasta water for later use, drain and rinse pasta. Set aside.

In large bowl, combine all remaining ingredients, except breadcrumbs. Toss in pasta and mix well. Add hot sauce as desired and add some pasta water if mixture seems too dry.

Place pasta mixture in casserole dish. In a separate bowl, mix breadcrumbs with garlic salt and parsley. Sprinkle breadcrumbs over top of pasta mixture and bake for 40 minutes or until top begins to turn golden brown. If casserole appears to be getting too dry before breadcrumbs are ready, simply pour ½ cup of pasta water around edges of pan. Remove from oven and let rest for 10 minutes before serving.

Hints:

- ◊ When cooking pasta, al dente means being firm to the tooth or having a little firmness to the pasta. Instead of relying on the clock, taste the pasta towards the end of the cooking time to determine the tenderness and firmness. There is a small moment between rawness and al dente, so be alert!
- ◊ Nutritional yeast has a nutty, cheese-like flavor. Many times it is substituted for Parmesan cheese in recipes.

Baked Pasta Casserole

This casserole can be easily assembled and baked. This is also good the following day.

- 8 ounces whole-wheat pasta *(penne, farfalle, fusilli, or macaroni elbow or your choice)*
- 3 cups broccoli florets, *fresh or frozen*
- 1 cup diced carrots, *fresh or frozen*
- 1 tablespoon oil or ¼ cup vegetable broth, *for sautéing*
- 1 small onion, *diced*
- 1 clove garlic, *minced*
- 1 jalapeño, *seeded, diced (optional)*
- 1 cup mushrooms, *chopped*
- 1 (28 oz) can stewed, *diced, or fire-roasted tomatoes*
- 1 tablespoon tomato paste
- ½ cup corn, *fresh or frozen*
- 1 zucchini, *diced*
- ½ cup of marinated artichoke hearts, *chopped*
- ½ teaspoon dried oregano or marjoram
- 1 tablespoons fresh basil, *chopped (optional)*
- 2 tablespoons capers, *drained*
- 1 teaspoon of Deb's Seasoning (page 269)
- 1 teaspoon of garlic salt
- 1 cup breadcrumbs for top
- ½ cup pine nuts, *toasted, chopped*
- 1 tablespoon parsley, *chopped*

Preheat oven to 350°F (175°C). Lightly oiled or spray with cooking oil a 10"×13" casserole dish.

Bring large pot of lightly salted water to a boil, add pasta and boil al dente, according to package instructions. Be careful not to overcook pasta; it will be cooking in oven later. Add broccoli and carrots to the pasta water for the last 4 minutes of the cooking time. Just before pasta is finished cooking, reserve one cup of the pasta water. Drain pasta and vegetables and run under cold water to stop cooking. Set aside.

Heat oil or vegetable broth in a large skillet and sauté onion, garlic, and jalapeño until tender. Drop mushrooms into onion mixture and cook for 3 more minutes, then add tomatoes with tomato paste, corn, zucchini, artichoke hearts, oregano, basil, capers, Deb's Seasoning, and garlic salt to skillet. Taste and add salt as desired. Next, toss in cooked pasta and add the pasta water as needed to thin. Transfer entire contents of skillet into casserole dish.

In a separate bowl, mix breadcrumbs together with pine nuts and parsley. Cover top of casserole with breadcrumb mixture.

Place in oven, uncovered, for 35-45 minutes or until bubbly and lightly browned. If dish seems too dry while cooking, add ½ cup of pasta water around the edges of the dish. Remove from oven and let flavors blend together for 10 minutes before serving.

Hint:

To make fresh breadcrumbs, cut away crusts of coarse textured bread. Crumble the bread into a food processor and pulse processor until bread reaches desired consistency. For dried crumbs, dry fresh crumbs in an oven set on 200°F (95°C) for about 30-45 minutes.

Matt's Pizza

Our family loves my son Matt's pizza. He can't make pizzas fast enough for us.

Pizza Dough
2 cups all-purpose flour
1 teaspoon salt
2 tablespoons Italian seasoning
1 packet instant active dry yeast
1 teaspoon sugar
¾ cup water
1 teaspoon of olive oil

Toppings
1 (16 oz) can pizza sauce
1 cup broccoli florets, *cut into bite-sized pieces*
1 cup canned artichoke hearts *(packed in water)*, *drained, chopped*
1 cup of fresh baby spinach leaves
1 cup black olives, *sliced*
1 cup chopped tomato
1 fresh or pickled jalapeño, *sliced or 1 teaspoon of red pepper flakes (optional)*
Salt, *to taste*
Freshly ground black pepper, *to taste*

Add flour, salt, Italian seasoning and active yeast in food processor or large bowl. In a separate bowl or cup, heat water to 120°F-130°F (50°C-55°C). Use an instant read kitchen thermometer to measure water temperature. Hot water from the tap will often suffice, but water that is too hot or too cold will prevent yeast from activating properly. Mix dry ingredients in processor or knead with your hands. Slowly pour in warm water.

Once the dough is well-blended and all dry ingredients are saturated, place in a non-porous bowl and cover with a dish towel. Place dough in a cool area, such as a countertop that is out of direct sunlight and away from a stove. Let dough rise for 15 to 20 minutes. Once risen, beat the air out of the dough and let rise again (typically, another 10 to 15 minutes).

While the pizza dough is rising, steam broccoli and cover artichoke hearts together in a medium saucepan for 3-5 minutes.

Preheat the oven to 425°F (220°C). Use a teaspoon of olive oil on a flat surface where dough will be rolled. With your hand, amply rub the oil over the surface. Using a rolling pin, work the dough to the desired rectangle or traditional circle shape. After rolling out the dough, carefully transfer to a non-stick 13" x 18" cookie sheet or a 16" round pizza pan. Spread sauce evenly on pizza dough.

When adding toppings, spinach should be the first layer. The remaining toppings can be added according to preference.

Bake for 18 to 22 minutes until edge of crust starts to turn brown.

Hints:

◊ For a change, try adding pesto instead of the pizza sauce to make a great tasting pizza. Try Sun-Dried Tomato Pesto (page 194), Olive Pesto with a Kick (page 206) or Chile Pesto (page 204).
◊ Tofu lovers should sprinkle Crumbled Tofu (page 233) over the top of pizza right before placing in the oven.

Veggie Pot Pie

These are really delicious and they fill the house with a scrumptious aroma! The recipe might seem complex, but it's simple once the pie crust is made. To simplify further, use store bought pie crusts.

1 tablespoon oil or ¼ cup vegetable broth, *for sautéing*
1 cup onion, *finely chopped*
1 cup celery, *finely chopped*
1 teaspoon garlic, *minced*
½ cup mushrooms, *chopped*
2 cups potatoes, *diced into bite-sized pieces*
4 tablespoons flour or cornstarch
1 teaspoon Deb's Seasoning (page 269)
Salt and pepper, *to taste*
Pinch cayenne pepper *(optional)*
2–3 cups vegetable broth
1 (10 oz) bag frozen peas and carrots
¼ teaspoon salt
¼ freshly ground pepper to taste
Pie crust top & bottom, *this can be bought or homemade (page 306)*

Preheat oven to 400°F (205°C).

Parboil-diced potatoes in water or vegetable broth until tender but not overcooked. Drain.

Place saucepan on medium heat. Add oil or broth and sauté onion, celery, and garlic, until translucent. Add mushrooms and potatoes and cook until golden color appears on onions.

Add flour and Deb's Seasoning with salt, pepper and cayenne to potato mixture in saucepan and stir for 2 minutes. Pour in 2 cups of broth and simmer until filling has thickened. Add in peas and carrots and more broth if mixture is too thick.

Roll out two pie crusts on a flat surface, cutting into the shape of your pie plate. You can use individual dishes called ramekins or a regular pie dish. Place bottom pie crust in pie plate and cook in oven for 10 minutes.

Be careful not to create a filling that is too thin. Remove pie crust from oven and fill with vegetable mixture. Top the pie with another layer of crust. Cut openings in top of crust to release steam.

Return pie to oven and lower oven temperature to 375°F (190°C). Bake for 35-45 minutes or until bubbly with a golden brown crust. If side of crust browns too fast, add foil around the edges and then remove foil before baking time is complete. Remove and let rest for 10 minutes. Serve hot.

Potatoes & Pepper Fajitas

This is a fun casual meal to share with a group. Everyone makes their own taco with any combination of toppings they like. Serve black beans and rice along with this to expand the meal.

- 4-5 red potatoes, *sliced*
- 2 cups vegetable broth plus water
- ¼ teaspoon salt
- 1-2 tablespoons oil or vegetable broth
- 1 onion, *sliced*
- 1-2 cloves garlic, *minced*
- 2 Poblano peppers, *seeded, sliced*
- 2 jalapeño peppers, *seeded, sliced*
- 1-2 teaspoons a grill seasoning
- Pre-made or packaged corn or flour tortillas

Place potatoes in saucepan with vegetable broth and water to cover. If vegetable broth is not salted, add salt to the cooking water. Boil until tender but not falling apart. Drain and set aside.

Bring a large skillet to medium-high heat, and add oil or vegetable broth. Sauté onion, garlic, Poblano peppers and jalapeño until tender crisp. Add potato slices and grill seasoning to skillet. Cook until potatoes are golden brown. Place on heated platter and serve.

Take a warm tortilla and fill with the potato mixture. Additional topping ideas include:

Black beans, avocados, salsa, Pico de Gallo (page 258), fresh chopped tomatoes, fresh jalapeño, diced onions, shredded lettuce or shredded cabbage.

Hint:

Poblano chiles are usually not very hot and very tasty. Their flavor improves with cooking.

Potato & Veggie Sausage Bake

This is a great brunch dish. Or, serve it for dinner with a salad. It can be changed up and added to with different vegetables or seasonings. You could omit the sausage or add tofu crumbles (page 233).

1 tablespoon canola oil
4 patties soy sausage, *if frozen, thawed, crumbled*
1 clove garlic, *finely minced*
1 container plain yogurt, *soy or coconut milk*
2 tablespoons chives, *chopped*
½ teaspoon Deb's Seasoning (page 269)
½ teaspoon any grill seasoning
Small or medium size red potatoes, *cut into similar sized slices (about 2 pounds, adjust for size of baking dish)*
1 cup onion, *minced*
1 jalapeño pepper, *finely diced*
1 cup mushrooms, *diced*
½ cup vegetable broth
Salt
Freshly ground pepper
Breadcrumbs for top *(optional)*
1 cup shredded soy cheese *(optional)*

Preheat oven to 375°F (190°C). Lightly oil a 10"× 10" baking dish or pan.

In a nonstick skillet add oil and crumble in soy sausage. Sauté until sausage is a little crispy. Add garlic to pan and cook for one minute, then set aside.

In a small bowl, mix yogurt, chives and seasonings and set aside.

Add a layer of potatoes to the bottom of the baking dish. Then add a third of the onion. Also add ⅓ of the jalapeño, sausage and mushrooms and a dash salt and pepper. Add another layer of potatoes, then another layer of soy sausage and vegetables. Repeat layers ending with potatoes on top. Pour ½ cup of vegetable broth evenly over top layer, and then pour the yogurt mixture over the entire dish.

Cover baking dish with foil and bake about 30-40 minutes, or until potatoes are done. Then remove foil and sprinkle breadcrumbs or soy cheese on top (if using). If potatoes seem to be dry, add ½ cup of water or vegetable broth around the edge of the dish. Cook 15 more minutes until top is golden brown. Remove from oven and let stand for 10 minutes before serving.

Hint:

A good topping mix is breadcrumbs, nutritional yeast with a ¼ cup of chopped walnuts or chopped herbs. You can mix in a little vegan butter but you do not need it.

Brown Rice & Vegetable Casserole

The possibilities for this casserole are endless. Change up the vegetables with any you may have on hand. The recipe is very flexible.

5 cups cooked brown rice
1 cup mushrooms, *sliced*
½ cup onions, *finely chopped*
2 cups broccoli florets
1 cup red bell pepper, *diced*
1-2 jalapeño peppers, *diced*
1 teaspoon chili powder
½ teaspoon salt
2 tablespoons vegan Worcestershire sauce
2 cups unsalted vegetable broth
½ cup breadcrumbs
2 tablespoons melted vegan butter *(optional)*
½ cup chopped almonds
2 tablespoons parsley, *chopped*
½ teaspoon ground black pepper
½ teaspoon celery salt

Preheat oven to 350°F (175°C). Lightly oil or use cooking spray on a 10"×13" casserole dish.

In a large bowl, add cooked rice, mushrooms, onions, broccoli, and peppers. Toss together. In another small bowl, mix the chili powder, salt (if vegetable broth is not salted), vegan Worcestershire and vegetable broth. Then, mix 1½ cup of the vegetable broth mixture to the rice and pour into casserole dish.

In a bowl, combine breadcrumbs, melted butter, almonds, parsley, pepper, and celery salt. Then spread the mixture over the rice and vegetables. If you feel mixture is too dry, pour the rest of the vegetable broth around the outside edge of the dish to add moisture.

Place in oven for 25-30 minutes or until top is golden brown and casserole is bubbly. Check for dryness during the cooking process and add water or broth as needed.

Remove and let stand for 10 minutes before serving.

Tofu with Kale, Carrots & Peanut Dressing
over Brown Rice

Great flavors! To expedite the time it takes to make this dish, chop ingredients before getting started.

- 1 (1 pound) package extra-firm tofu, *drained and squeezed dry*
- 4 cups cooked brown rice (page 174), *or a bag frozen brown rice*
- 1 large bunch kale, *tough spines over ¼" removed, leaves chopped*
- 2 carrots, *peeled, julienned*
- Peanuts, *chopped for topping (optional)*
- Toasted sesame seeds for topping *(optional)*
- Green onions, *slivered and chopped for topping (optional)*

Squeeze excess water from tofu and pat dry. Cut into cubes and then place in a shallow container with a top. Mix marinade ingredients (see below) and pour over tofu. Cover container and roll tofu around in marinade. Place in refrigerator and marinate for at least an hour, if not overnight.

Mix together ingredients for peanut butter dressing (see below) and set aside. If dressing seems too thick, just add water a tablespoon at a time until dressing becomes fluid.

Prepare vegetables for cooking. Tofu can be cooked while kale and carrots are steaming so all is hot and ready at the same time.

Heat nonstick skillet to medium-low heat. Drain marinade off of tofu and save. Add tofu to skillet and brown on each side. Add remaining marinade and heat.

Steam kale and carrots in steamer basket for 5 minutes. Remove kale and carrots from pan and place in bowl and add 2 tablespoons of peanut dressing at a time and toss. Keep adding until a light coating of dressing has covered the vegetables.

Put kale and carrots with dressing over brown rice then add tofu and any remaining marinade from the skillet. Top with chopped peanuts, or sesame seeds or green onions and enjoy!

Spicy Marinade

- 1 tablespoon sesame oil
- 3 tablespoons soy sauce
- 2 tablespoons rice vinegar
- 1 tablespoon agave nectar or sugar
- ½-1 teaspoon chili oil
- 2 tablespoons vegan Worcestershire
- 1 tablespoon oil or ¼ cup vegetable broth

Peanut Butter Dressing

- 3 tablespoons peanut butter, *creamy or crunchy*
- ¼ cup warm water
- 2 tablespoons soy sauce or tamari
- 1 tablespoon chili sauce or ketchup
- ½ teaspoon chili oil or red pepper flakes
- 1 teaspoon agave nectar or sugar

Sautéed Mushrooms & Tofu with Rice Noodles

This is a delicious meal. Add steamed broccoli at the end with the noodles for great flavor.

1 package firm tofu, *drained and cut into cubes*
5-6 tablespoons soy sauce or tamari
1 teaspoon mirin or brown sugar
1-2 teaspoons roasted sesame oil
2 teaspoons chili paste or sauce
8 ounces rice noodles
1 tablespoon canola or peanut oil
2 cups broccoli florets *(optional)*
4-5 cups mushrooms, *sliced, this can be a mix*
½ cup shallots, *finely diced*
1-2 jalapeño or Serrano peppers *finely diced*
3 tablespoons garlic, *finely chopped*
1 bunch green onions, *sliced*
½ teaspoon salt
Freshly ground pepper, *to taste*

Preheat oven to 350°F (175°C).

Drain tofu and squeeze out excess water. Cut into cubes and place in a flat dish. To make the marinade, mix soy sauce, mirin, sesame oil, and chili paste together. Pour sauce over tofu and gently toss. Let tofu sit for one to four hours. The longer tofu marinates, the better it tastes.

When ready to cook, spray baking pan with canola cooking spray and remove tofu from marinade, reserving the marinade mixture. Place tofu onto baking pan in a single layer with cubes not touching. Bake tofu for 15 minutes, turn over and cook for 10 minutes more, until both sides are browned. Remove and set aside.

If using rice noodles, heat water to hot, but not boiling. Pour hot water over noodles and let stand in a bowl for 10 minutes or until soft, then rinse and drain noodles.

If using broccoli, steam for 5 minutes, remove and rinse with cold water and drain.

Chop the garlic, shallots, green onions, and jalapeño peppers and set aside. Heat a large non-stick skillet to medium-high. Heat 1 tablespoon of canola or peanut oil in skillet, then add mushrooms, shallots, and jalapeño pepper. Stir often, until the mushrooms release their juices and are brown, about 2-3 minutes. Stir in garlic and then add the tofu, the saved marinade, broccoli and noodles. Gently toss everything together. Taste for seasonings. Pour into large, warm bowl and top with green onions. Serve.

Stir Fry with Soba Noodles

This is an excellent stir-fry dish. The key is to have all your ingredients prepared beforehand. The tofu used here should be marinated and baked before you begin. When serving a large crowd, consider making two separate dishes- one dish without the hot peppers for the children and one nice and spicy for adults.

- 1 pound Baked Tofu (page 229), *marinated and cut into bite-sized pieces*
- 4 cups shredded cabbage
- 1 cup sliced mushrooms
- 1 cup grated carrots
- ¼ cup red bell pepper strips
- 3 baby bok choy, *chopped*
- 1-2 jalapeños or other hot peppers, *to taste*
- ½ cup sliced green onions
- ¼ cup soy sauce or tamari
- ¼ cup vegan Worcestershire sauce
- 3 tablespoons ketchup
- 3 tablespoons mirin
- 2 teaspoons toasted sesame oil
- 2 tablespoons chili paste
- Dash hot chili sauce, *to taste*
- 1 teaspoon minced ginger *(optional)*
- 1 (12 oz) box soba noodles
- 1 tablespoon oil or ¼ cup vegetable broth, *for sautéing*
- Cashews, *chopped, for garnish (optional)*

Prepare all vegetables before you begin. Tofu should already be baked and ready to use.

Prepare cabbage, mushrooms, carrots, bell peppers, bok choy, jalapeños, green onions and toss together in a large bowl.

Combine soy sauce, Worcestershire sauce, ketchup, mirin, sesame oil, chili paste, hot chili sauce, and ginger, together and set aside.

Bring large pot of water to boil to cook the soba noodles. Right before you put noodles in to cook, start heating the wok or cooking pan to medium-high heat. Do not put oil or vegetable broth in yet. Cook soba noodles for 4 minutes, check for doneness, drain, rinse and set aside.

The next part goes very fast, so be ready! Add 1 tablespoon of oil or vegetable broth to hot wok and then add all the vegetables together at the same time. Using tongs, toss veggies continually about 2-3 minutes. The vegetables should be tender crisp not limp or rubbery. Add noodles, soy sauce mixture and tofu to stir-fry mixture in wok. Toss all together. Turn off heat. Serve in warm bowls or plates and top with cashews.

Hints:

- ◊ One pound of tofu might not be needed; it depends on how many are being served. Adjust accordingly and save the remaining tofu in the refrigerator for further use on salads or sandwiches.
- ◊ You can buy tofu with different textures from silken to super-firm. Buy extra-firm or super-firm to use in a stir-fry and for sautéing or grilling. Silken tofu is great for sauces or pies.

Tofu Stir-Fry

This is quick. Have all ingredients ready to cook before you begin.

- 1 tablespoons canola or peanut oil
- 1 package tofu, *extra firm, drained, pressed, cubed*
- 1 clove garlic, *minced*
- 1 carrot, *peeled, diced*
- 1 shallot, *diced*
- 1 cup mushrooms, *stems removed and sliced or diced*
- 1 cup snow peas
- Pinch red pepper flakes, *to taste*
- ½-1 teaspoon ginger, *minced (optional)*
- 3 cups brown rice, *cooked*
- 2 tablespoons soy sauce

Heat wok or large skillet to medium high. After a few minutes of heating, add oil. Put tofu in skillet and let brown before flipping to the other side. When all sides of the tofu are lightly browned, toss in garlic, carrots and shallots. Toss and cook for one minute then add mushrooms, snow peas, red pepper flakes and ginger for one minute. Add rice. Let rice begin to brown and add soy sauce. You can add a little water to loosen the mixture when it begins to stick to pan. Remove from heat and serve in a warm bowl.

Hint:

Keep your ginger in a plastic bag in the freezer. Use a zester or fine mesh grater to zest as much as you need and return to freezer.

Chapter Eight

Tofu, Beans and Peas

- Tofu seems to be intimidating at first, but you will grow to love it as a versatile source of protein. Like a blank canvas, tofu takes on flavors from marinades and sauces and can be any texture you crave, from soft and creamy to crunchy. It can be baked, fried, grilled, crumbled and pureed. Start slow and soon you will be a tofu fan.

- Frozen tofu has dryer, crispier texture once cooked. Plan ahead to thaw the tofu before use. Remove the tofu from the freezer and let it thaw in the refrigerator (which takes several days) or by putting the frozen package in a bowl of hot water. Keep draining tepid water and adding hot water until the tofu is ready to remove from the package and place in a colander to drain and finish thawing.

- Epazote is a Mexican herb that is grown in the U.S. and in Mexico. It is never eaten raw. There is a Mexican folk saying that when added to beans it controls flatulence. It does change the taste a little, but if you have the problem, you might give it a try.

Baked Tofu

The fact that the crunchy texture of this dish is achieved without frying in oil makes this my favorite way to prepare tofu. Besides, the taste is changed just by changing the marinade. You can even use barbecue sauces or salsas.

1 package tofu, *in water, firm, or super-firm*
Marinade *(a selection of possible marinades appear on page 230.)*

Preheat oven to 350°F (175°C).

Drain and squeeze excess water from the tofu by hand. Remove as much water as possible by wrapping the tofu in a cloth or paper towels and placing a heavy object, such as a heavy skillet, pot or heavy can of beans, on top for 15-30 minutes. Once drained, cut tofu into slabs, sticks or cubes.

Place tofu in a flat dish and pour marinade over the top. The firmer tofu tends to fall apart easily before it is cooked (especially if it is cut too thin), so gently flip slices to their other side to coat tofu in marinade. Cover dish and place in refrigerator to marinate from an hour to overnight; the longer the tofu is allowed to soak up the flavors, the better it will taste.

When ready to cook, remove tofu from marinade but save marinade for further use. Place tofu in a single layer on a non-stick baking pan and where pieces are not touching. Bake for 15 minutes. Flip tofu to opposite side and bake for an additional 15 minutes until it is crispy around the edges, but not dried out. Remove tofu and set aside.

Baked tofu can be refrigerated for several days. In fact, it is nice to have it available for a sandwich, salad or for use in another dish.

Grilled Tofu

Instead of baking, tofu can be grilled. Follow the same steps as above for removing excess moisture from the tofu. The cut into ½" thick slabs and place in a marinade of your choice for 30 minutes.

Place tofu on a lightly oiled vegetable grill pan. Grill until browned with a slight crust, about 5 minutes per side. The left over marinade can be brushed on tofu during cooking for an added glaze. Garnish with sliced scallions.

Basic Marinade

This a good basic marinade that goes well with stir-fry.

- ½ cup soy sauce or tamari
- 3-4 tablespoons rice vinegar
- 1 teaspoon agave nectar or mirin
- 2 teaspoon chili paste or sauce
- Dash roasted sesame oil

Chili Marinade

This is a spicy marinade that goes well with Mexican influenced dishes.

- ½ cup soy sauce or tamari or beer with 2 tablespoons soy sauce
- 3 tablespoons rice vinegar
- 2 teaspoons chili paste
- ½ teaspoon chili powder
- ½ teaspoon cumin
- ½ teaspoon red pepper flakes

Tomato Marinade

This is a good marinade for pasta dishes. You can add as much garlic as you like.

- ½ cup wine or vegetable broth
- 3 tablespoons red wine vinegar
- 2 tablespoons olive oil
- 2 tablespoons tomato paste
- 2-4 cloves garlic, *crushed*
- 2 tablespoons soy sauce

Marinade With Garlic

This is a great basic marinade that goes well with a stir-fry.

- ⅓ cup soy sauce or tamari
- 2-3 cloves garlic, *minced*
- 2 teaspoons toasted sesame oil
- 1 tablespoon rice vinegar
- 2 tablespoons mirin

Create Your Own Marinade

Tofu is a blank canvas and will take on any flavor it is marinated in, so be creative in adjusting the suggested marinades above by substituting or adding any of the following ingredients:

Wine
Beer
Vegetable broth
Any flavor vinegar
Any flavored oil
Tomato paste
Grated ginger
Fruit juices
Fresh or dried herbs
Smoked or regular paprika
Hoisin sauce
Mirin
Salsas
BBQ sauces

Hints:

◊ Frozen tofu has a drier, crispier texture once cooked. Plan ahead to thaw the tofu before use. Remove the tofu from the freezer and let it thaw in the refrigerator (which takes several days) or by putting the frozen package in a bowl of hot water. Keep draining tepid water and adding hot water until the tofu is ready to remove from the package and place in a colander to drain and finish thawing.
◊ Soy sauce is lighter and less overpowering in flavor than Tamari.

Cornmeal-Crusted Tofu

Try this crunchy treat as a side for greens. It also goes well with beans and rice. You can marinade the tofu before you coat it with cornmeal, although it is also quite good without it. Marinading will add an extra depth of flavor to the tofu.

- 1 pound package firm or extra firm tofu, *drained, cut in ½"-thick slices*
- 1 cup fine or medium ground cornmeal
- 1 tablespoon fresh chives, *finely minced* (optional)
- Fresh ground pepper
- ½ teaspoon red pepper flakes
- 1 teaspoon Deb's Seasoning (page 269)
- 4 tablespoons chili sauce or vegan Worcestershire sauce
- 1 tablespoon oil for cooking

Drain and squeeze excess water from the tofu by hand. Remove as much water as possible by wrapping the tofu in a cloth or paper towels and placing a heavy object, such as a heavy skillet, pot or heavy can of beans, on top for 15-30 minutes. Once drained, cut tofu into ½"-thick slabs.

Combine cornmeal with chives, fresh ground pepper, red pepper flakes and Deb's Seasoning in a pie plate. Put chili sauce or Worcestershire sauce in another pie plate. Dip each slice of the tofu in chili sauce or Worcestershire sauce and then coat both sides with the cornmeal mixture.

In large skillet, heat oil over medium heat and sauté tofu until golden brown, about 5 minutes per side. Place on paper towels to drain excess oil and then serve.

Broiled Tofu

This is a quick way to add crunchy texture to your tofu before adding it to a dish, such as stir-fry.

- 1 pound firm or super-firm tofu, *drained, cut into 1" cubes*

Place tofu on a lightly oiled baking sheet and place under broiler for 15 minutes or until golden in color. Turn each piece midway through cooking time to have even browning.

Crumbled Tofu

Tofu crumbles can be used in sauces, tacos, chili, Sloppy Joes (page 92), pastas or as topping for pizza (the list goes on and on). A lot of seasoning is required in the crumbled tofu for the flavors to hold up in many recipes, and, to keep their crunch, crumbles should be added at the very end of preparing your final dish.

1 package extra firm or super extra firm tofu, *water-packed*

Suggestions for Seasonings:
Taco seasoning
Deb's Seasoning (page 269)
Grill mix
Curry mix
Italian mix
Garlic or onion powder
Dry salad or dip mix that comes in packages
Salt and pepper

Place the tofu in the package in your freezer for at least one day. Freezing the tofu makes its consistency drier and chewier. Remove the tofu from the freezer and let it thaw in the refrigerator (which takes several days) or by putting the frozen package in a bowl of warm water. When the frozen water in the tofu package has melted enough to remove the tofu, remove the tofu from the package and place in a colander to drain until thawed completely.

Drain and squeeze excess water from the tofu by hand. Remove as much water as possible by wrapping the tofu in a cloth or paper towels and placing a heavy object, such as a heavy skillet, pot or heavy can of beans, on top for 15-30 minutes.

Crumble tofu into a bowl with seasoning. Toss around until well coated. Crumbles can be cooked at this time or stored in the refrigerator for a couple of days.

Tofu crumbles are great when dried in the oven. To do this, spread crumbles on a non-stick baking sheet. Place in a 250°F (120°C) oven for about 1 hour or until golden brown. Stir crumbles about half way through to make sure the ones around the edges do not get too brown. Remove and cool. If not using right away, store in an airtight container in the refrigerator.

Making your own crumbles is so much tastier than those purchased at a typical grocery store.

Tofu with Teriyaki Sauce

So simple and fast! The crispy tofu with the sauce is great served over rice or noodles with a side of broccoli.

1 package super-firm water packed tofu, *drained, squeezed excess moisture*
Cornstarch or arrowroot for coating tofu
2 tablespoons canola oil
4 tablespoons soy sauce
3 tablespoons mirin
1-2 teaspoons chili paste
1 teaspoon sugar
2 tablespoons green onions, *chopped*

Drain and squeeze excess water from the tofu by hand. Remove as much water as possible by wrapping the tofu in a cloth or paper towels and placing a heavy object, such as a heavy skillet, pot or heavy can of beans, on top for 15-30 minutes.

Slice the tofu into ½" slabs and then lightly coat with the cornstarch or arrowroot.

Heat skillet to medium and add oil. Sauté the tofu until brown on both sides. Remove tofu and pour off any left oil that is in the skillet. Add soy sauce, mirin, chili paste and sugar to skillet and bring to a boil. Turn off heat and add tofu back to the skillet with the soy sauce mixture. Gently turn tofu to cover with the sauce. Serve over rice on a warm plate. Top with green onions as a garnish.

Hint:
Arrowroot browns quickly and produces a golden crispy coating when sautéing tofu.

Sautéed Tofu

You can use it in pastas, on sandwiches, in stir-fry or on your salads. Change your seasonings to suite your taste.

- 1 package of firm or super firm tofu in water, *drained*
- 2 teaspoons canola oil
- 2 tablespoons of Vegan Worcestershire sauce or soy sauce or tamari or salsa, BBQ sauce or any other favorite sauce
- Salt
- Freshly ground pepper

Drain and squeeze excess water from the tofu by hand. Remove as much water as possible by wrapping the tofu in a cloth or paper towels and placing a heavy object, such as a heavy skillet, pot or heavy can of beans, on top for 15-30 minutes. Cut tofu into ½" slabs or cubes.

Heat the oil in a nonstick skillet to medium. Add tofu and salt. Cook until golden brown on one side and then flip. Cooking takes about 10 minutes.

Add sauce of choice and continue cooking until the sauce evaporates and the tofu is glazed. Season with salt and freshly ground pepper as desired and serve.

Battered Tofu

- 1 pound of firm or super-firm tofu, *drained, cut into slabs*
- 1 cup of all-purpose flour or cornmeal
- 1 tablespoon of arrowroot
- ¼ cup of nutritional yeast
- ⅛ teaspoon freshly ground black pepper
- ½ teaspoon garlic powder
- 1 teaspoon of Deb's Seasoning (page 269)
- ½ cup of soy sauce or vegetable broth
- 2 teaspoons of oil, *for cooking*

Drain and squeeze excess water from the tofu by hand. Remove as much water as possible by wrapping the tofu in a cloth or paper towels and placing a heavy object, such as a heavy skillet, pot or heavy can of beans, on top for 15-30 minutes. Cut tofu into ½" slabs.

Combine flour or cornmeal, arrowroot, nutritional yeast, black pepper, garlic powder and Deb's Seasoning in a pie plate.

In a separate bowl, take the tofu slabs and place them in the soy sauce or vegetable broth to soak for a few minutes.

Coat both sides of the tofu slabs in the pie plate with the dry ingredient mix and set aside. Heat oil in large skillet at medium heat. Cook tofu about 4 minutes on each side or until golden brown. Place on paper towels to drain of any excess oil.

Baked Beans

How can we have a backyard party or picnic without Baked Beans?

1 pound of dry Navy beans, *washed and soaked overnight*
1 (15 oz) can of tomatoes
1 teaspoon of salt
1 cup of onion, *diced and separated into two parts*
½ cup red bell pepper, *diced*
2 stalks of celery, *diced*
1 clove of garlic, *minced*
1 can of tomato sauce or 1 can of RO*TEL® tomatoes
½ cup of molasses
½ cup of catsup
¼ cup of prepared mustard
1 tablespoon of vegan Worcestershire sauce
2 teaspoons of red wine vinegar, *or your choice*
1 jalapeño, *diced (optional)*
½ teaspoon of seasoned salt
½ teaspoon of pepper
1 small onion, *thinly sliced*

Wash and soak beans overnight. Pour off soaking water and place beans in 10 quart pot with fresh water. Bring to a boil over medium-high heat. Add tomatoes, one teaspoon of salt, and ½ cup of the onions. Cook over medium-low heat for about 2 hours, until soft. When beans are tender, pour off at least half of the cooking water.

Preheat oven to 350°F (175°C). Lightly spray casserole dish or pan with canola cooking spray.

Combine all of the remaining ingredients, including the remaining uncooked onions, with the Navy beans in a large bowl and mix well. Pour mixture into casserole dish and cover top with the sliced onions. Cover dish with foil and bake for 30 to 45 minutes.

Remove foil and bake for additional 30-45 minutes. When the beans are done, they will appear bubbly, the onions will be golden brown and the sauce will thicken. Do not overcook or the sauce will dry out!

Remove from oven and cover lightly until you serve.

Hint:

To save time soaking and cooking dried beans, use 4 (14.5oz) cans of Navy beans. Rinse the canned beans and then follow remaining instructions. Faster and almost as good.

Black Beans

This recipe makes a large pot of beans but the leftovers hold up well to freezing for future needs, such as Black Bean Dip (page 264).

12 cups of water
3-4 cups of dry black beans, *sorted and rinsed*
1 onion, *finely chopped*
1-2 jalapeño peppers, *seeded and finely chopped*
1 teaspoon of salt
3 Roma tomatoes, *chopped*

Soaking the beans prior to cooking would speed up the cooking time but is optional. To soak beans wash beans checking carefully for shriveled beans and rocks. Cover and soak for an hour to overnight. Be sure to pour off the soaking water, rinse well and start the cooking process with clean water.

Add water to large pot over medium-high heat and add beans. Bring beans to a boil for 10 minutes, skimming off any foam that collects on top.

Add onion and jalapeño pepper. Lower heat to medium-low and simmer, about 45 minutes, until beans are close to being tender. Add salt plus tomatoes and partially cover the top of the pot. Turn heat down to low and continue to simmer until beans are tender. Turn off heat, cover and let beans sit until ready to serve.

Hint:
Overall cooking time depends on the age of the beans and the hardness of your water.

Refried Black Beans

So good! Try these as a side dish or on burritos, enchiladas, and tacos or in the Black Bean Layer Dip recipe. You can use pinto beans in place of the black beans in this recipe.

1 small onion, *diced*
½ teaspoon cumin
1-2 jalapeño or Serrano peppers, *seeded and finely diced*
1-2 cloves garlic, *minced*
3-4 cups black beans, *canned, rinsed, drained or homemade*
2 tablespoons canola oil
Salt, *to taste*
Freshly ground pepper, *to taste*
1½ cups water

Heat a large skillet to medium heat and cook onions with oil until tender and then add jalapeño and garlic and continue to cook until onions are slightly golden brown. Add cumin and stir into mixture. Bring heat up to medium-high and stir the beans into the mixture. Add 1½ cups of water to canned beans or 1 cup of water to homemade. Bring mixture to a boil, then lower the heat and simmer for 15 minutes.

When the liquid has reduced to half, mash beans until beans are smooth or consistency is as desired. This step can be done by hand or beans can be pureed in a food processor. Continue to cook for 5 more minutes. If beans become too dry, add a small amount of water. Add salt and pepper to taste. Serve.

Easy BBQ Beans

These beans are great for backyard gatherings. It just takes a couple of minutes to throw together and can be cooking while you are preparing other dishes. Make beans as spicy as you like but keep the little kids in mind.

- 2 cans vegetarian baked beans, *depending on size crowd*
- 1 (15 oz) can tomatoes, *stewed or diced, drained*
- ½ cup catsup
- 1 cup onion, *finely diced*
- ½ cup red bell pepper, *diced*
- ½ cup celery, *diced*
- 1 jalapeño, *diced (optional)*
- 1 clove garlic, *minced*
- 1 tablespoon molasses *(optional)*
- 1 tablespoon prepared mustard
- 1 tablespoon vegan Worcestershire sauce
- ½ teaspoon seasoned salt
- ½ teaspoon freshly ground pepper
- 1 tablespoon horseradish *(optional)*
- 1 small onion, *thinly sliced*

Preheat oven to 350°F (175°C). Lightly spray cooking dish or pan with canola cooking spray.

In a large bowl, mix all ingredients together except the sliced onions. After combining ingredients, place in casserole dish or pan and top with sliced onions.

Bake covered for 30 minutes and then uncovered for 30-45 minutes, until bubbly and thickened.

Butter or Large Lima Beans

The thick sauce that butter beans make after they are cooked is scrumptious. My mom made the best ever! Here is my take on hers:

4-5 cups dry butter or large lima beans, *rinsed and sorted*
1 medium onion, *diced*
1 teaspoon salt
Freshly ground pepper, *to taste*
2-3 tablespoons of fresh parsley, *chopped*

Place beans in large pot and soak for 30 minutes. Drain and add fresh water and bring to a boil over medium-high heat. Cook for 15 minutes and lower heat to simmer.

Add onion and salt then cook for 30 more minutes until beans are beginning to become tender, soft and creamy in the middle. Taste for salt, add pepper to taste and chopped parsley. Cover and turn off heat. Reheat before serving.

Hints:

- If the loose skins on the beans bother you, drain beans but reserve the broth. Then run your fingers through the beans to loosen and remove the skins. This is a tedious step but it does make the beans silky and easier to digest. Just pour broth back over beans and heat on simmer until they are hot.
- Butter beans tend to get mushy after they have been frozen so I don't recommend freezing.

Deb's Pinto Beans

Everyone loves this recipe. The best part is that no oil is added or needed.

4½ cups of dried pinto beans
1 large onion, *finely chopped*
1 teaspoon of Deb's Seasoning (page 269)
1 teaspoon of grill seasoning
Tabasco® pepper sauce, *to taste*
1 teaspoon salt
Freshly ground black pepper, *as desired*

Rinse beans well and be sure and look for rocks. Place in large pot, cover with fresh water and soak for 30 minutes to overnight. Soak for at least an hour. Remember that the beans will get 2-3 times larger once they are soaked. Pour off water, add fresh water and then over medium heat, bring to a full boil for 30 minutes. Keep adding water if the level goes below the beans to make sure they do not dry out and burn. Once the beans have reached their full size, add chopped onion, seasonings, one teaspoon of salt and freshly ground pepper.

Reduce heat to low, partially cover and simmer for about 1-1½ hours, until beans are tender, creamy and soft inside but not falling apart. When beans are done, taste and add Tabasco® sauce if more heat is needed.

Hint:

Find your favorite seasonings or seasoning blends so you always have the flavors you love on hand. There are many tasty grill seasonings. Buy a couple and experiment until you find the combinations that you like most.

Red or Kidney Beans

When I cook beans I always make a large pot so I can freeze extras in small containers. A dinner of rice and kidney beans is delicious and easy.

4½ cups of dry small red or kidney beans, *washed and well sorted*
1 medium onion, *diced*
1 teaspoons grill seasoning
Deb's Seasoning (page 269)
1 teaspoon salt
Freshly ground pepper, *to taste*
Dash of Tabasco®

Place dry beans in large bowl or pot, cover with fresh water and soak for at least one hour. Plan on beans getting 2-3 times larger in size. After soaking, drain water and pour beans into large saucepan with enough fresh water to cover them. Bring to boil over medium-high heat for 30 minutes. Keep adding fresh water to maintain level of water to cover beans.

Add chopped onion and seasonings and turn to low heat. Simmer about one hour, until beans are tender, soft and creamy inside but not falling apart. Test beans for tenderness and add salt and pepper. Add Tabasco® or red pepper flakes for spice. When done, turn off burner, cover. Heat up to serve.

Hint:

Epazote is a Mexican herb that is grown in the U.S. and in Mexico. It is never eaten raw. There is a Mexican folk saying that when added to beans it controls flatulence. It does change the taste a little, but if you have the problem, you might give it a try.

Red Beans & Broccoli

Easy to make and even better the following day! Red beans and broccoli makes a main dish or side dish.

2 cups broccoli florets
1 tablespoon oil or ¼ cup vegetable broth
1 small red onion, *thinly sliced*
½ red bell pepper, *seeded and thinly sliced*
1½ cloves garlic, *minced*
1 (15 oz) can kidney beans, *drained and rinsed*
2 tablespoons parsley, *chopped*
½ cup vegetable broth
½ teaspoon red pepper flakes
Salt and ground pepper, *to taste*

In a large pot of boiling water, cook broccoli 2-3 minutes until it is bright green. Drain the broccoli, run under cold water to stop the cooking and set aside.

Heat oil or vegetable broth in large skillet and sauté onion, pepper, and garlic and cook until tender. Add broccoli, beans, vegetable broth, parsley and red pepper flakes. Taste for salt and pepper and cook until all is heated through. Serve over rice or your favorite pasta.

White Beans

Navy or Cannelloni
4-5 cups dry white beans, *washed and sorted*
1 medium onion, *diced*
1 bay leaf
½-1 teaspoon thyme
1 teaspoon salt
Freshly ground pepper

In large pot, parboil beans for 10 minutes, drain, rinse, and add fresh water.

Turn heat to medium-high and bring to boil for 15 minutes. Add onion and lower heat to medium-low and cook for 30 minutes or until beans are tender, soft and creamy inside.

Turn heat to low and simmer. Add thyme, bay leaf, salt and pepper. Simmer for 15 minutes and check for taste and tenderness. Turn off heat, remove bay leaf and cover until ready to serve.

> ### *Hint:*
> The reason you parboil the beans in this recipe is to jump start the cooking process since you are not soaking first. You can also parboil some vegetables to remove the bitter taste or soften for regular cooking.

Red Beans & Rice

½ cup vegetable broth or water
2 cups brown rice
1½ cups red onion, *chopped*
3 garlic cloves, *minced*
½ cup celery, *chopped*
½ cup green bell pepper, *diced*
1 cup carrots, *peeled and finely diced*
1 jalapeño pepper, *seeded and minced*
1 tablespoon cumin
1½ teaspoons coriander
2 teaspoons chili powder
1 teaspoon smoked paprika or regular paprika
4 cups vegetable stock, *unsalted*
1 bay leaf
1½ cups cooked red beans
1½ cups fresh tomatoes, *chopped,* or 1 (14.5 oz) can stewed tomatoes, *drained*
½ cup corn, *fresh or frozen*
1 teaspoon salt
Ground pepper, *to taste*
Pinch cayenne pepper
3 tablespoons fresh parsley, *chopped*

In a large, deep sided skillet, add either ½ cup of vegetable broth or water over medium-high heat. Add rice, onion, garlic, celery, bell peppers, carrots, jalapeño, cumin, coriander, chili powder and paprika. Stir until lightly browned.

In another pot, bring 4 cups of vegetable broth and bay leaf to a boil. Add to rice mixture. Cover, lower heat and simmer for 15 minutes.

Add beans, tomatoes, corn, salt, freshly ground pepper and cayenne. Stir, cover and simmer for 25 more minutes, or until liquid is absorbed. Remove from heat and remove bay leaf. Taste for seasonings and add parsley.

Serve with a green salad or top with fresh chopped onions, tomatoes, and diced jalapeños.

Black-Eyed Peas

Spice this recipe up with pepper sauce or a couple of chopped hot peppers.

2 cups black-eyed peas, *fresh*
1 quart water
1 onion, *diced*
1 small green pepper, *diced*
1 celery rib, *finely diced*
½ teaspoon red pepper flakes
1 teaspoon Deb's Seasoning (page 269)
½-1 teaspoon salt
Ground pepper, *to taste*
Pepper sauce *(optional)*

Add peas to soup pot with water and bring to boil over medium-high heat. Add onion, green pepper, and celery and cook for about 10 minutes.

Add pepper flakes, seasoning and salt then lower heat to simmer. Partially cover pot and cook for about 30 minutes.

Taste for salt, add pepper and cook until peas are tender. Turn off heat and let flavors marry for a while. Check for seasonings and add pepper sauce to taste. Preheat before serving.

Crowder or Cream Peas

We always grow peas in our garden, so I cook them often during the peak season.

Fresh peas, *washed*
½ onion, *chopped*
1 jalapeño pepper, *seeded, finely diced*
½-1 teaspoon salt, *to taste*
Freshly ground pepper
Pepper sauce (*optional*)

Cover peas with fresh water. Add chopped onion and bring to boil on medium-heat. Cook for 30 minutes until water begins to turn brown in color. Watch and stir often because water will evaporate and you will burn your peas!

When peas begin to soften, turn down to low and add salt. When you feel peas are done, taste for salt and black pepper. Turn off heat and cover. Reheat right before serving. Taste again and add desired amount of pepper sauce if more spice is desired.

Chapter Nine

Sauces, Dips, Gravies and Extras

Kitchen Tips

- Be creative with plain vegan yogurt or vegan sour cream for dips and dressings. You can add so many different combinations of fruits, vegetables or seasonings, including packaged seasonings that will do the work for you.

- To reduce heat in chiles, cut out the membranes and seeds from inside. After handling cut peppers, be certain to wash your hands, knives and cutting boards with soap. Pepper juice burns and can be dangerous if rubbed into eyes.

- If you feel that your limes or lemons are not juicy enough, just pop them in the microwave for 10 seconds at highest power setting. It makes them release their juices.

- Tomatillos have a sticky coating under their husks. Before cooking, remove husks, and then wash the coating off with running water.

- Serrano peppers tend to be hotter than jalapeños.

- To make fresh breadcrumbs, cut away crusts of coarse-textured bead. Crumble the bread into a food processor and pulse to the desired consistency. For dried crumbs, dry fresh crumbs in an oven set on 200°F (95°C) for about 30-45 minutes.

Caramelized Onion Gravy

If you like sweet caramelized onions, you will love this on everything!

1 tablespoon of vegan butter or ¼ cup of vegetable broth
1 onion, *sliced*
1½ cup of red wine
¼ teaspoon salt
Freshly ground pepper, *to taste*

In a medium skillet, heat vegan butter or vegetable broth to medium low. Add onions and cook at a slow heat until browned and tender. Stir occasionally. The longer the onions cook, the sweeter they become.

Add the red wine and simmer until liquid has reduced by half and thickened. Taste and add desired salt and pepper. Serve.

Enchilada Sauce

This is good on enchiladas or tostados or anything! Simple to make!

4 cups of vegetable broth
5 tablespoons of mild chili powder
½ teaspoon of garlic salt
1 teaspoon of cumin
4 tablespoons of cornstarch with 2 tablespoons of water

Combine vegetable broth, chili powder, garlic salt, and cumin and bring to boil. Mix cornstarch with water and make a paste then add to broth. Boil hard for 1-5 minutes until it thickens. Turn off heat and cover for a few minutes to let the flavors blend together. Heat before serving.

Cashew Cream

This can be used like you would a heavy cream. It can be used in many different dishes including soups, casseroles and sauces. Just adjust the thickness of the cream by the amount of water that you add when blending. It is easy to make and can be stored in the refrigerator for a couple of days and even frozen for a couple of months. Just thaw and put back in the blender to get rid of the lumps. To get the best results, soak cashews overnight in the refrigerator.

1 cup of whole raw cashews
Water to cover

Place cashews in a container with a top and cover with water. Store overnight in the refrigerator.

When you are ready to blend, pour off soaking water and cover cashews with fresh water so that the water just covers the top of cashews. Place cashews and water in blender and blend until smooth and graininess is eliminated. Adjust the amount of water as needed. If you want a thinner cream or to make cashew milk add more water. Refrigerate until needed.

Hint:

If you need the cashew cream right away you can bring the cashews and water to a boil, then remove from heat and let soak for an hour before blending.

Mushroom Gravy

Delicious! You can use this savory gravy on so many things!

- 1 tablespoon of vegan butter or oil or ¼ cup of vegetable broth
- 2 cups of mushrooms, *any type or combination, without stems, finely chopped*
- 3 tablespoons of flour or cornstarch
- 2 teaspoons of tamari or soy sauce
- Fresh ground pepper to taste
- 2 cups of vegetable stock
- Salt, *depending on taste*

Sauté mushrooms in butter, oil or vegetable broth. Add flour and cook for 3 minutes. Then add tamari and pepper and stir. Add vegetable broth a little at a time, stirring constantly until gravy is thick. Taste for salt. Serve hot. This will keep a couple of days in the refrigerator and heats up nicely in the microwave.

Vegetable Gravy

A light, but full-flavored, gravy made with onions and celery. Perfect addition to Smashed Potatoes (page 163), Rusty's Mashed Potatoes (page 162) or Cornbread Dressing (page 281).

- 1-2 tablespoons oil or ½ cup vegetable broth
- 2 shallots, *finely minced*
- ¼ cup onion, *finely diced*
- ¼ cup celery, *finely diced*
- 1½ cups mushrooms, *chopped*
- ¼ cup cornstarch mixed in ¼ cup water or broth
- 3 cups Not-Chicken Vegetable broth
- Salt
- Pepper

Heat a skillet to medium. Add oil or broth and cook shallots, onions, celery and mushrooms until tender. Add cornstarch mixture, salt and pepper and stir until it is well mixed with the onions, shallots and celery mixture. Cook for a few minutes then add 3 cups of vegetable broth. Stir until gravy thickens, about 20 minutes. Taste and add salt and pepper as needed.

This is a hearty-tasting gravy. Mushrooms can be omitted from the sauté if you want a lighter taste.

Quick Peanut Sauce

This nutty flavored sauce is great over kale, tofu or brown rice.

½ cup natural peanut butter
2 tablespoons rice wine vinegar
1 clove of garlic, *minced*
2 teaspoons soy sauce or Tamari, *to taste*
1 teaspoon light brown sugar or 2 teaspoons agave nectar
½ teaspoon red pepper flakes or ½ teaspoon chili oil or 1 teaspoon of Sambal chili paste
1 cup hot water
¼ teaspoon salt

Combine all the ingredients except salt in a bowl, adding hot water to create the desired consistency. Taste for salt or seasonings. Add salt only if needed.

Black Bean Salsa

Prepare this salsa ahead of time so the flavors can marry. Great to use for many things but perfect with a big bowl of tortilla chips!

1 (15 oz) can black beans, *drained, rinsed*
1 avocado, *peeled, pitted, diced*
½ cup corn, *fresh or frozen, cooked*
½ cup bell pepper, *any color, finely diced*
½ cup onion, *finely diced*
1 jalapeño, *seeded, finely diced*
Juice of one lime
3 tablespoons any prepared salsa
Salt, *to taste*

Mix all ingredients. Add salt as desired. Refrigerate until you are ready to serve.

Hint:

If you feel that your limes or lemons are not juicy enough, just pop them in the microwave for 10 seconds at highest power setting. It makes them release their juices.

Ranchero Salsa

Use this rich sauce for dipping or pouring over enchiladas or tostadas. This is a basic recipe that you can add more heat or garlic to depending on your tastes. This makes about 4 cups.

4 large tomatoes
1-2 Serrano chiles or jalapeño
½ cup onion, *finely diced*
1 clove of garlic
Salt and pepper, *to taste*

Preheat oven to broil.

First, you need to blister the tomatoes and Serrano chiles under a broiler. Place them on a cooking pan, about 4" from the top of the oven. Using tongs, turn often for about 3-4 minutes until tomatoes and chiles are blistered all over. Cut off stems and remove seeds from chiles (unless you want the salsa to be really hot). If you would prefer a less smoky-tasting sauce, the skins can be removed from the chiles and tomatoes.

Pulse blistered tomatoes and chiles in a food processor along with the onions and garlic. This mixture can be as smooth or chunky as you prefer. Taste for salt and pepper.

Heat a skillet to medium-high. Add blended mixture to the skillet and lower the heat to medium-low. Cook for about 5-8 minutes until bubbly. Serve warm or cold.

Hint:

To reduce heat in chiles, cut out the membranes and seeds from inside. After handling cut peppers, be certain to wash your hands, knives and cutting boards with soap. Pepper juice burns and can be dangerous if rubbed into eyes.

Black-Eyed Pea Salsa

It is an old Southern saying that, if you eat black-eyed peas on New Year's Day, it will bring you luck and money. I can't promise either with this recipe, but it is great as a side dish, served as a dip with pita chips, or as a main dish served over Green Rice (page 176).

- ¼-½ cup balsamic or rice vinegar
- 1 tablespoon olive or canola oil
- 1 teaspoon salt
- ½ teaspoon pepper
- 2 cans (15 oz) of black-eyed peas, *rinsed and drained*
- 1½ cups bell peppers, *diced (this can be a mix of color)*
- ½ cup red onion, *finely diced*
- ½ cup cherry tomatoes, *chopped*
- 1-2 jalapeños, *seeded, finely diced*
- 1 tablespoon fresh parsley, *chopped*

Use a whisk to combine all dressing ingredients in the serving container you plan to use. Add all other ingredients and toss well. Taste for seasonings. Refrigerate at least 2 hours.

Hint:
Black-eyed peas can be substituted by any bean you would prefer.

Corn Salsa

This is colorful and crunchy and a great side dish, dip or salad.

- 2 cups fresh whole kernel corn or frozen, *cooked*
- 2 tomatoes, *diced*
- 1 jalapeño pepper, *seeded, finely diced*
- 3 green onions, *sliced*
- ½ cup red onion, *finely diced*
- ¼ cup fresh parsley, *chopped or cilantro*
- ¼ cup red bell pepper, *diced*
- 1 can (4.5 oz) chopped green chiles, *with liquid*
- 1 teaspoon olive oil *(optional)*
- ⅓ cup red wine vinegar, *or any vinegar you have on hand*
- 2 tablespoons fresh lemon juice
- ½ teaspoon cumin
- ¼ teaspoon salt
- ¼ teaspoon pepper
- Hot sauce to taste

Combine all ingredients and toss. Cover and refrigerate at least 2 hours (if not overnight).

Hint: Look for a variety of sweet onions like Vidalia or Maui to use in this salsa.

Guacamole

Most people overwork guacamole—keep it simple, fresh and wonderful. Plan on half of an avocado per person with one whole one for the bowl. It really depends on how hungry your crowd is. Adjust ingredients according to the number you are serving.

6 avocados
¼-½ cup red onion, *finely diced*
1 large or 2 medium tomatoes, *finely diced*
1-2 fresh jalapeño, *seeded, finely diced*
2 fresh limes, *one for salad and one for top*
Salt, *to taste*

Peel and remove seeds from avocados and place in a non-metal bowl. Add onions, tomatoes, jalapeños, juice of one lime and salt. Do not mash; mix in a cutting motion with a knife! You want to end up with chunks of avocado in mixture not mushy and smooth. Taste and adjust quantity of jalapeño, salt, and lime juice to match your tastes. If you are satisfied, squeeze more lime juice on top, cover with plastic wrap, and refrigerate until ready to serve.

Pico de Gallo

You can use this as a dip or to top anything when you want to add a little heat. Especially great when the tomatoes are in season.

3 large fresh tomatoes, *diced*
1 small onion, *finely diced*
1-2 jalapeños or Serrano peppers, *finely diced*
¼-½ cup parsley or cilantro, *chopped*
3-4 tablespoons of fresh lime juice
½ teaspoon salt, *to taste*
¼ teaspoon ground black pepper

Remove seeds of the peppers before dicing if you want a milder Pico de Gallo dip. Combine all ingredients in a bowl. Taste and adjust salt or pepper content. Refrigerate until needed.

Tamari Sauce

This sweet, spicy sauce is great for dipping raw or grilled vegetables, over rice or for stir-frys.

½ cup tamari or soy sauce
2 tablespoons rice vinegar
2 tablespoons agave nectar
1 clove garlic, *finely minced*
2 tablespoons shallots, *finely minced*
½ teaspoon ginger, *minced (optional)*
Red pepper flakes, *to taste*

Mix all ingredients in a saucepan. Simmer over low heat about 15 minutes. Let cool.

Sesame Sauce

This is really good on any grain or rice.

3 ounces silken tofu
¼ cup tahini
1-2 cloves garlic, *chopped or 3 cloves roasted garlic*
3 tablespoons lemon juice
1 teaspoon roasted sesame oil
½ teaspoon cayenne pepper, *for spice*
½ teaspoon salt
Freshly ground pepper
1 teaspoon fresh parsley, *chopped*

Place all ingredients in a blender or food processor and blend until well combined. Use water to thin to the desired consistency. Taste for salt and seasonings. More lemon juice can be added if desired. Serve room temperature. Keep leftovers in the refrigerator.

Veggie Sausage & Cream Gravy

The secret to this gravy recipe is to use ample ground pepper.

- 1 tablespoon canola oil
- 4-6 vegan sausage patties, *crumbled, if frozen let thaw*
- 2 tablespoons vegan butter
- 3 tablespoons all-purpose flour
- ½ teaspoon salt
- ¼ teaspoon pepper to taste
- 2-3 cups unsweetened almond milk
- ¼ cup cashew cream, page 252 *(optional)*

In medium skillet, heat oil to medium-high and add crumbled sausage. Cook until sausage is crispy stirring often. Remove sausage and set aside.

Using the same skillet, turn heat to medium-low and add vegan butter. When the butter has melted and is bubbly, add flour with salt and pepper. Mix thoroughly together. Stir continuously while cooking until the flour turns golden brown Add almond milk and stir often until mixture begins to thicken (about 10 minutes).

Add sausage crumbles and stir in cashew cream, if using.

Check for salt and pepper. Then serve over hot Easy Biscuits (page 279).

Hint:

Because of the lack of fat, almond milk will not get as thick as dairy milk. However, an acceptable thickness can be achieved with a few more minutes of cooking. The cashew cream helps add creaminess and thickness to the gravy, but an excessive amount will make the gravy fluffy.

Verde Sauce

This tangy green sauce is addictive. Add it to enchiladas, tacos, burritos and potatoes or use it as a dipping sauce for tortillas.

12 tomatillos, *husked, washed, cut in half*
1 small onion, *slices*
1 clove garlic, *whole, unpeeled*
2 jalapeño or Serrano chiles
½ cup fresh parsley or cilantro, *chopped*
½ teaspoon salt, *to taste*
Freshly ground pepper, *to taste*

Preheat oven to 425°F (220°C).

Place tomatillos, onion, garlic and jalapeño on a non-stick baking pan. Bake until vegetables are blistered and tender crisp.

Remove garlic from the pan and peel. Remove stems and cut the peppers open and remove seeds (unless you want the sauce to be really spicy). Place all ingredients in food processor and pulse until well blended. Taste for salt, pepper and stir in parsley or cilantro.

Hints:

◊ Tomatillos have a sticky coating under their husks. Before cooking, remove husks, and then wash the coating off with running water.
◊ Serrano peppers tend to be hotter than jalapeños.

Nutty Miso Dressing

There are many different recipes for this nut sauce. This is a good, basic recipe I got from an old friend years ago. Just by changing the choice of nut creates a totally different dressing. Use it as a sauce or dressing for salads and steamed vegetables or as a simple dip.

1 cup walnuts, roasted cashews or roasted almonds
1 cup water
¼ cup white miso
2 tablespoons lemon juice or vinegar
A touch salt or a teaspoon soy sauce
Pinch of red pepper flakes

Put all ingredients in a blender or food processor and blend until very smooth. A sprinkle of salt or soy sauce and red pepper flakes can be added for taste.

Hint:

Miso paste is made from soybeans. There are different types of miso. I prefer to use white miso when making dressings or sauces and brown rice miso and light yellow miso when making soups. These tend to be milder in flavor than some of the other types.

Black Bean Layer Dip

Who doesn't love this? You just need a big basket of tortilla chips.

1 tablespoon Taco Seasoning (page 269)
2 cups vegan sour cream
3 tablespoons lime juice
2 cups refried black beans (page 239)
½ cup fresh salsa or jarred
1 (4 oz) can chopped green chiles, *mild or hot*
½ teaspoon salt
3 avocadoes, *peeled, pitted, and chopped, or 2 cups guacamole (page 258)*
2 cups vegan cheese *(optional)*
1 cup red onion or green onions, *diced*
2 cups tomatoes, *diced*
1-2 jalapeños, *finely diced*

Mix taco seasoning with sour cream in a bowl and set aside. In a separate bowl, toss the lime juice and salt with avocados and set aside. Spread the black beans in the bottom of a 9"×9" baking dish. Top the layer of refried beans with the sour cream mixture and then spread the chiles over the layer of sour cream. Spread avocados evenly over the chiles. Sprinkle cheese, if using, and salsa over avocados. Top with fresh onions and tomatoes. Refrigerate until ready to serve.

Hint:

Push the skin of an avocado to determine ripeness. If it yields slightly it is ready to use. Do not use soft or mushy ones.

Chili Peanut Dip

1 cup of natural peanut butter
1 tablespoon of soy sauce
4 tablespoons of lime juice
¼ cup of hot water
1-2 jalapeños, *finely diced*
5 green onions, *white parts thinly sliced, chopped*
Salt, *to taste*

First, mix peanut butter with soy sauce and lime juice, thinning with hot water a little at a time as needed. Mixture should be thick but not gooey. Stir in jalapeños and onions and salt to taste. Check seasonings to see if more lime juice is needed.

Black Bean Dip

1 teaspoon canola oil
¼ cup onion, *finely diced*
1-2 jalapeños, *seeded, finely diced*
½ teaspoon ground cumin
Sprinkle of cayenne
2 cups black beans, *canned or homemade (page 238), drained*
¼ cup water or saved bean broth
Juice of one lime
Salt

In small skillet over medium heat, add oil and sauté onions and jalapeño for 1 to 2 minutes. Stir in cumin and cayenne. Remove from heat.

Add beans and bean broth to onion and pepper mixture in food processor. Pulse until not quite smooth. Add lime juice and salt. Taste and adjust flavors.

Hint:

Jalapeños have been bred to be milder than they used to be. To find a hot one, you really must taste. If you want more heat, just leave in the seeds and membranes.

Chive Aioli Dip

I love this in the spring when my herb garden is full of fresh chives. Makes a great, fresh-tasting dip to be served with crackers, chips or crudités. This can also be made with fresh basil or with a little freshly-grated horseradish stirred in.

¾ cup vegan mayonnaise
1 clove garlic, *finely minced*
¼ cup chives, *sniped with kitchen scissors*

Combine ingredients. Taste for seasonings you might like to add like freshly ground pepper. This can be refrigerated for several days.

> *Hint:*
> Aioli is the French word for garlic.

Cucumber Walnut Yogurt Dip

Serve with crudités, crackers, or pita chips.

One dash of ground cumin
½ cup cucumber, *seeded, quartered, sliced*
¼ cup walnuts, *finely chopped*
1 tablespoon fresh lemon juice
1 cup plain soy or coconut milk yogurt
½ teaspoon garlic salt
⅛ teaspoon freshly ground black pepper

Stir all ingredients together in small bowl. Taste for seasonings. Top with additional walnuts.

> *Hint:*
> The English Hot House cucumber has a mild flavor and the seeds are small; the skin is also thin and does not need to be peeled.

Avocado Jalapeño Yogurt Dip

Makes a creamy and zesty dip. Serve with tortilla chips.

1 avocado, *peeled, pitted and cut into chunks*
½ cup plain soy or coconut milk yogurt
2 teaspoons lime juice
½ teaspoon salt
1 small fresh jalapeño, *seeded, finely chopped*
½-1 teaspoon Deb's Taco Seasoning
    (page 269)

In small bowl, mash avocado, yogurt, lime juice and salt together. Combine until smooth or leave a few avocado chunks. Stir in jalapeño.

Hint:
Be creative with plain vegan yogurt or vegan sour cream for dips and dressings. You can add so many different combinations of fruits, vegetables or seasonings, including packaged seasonings that will do the work for you.

Roasted Almonds, Walnuts, Cashews or Peanuts

Preheat oven to 300°F (150°C).

Spread nuts out in a single layer on a baking sheet. Cook for 9-20 minutes, depending on the nut. You can tell when it is ready by the nutty smell. Remove and cool. Roasted nuts can be kept in the freezer in a plastic bag for months.

You can roll nuts around in 1 teaspoon of oil before roasting and then sprinkle with coarse sea salt or other seasonings when finished cooking.

Toasted Pine Nuts

Place nuts in a dry skillet over medium heat and cook until lightly brown in color. Shake and stir often. When you can smell the nuts they are done or close to it. Remove and cool. Roasted nuts can be kept in the freezer in a plastic bag for months.

> **Hint:**
> Keep nuts stored in your freezer in a sealed plastic bag or container. Just take out the amount needed and toss directly into your dish.

Roasted Edamame

When you offer these for an appetizer, they disappear fast. Make plenty.

1 bag of Edamame, *shelled, frozen*
1-2 teaspoon olive oil
¼ teaspoon sea salt
Fresh ground pepper *(optional)*

Preheat oven to 375°F (190°C).

Let edamame thaw for a few minutes and then dry off with paper towels. Toss in a bowl with 1-2 teaspoons of olive oil, sea salt and pepper. Spread out in a single layer on a baking sheet pan. Cook for 35 minutes, stir around a couple of times during cooking time. When they are firm and golden in color, remove from oven. Taste for salt. Serve.

Fried Capers

These fried capers add a lot of crispy crunch and flavor when used for a garnish.

2 tablespoons of capers, *drained*
1 teaspoon of canola oil

In small skillet, heat teaspoon of oil over medium-high heat. Add the capers and cook until crisp, 1 to 2 minutes. Remove and put on a paper towel until ready to use.

Hint:

Non parell capers are small pickled capers from Province, France. They are considered the best capers because they come from that region. Non parell means "without equal" in French.

Deb's Seasoning

The great thing about this recipe is seasoning can easily be added or taken away to suit your tastes. It is a good basic start. You can decide how much heat you want to add or how much, if any, salt you want to add. If you find that you always like to add fresh garlic and onion to your dishes, you can leave the garlic and onion powder out of the recipe. There are many other great products available and worth trying, but stay aware of the amount of salt used.

1 tablespoon of paprika
1 tablespoon of marjoram
1 tablespoon of garlic powder
1 tablespoon of onion powder
1 teaspoon of cumin
1 tablespoon of thyme
1 teaspoon of ground fennel seed
1 teaspoons of cayenne pepper
½ teaspoon of salt *(optional)*

½ teaspoon of red pepper flake or powder *(optional)*
1 teaspoon of celery salt
½ teaspoon of black pepper

Mix all ingredients together in a plastic bag or jar. Will stay fresh for up to 3 months.

Deb's Taco Seasoning

Many pre-packaged taco seasonings contain dairy product. Making your own taco seasoning is very easy.

½ teaspoon of garlic powder
½ teaspoon of onion powder
2 tablespoons of chili powder
2 teaspoon of paprika
2 teaspoons of ground cumin
¼ teaspoon of cayenne pepper
½ teaspoon of red pepper flakes *(optional)*

½ - 1 teaspoon salt
½ teaspoon of pepper

Mix together thoroughly and store in a tight container. Will stay fresh for up to 3 months.

Homemade Croutons

These are basic croutons. Be creative with your own!

- 2 cups of French bread or any non-dairy bread you like
- 1 tablespoon of vegan butter, cooking spray or olive oil
- ¼ teaspoon of garlic, *finely minced*

Preheat oven to 350°F (175°C).

Cut bread into 1" cubes, without crust. Mix melted vegan butter or olive oil with the garlic. Toss bread with mixture and add freshly ground pepper to taste. Bake 5-10 minutes until they are golden and crisp.

For a lighter version, sprinkle bread with garlic and use a light coat of canola oil cooking spray instead of vegan butter.

Variation:

There are many different herbs and seasonings that can be used. Just a few would include a sprinkle of cayenne pepper, parsley, finely minced, basil, minced or dried, chives, a seasoning salt like Tony Chachere's, flavored pepper, or a teaspoon of an Italian herb. Different breads can also make a big difference it the taste.

Hint:

To make fresh breadcrumbs, cut away crusts of coarse-textured bead. Crumble the bread into a food processor and pulse to the desired consistency. For dried crumbs, dry fresh crumbs in an oven set on 200°F (95°C) for about 30-45 minutes.

Masa Dumplings

These are corn flavored little dumplings that are great to eat with soups, Place on top as a garnish or put in the bottom of the bowl and pour soup over.

1 cup Masa Harina *(corn tortilla mix)*
1 teaspoon baking powder
2 teaspoons ground pure red chile pepper
    (not chili powder)
1 teaspoon salt
1 tablespoon oil
½ cup water

Stir Masa, baking powder, chili and salt together with fork. Mix in oil and water a little at a time, making sure you do not get too much, until dough comes together. Gently form into a small ball. Break off pieces of dough and roll into marbles.

Pour oil in skillet and heat to medium high. When hot, add balls and cook for several minutes, rolling them around in the pan, until golden. Remove to a paper towel covered plate to drain.

Maple-Glazed Pecans

Texas wouldn't be Texas without pecans. These are great for any gathering and are also appreciated small gifts for the holidays. I have used them for a light dessert and on salads.

2 cups raw pecans
¼ cup maple syrup
¼ cup sugar
Sea salt

Preheat oven to 350°F (175°C).

Spread pecans on baking pan and toast until lightly browned, about 8 minutes. Set aside.

Bring syrup and sugar to a boil in a saucepan over medium heat, stirring often. Boil for 2 minutes and then add pecans. Stir with a wooden spoon to totally coat pecans. Spread pecans on baking pan to cool. Sprinkle with coarse sea salt to taste.

Pita Toasts

3 pita breads
2 tablespoons vegan butter, *room temperature*
1 tablespoon fresh parsley, *minced*
1 teaspoon fresh chives
2 teaspoons fresh lemon juice
1 clove garlic, *minced*
Salt and pepper, *to taste*

Preheat oven to 425°F (220°C).

Cut pita into quarters. Blend the butter with other ingredients and let stand room temperature for 15 minutes. Spread on inside of bread.

Place pita quarters in a single layer on a baking sheet pan. Bake for about 5 minutes or until crisp. Remove from oven and serve warm.

Tortilla Strips

There are many uses for these strips like soups, salads and even tossed on top of enchiladas or a casserole.

Corn tortillas
Oil or canola cooking spray

Preheat oven to 425°F (220°C).

Lightly brush tortillas with oil or use canola-cooking spray. Stack together and cut into wedges or strips. Separate into a single layer on a baking sheet pan. Bake, tossing occasionally, until crisp. Remove and lightly salt.

Chapter Ten

Breads, Muffins and Breakfast

Kitchen Tips

FLOURS AND CORNMEALS—Bob's Red Mill® coarse or medium ground cornmeal has great corn flavor and texture. Or, Arrowhead Mills® regular yellow cornmeal is preferred for texture and taste. Masa Harina De Maiz® is flexible to use for tortillas, to thicken soups or for masa dumplings. For baking, King Arthur bleached or unbleached all-purpose and whole-wheat pastry flour seems to work best, often mixing the two in equal parts.

BAKING POWDER—Make sure to look for a double-acting aluminum-free baking powder, like Rumford.

BAKING SODA—Not just for baking, baking soda can be used for cleaning and refreshing a freezer or refrigerator. Arm and Hammer is an old stand-by, but Bob's Red Mill Aluminum Free Baking Soda works just as well.

CORNSTARCH—This grain starch, made from ground corn kernels, has a cloudy appearance when added to water and a cereal-like taste when cooked. Use it to thicken soups, puddings and gravies.

ARROWROOT—Extracted from the roots of the arrowroot plant, this tuber starch stays clear when added to water and has a neutral taste. Good for puddings and cakes. It gives a silky gloss to the appearance of food.

CHOCOLATE—Ghirardelli® unsweetened is great for cocoa and semi-sweet or Double Chocolate chips for baking. Use Ghirardelli® Hot Chocolate in Mocha or Double Chocolate for a smooth, rich taste. Ah!laska Chocolate syrup® works well for topping ice cream or desserts.

VANILLA EXTRACT—Mexican vanilla extract is a favorite due to its consistent and strong flavor. Try Citlali brand, which has a complex depth of flavors.

Egg Substitutes

The hardest ingredient to substitute in baking is eggs, but don't give up. There are many options available.

GROUND FLAXSEEDS—One tablespoon of ground flaxseeds plus two tablespoons of water replaces one egg. Beat together with a fork until it becomes gooey, much like an egg white. It works best in things like pancakes, whole-grain items such as cornbread, oatmeal cookies, apple cakes or hearty breads. Flaxseeds have an earthy, nutty taste. Whole Foods sells bags of ground flaxseed (either 365® or Spectrum®) in the area where vitamins are sold.

SILKEN TOFU—One-fourth of a cup of blended, silken tofu equals one egg. Blend in blender to smooth and cream. Usually requires a bit of non-dairy milk to smooth the texture. Silken tofu works best in dense cakes and brownies. It is also great in creamy pies and puddings. If you are trying it in a new recipe, go light at first as to not weigh the recipe down with too much of a tofu-like taste. Silken tofu is good if the recipe has strong flavored seasonings, but be cautious in using when recipe has a light, delicate flavor!

BANANA—One-half of a mashed banana equals one egg. Bananas work well as an egg replacer making things nice and moist. Of course, they have a banana flavor so they work best in breads, muffins, cakes and pancakes. Make sure bananas are ripe and are not green. This works best when used with baking powder or baking soda in a recipe.

BAKING POWDER—Baking powder is also a good egg replacer. 1½ teaspoons of baking powder equals one egg. This is an easy way to replace eggs in many recipes on most occasions. However, you must usually add a little more oil or liquid to the recipe to make it work.

ARROWROOT—Two tablespoons arrowroot plus ¼ cup of water equals 1 egg. This is another good way to replace an egg in baked goods.

PLAIN YOGURT, SOY OR COCONUT MILK—One-half of a cup of yogurt equals one egg. Using yogurt as an egg substitute does work and works well. Use this in recipes for a neutral taste and a creamy, richness.

ENER-G EGG REPLACER—Mix it up at the beginning of your recipe. It needs a few minutes to get foamy. Product can be inconsistent.

SOY FLOUR—One tablespoon of soy flour with 1 tablespoon of water can act as an egg substitute. Practice caution in using with delicate-tasting recipes as soy flour may have a strong taste that can be overpowering in some recipes.

APPLESAUCE—Use 3-4 tablespoons in baked goods. This can work well if the flavor works in your recipe.

Dairy Alternatives

Many non-dairy options are available: yogurts, cream cheeses, whipped creams, creamers, half-and-half, sour creams and puddings. Just check the labels to ensure that the product is vegan.

BUTTERMILK—The following is a simple recipe substitution for buttermilk that can be used to create light, moist and tender baked goods. Use 1 cup of unsweetened non-dairy milk and add one tablespoon of apple cider vinegar to mimic buttermilk. Let set for a few minutes before adding to your recipe.

MILK—Unsweetened ALMOND MILK is creamy and smooth in taste. The 365 Brand® almond milk from Whole Foods has a great thickness for baking. Rice Dream Original rice milk is thinner than almond milk, but works well in some batters, like Okra Cakes (page 128). Avoid sweet or flavored milks which can change the taste of baked goods.

BUTTER & OIL—Earth Balance vegan butter has a nice, neutral taste. To substitute oil for butter, use one-third cup of oil for one half cup of butter. Using canola oil, try to use the least amount possible in a recipe to achieve the desired result. Another substitution for oil or butter in baked goods is pureed prunes or

apples. Just buy a jar of pureed baby food and use to replace fat in a recipe. This substitution only works best if prune or apple flavors enhance the recipe (e.g., cakes and breads).

WHIPPED CREAM—Healthy Top by Mimic Creme is a brand which has a creamy texture and taste. Unfortunately, it is often difficult to find in the stores, but it can be ordered online.

CREAM CHEESE—There are many different brands of good tofu cream cheese. Tofutti is good with a consistent texture and flavor.

Sweeteners

There are several alternatives to white sugar, including: organic cane sugars, such as beet or cane sugar, raw sugar, brown sugar, maple syrup, agave nectar, molasses, barley malt and brown rice syrup. Some refined white sugar products can be processed with animal bones, so be sure to do your research.

AGAVE NECTAR is a natural sweetener that comes from the agave cactus. It is low in sucrose and has a low glycemic index. It has slightly more calories than sugar by volume but is 25% sweeter, so you use less. Use it in desserts or your morning oatmeal.

BARLEY MALT is a low sucrose sweetener that comes from whole barley.

BROWN RICE SYRUP, as the name implies, is a natural sweetener made from fermented brown rice.

BROWN SUGAR is really just refined sugar with a little bit of molasses added. Once again, check your brands to determine if product is vegan friendly.

MAPLE SYRUP is great for baking and for pancakes.

MOLASSES is a thick robust-tasting syrup produced during the refining of sugarcane or sorghum, varying in color from light to dark brown. Great for baking, but a little goes a long way. Sorghum molasses is versatile while Blackstrap can sometimes have a bitter taste.

CANE and **EVAPORATED CANE SUGAR** for baking. Vegan refined cane sugar is available at natural food stores. Although a little less sweet, evaporated sugar is similar to white sugar with less processing.

CONFECTIONERS' SUGAR OR POWDERED SUGAR is a combination of ground sugar and cornstarch useful for making icing. Be certain your brand is vegan.

STEVIA—A powdered extract from the stevia plant, stevia is a zero-calorie sugar substitute. It is much sweeter than sugar. Some brands can have an aftertaste but many do not. One-half of a cup of sugar equals 3½ tablespoons of stevia.

TURBINADO SUGAR is a coarse, unrefined sugar sprinkled on cookies or cupcakes for a sweet crunch.

Jen's Apple Spice Bread

Moist, flavorful and slightly sweet. This bread fills the house with wonderful aromas. It is so good!

- ¼ cup vegan butter
- ½ cup sugar
- 1 container plain yogurt, *soy or coconut milk*
- 2 teaspoons ground flaxseed
- 1 teaspoon vanilla
- 1 cup unsweetened applesauce
- 1 cup all-purpose flour
- 1 teaspoon baking soda
- ½ teaspoon salt
- ½ teaspoon cinnamon
- ⅛ teaspoon ground cloves
- A touch nutmeg
- ½ cup raisins
- ½ cup pecans, *chopped*

Preheat oven to 350°F (175°C). Lightly oil an 8"×8" or 9"×9" pan.

Cream vegan butter and sugar together. Add yogurt, flaxseeds, and vanilla and beat well. Add applesauce.

Combine flour, baking soda, salt, cinnamon, cloves, nutmeg and stir into cream mixture. Stir in raisins and pecans. Pour mixture in prepared pan and bake for 25-30 minutes, until toothpick comes out clean from center. Let cool for 10 minutes before serving.

Banana Bread *with Coconut & Pistachios*

Moist and rich, this bread is perfection when warm from the oven. Pistachios add an enticing flavor and aroma to this tender and cake-like bread.

1½ cup unsweetened almond milk
2 teaspoons apple cider vinegar
2½ cups all-purpose flour or whole wheat
1½ teaspoons baking powder
½ teaspoon baking soda
1 teaspoon salt
⅓ cup vegan butter
1 cup sugar
½ cup plain yogurt soy or coconut
1 teaspoon vanilla
2 large bananas, *mashed*
½ cup shredded coconut
½ cup pistachios, *chopped, roasted*
¼ cup confectioner's powdered sugar (*optional*)
¼ cup coconut flakes, *toasted, optional*

Preheat oven to 350°F (175°C). Spray bread pan with canola oil cooking spray.

Mix milk and apple cider vinegar together and set aside. Mix together flour, baking powder, baking soda, and salt.

In separate bowl beat vegan butter and sugar until fluffy. Add yogurt, milk mixture and vanilla. Pour wet mixture into dry ingredients and mix. Stir in bananas, coconut and pistachios. Pour into bread pan or pans. This makes two medium loaves or 4 mini loaves or muffins.

Bake 40 minutes or until golden brown and a toothpick comes out clean. Top can be sprinkled with powdered sugar or toasted coconut.

Hint:

When bananas are ripe and you are not going to use right away, peel, slice or leave whole, wrap in wax paper, then foil and freeze. Use for smoothies or thaw for banana bread or muffins.

Easy Biscuits

Not your Grandmother's recipe but…their great flavor is worth trying. Try topping them off with Veggie Sausage with Cream Gravy (page 260).

- 3¾ cups all-purpose flour
- 2 tablespoons baking powder
- 1½ teaspoons salt *(optional amount)*
- 8 tablespoons vegan mayonnaise
- 3 tablespoons vegan butter
- 2 cups almond, *soy or rice milk, unsweetened*

Preheat oven to 425°F (220°C). Spray two muffin pans with cooking spray.

Mix flour, baking powder and salt. Cut in vegan mayonnaise and vegan butter and mix until flour mixture creates pea-size crumbles. Add small amounts of milk a teaspoon at a time and mix. If mixture is too dry, add a little more milk or mayonnaise, dough should not be too wet. Try not to overwork dough. Fill muffin pans halfway. Bake 12 minutes or until golden brown. Check center with toothpick. Do not overcook because it makes the biscuits too dry. Serve hot.

Cornbread

If you were raised was raised on crispy cornbread, this recipe is ideal. If you prefer sweetness to your cornbread, just add a little agave nectar or honey.

- 1-2 tablespoons canola oil
- 1½ cup unsweetened almond milk or rice milk
- 2 teaspoons apple cider vinegar
- 1 cup yellow cornmeal
- ¼ cup coarse-ground cornmeal
- ¾ cup all-purpose flour or whole wheat
- 2 teaspoons baking powder
- 1 teaspoon baking soda
- 1 teaspoon salt
- 1 container plain soy yogurt or coconut milk yogurt
- 1 jalapeño, *seeded and minced (optional)*
- ½ red bell pepper, *finely chopped (optional)*
- 1 cup corn, *fresh or frozen (optional)*

Preheat oven to 425°F (220°C). Add 1 tablespoon of oil to bottom of cast iron skillet or 9" baking pan and preheat while mixing cornbread.

Mix almond milk or rice milk with vinegar and set aside. Combine all dry ingredientsin a medium-size bowl. Then add yogurt, almond (or rice) milk and vinegar. Mix well. Stir in jalapeño, red bell pepper and corn.

Remove pan or skillet from oven, pour in mixture and return to oven. Be careful not to burn yourself on the hot pan or skillet in this process. Cook for 20-30 minutes or until top is light brown in color. Remove and let cool for 10 minutes before serving.

Variation: Simple Cornbread

This recipe can be used for Cornbread Dressing (page 281). Preparation is identical to the instructions above.

- 1 cup yellow cornmeal
- 1 cup all-purpose flour
- 2 teaspoons baking powder
- 1 teaspoon baking soda
- 1 teaspoon salt
- 1 container plain soy yogurt or coconut milk yogurt
- 1 cup unsweetened almond or rice milk
- 1-2 tablespoons oil for iron skillet or pan

Cornbread Dressing

It took me a couple of Thanksgivings to perfect this recipe. Take time to adjust the flavorings to suit your family. This recipe is for one 10"×13"×2" casserole dish of dressing. To double the recipe, use two individual dishes since mixing a large batch tends to make the dressing mushy, losing the fluffy texture the dressing should have after cooking. You can cook the cornbread and crumble it the day before you plan to use it to save time the next day. Day-old cornbread also becomes dryer and coarser in texture which adds to the dressing. Plan on preparing one recipe of cornbread per baking dish of dressing.

- 2 tablespoons oil
- 1½ cups celery, *finely chopped*
- 1 cup onions, *finely chopped*
- 1 pan Simple Cornbread (page 280)
- 1 cup fresh bread, *dried, crumbled, fresh tastes better*
- 8 saltine crackers for extra crunch, *crumbled*
- 1 tablespoon poultry seasoning
- 2 teaspoons sage, *dried or fresh, to taste*
- Salt, *to taste*
- Freshly ground pepper, *to taste*
- 2-3 cups salted vegetable broth for moisture
- Vegan butter, *for top (optional)*
- Serve with Vegetable Gravy (page 253)

Preheat oven to 375°F (190°C). Lightly oiled 10"×13" baking dish or pan. In a medium-sized skillet, warm oil on medium heat. Sauté celery and onions until tender crisp. Remove from heat. Set aside.

Mix cornbread, crumbled bread and crumbled saltines in a large bowl. Add bread mixture to oiled baking dish. Pour the celery and onion mixture, along with the oil, over the cornbread mixture. Toss in 1 tablespoon of poultry seasoning, 1 teaspoon of sage, salt and pepper. Pour 1 cup of the vegetable broth and stir ingredients together with a fork, but do not over-stir. A light fluffy texture is desired, not a mushy or densely packed one, so remaining broth should be added one tablespoon at a time to avoid over-saturating the dressing. Taste as you go to make certain you have enough salt, sage, and poultry seasoning to meet your taste requirements. Let dressing rest for a few minutes then taste again.

When you are satisfied with the taste and consistency, slightly even out the dressing in the pan but do not pack it down, keep it fluffy, then dab four or five small chunks of vegan butter around on the top which will give a golden crunch to the top of the dressing. Cover and place in oven for 25 minutes. Uncover the pan and continue to bake for approximately 20 minutes or until the top is golden brown.

Hints:

- Apple cider vinegar is milder and sweeter than most vinegar. Good cider vinegar is slightly cloudy, like fresh cider and has a fruity, apple flavor.
- When you know you are going to make dressing the next day, cut up and refrigerate onions and celery in plastic bags, bake the cornbread, and dry out the fresh bread in a covered bowl on the counter the day before. It is far less stressful to have everything ready to go.

Lemon Bread

This is a quick, simple bread to make for breakfast or a snack. Everyone loves this, so make two! The recipe below is wonderful served plain but simple lemon syrup can be poured over the top or a Glaze With Lemon Zest (page 331) can be added for a sweet icing.

- 3 cups all-purpose flour or whole-wheat pastry flour or combination
- 1½ cups sugar
- 2 teaspoons ground flaxseeds
- 1½ teaspoon baking powder
- 1 teaspoon baking soda
- 1 teaspoon salt
- 2 tablespoons lemon zest
- 1 cup unsweetened almond milk
- 1 plain yogurt, *coconut milk or soy*
- ¼ cup fresh lemon juice
- ¼ cup canola oil
- 2 teaspoons rice vinegar

Preheat oven to 350°F (175°C). Lightly oil an 8"×4" bread pan.

Combine flour, sugar, flaxseeds, baking powder, baking soda, salt, and lemon zest. Whisk together milk, yogurt, lemon juice, oil, and vinegar. Stir into dry mixture until just combined.

Pour into bread pan and bake for 50 minutes, until top is golden and toothpick comes out clean from center. Poke holes in bread after it has finished cooking and drizzle syrup over the top. Let cool for 15 minutes before removing from pan. Cool on rack before slicing.

Lemon Syrup

You can make simple lemon syrup by mixing ¼ cup of sugar with 2 tablespoons of fresh lemon juice.

Simple Bread

Mouth-watering! This is a simple bread to pull together. Hearty, flaky and crusty and amazing how easy. This is great with soups. Any herb can be added for a different flavor but go lightly not to overpower the bread.

- 1½ cup unsweetened almond milk *(or any unsweetened non-dairy milk)*
- 3 tablespoons vinegar, *apple cider or plain*
- 4 cups all-purpose flour
- 1½ teaspoon baking soda
- 1 teaspoon baking powder
- 1 teaspoon salt
- ¼ cup vegan butter

Preheat oven to 400°F (205°C). Spray a cast iron skillet or 9"×9" baking pan with canola cooking spray.

Mix milk with vinegar and set aside. Mix flour, baking soda, and baking powder and salt together. Work vegan butter into flour mixture with fingers until crumbly. Pour milk mixture into flour and stir until just mixed.

Put dough onto floured surface and knead together with extra flour but do not overdo flour or kneading. Form into round disk-like loaf and place in skillet or baking pan. Cover loosely with foil and bake 30 minutes.

Remove foil and cook 15 more minutes until bread is nice and golden brown. Let cool for a few minutes before cutting.

Hint:

For hearty and healthful bread just add in ½ cup of chopped, cooked spinach and a ½ cup of chopped, toasted walnuts to the batter right before you pour into pan.

Zucchini Bread

An old favorite revisited.

- ½ cup unsweetened almond milk
- 1 tablespoon apple cider vinegar
- 3 cups all-purpose flour or whole-wheat pastry flour
- 2 teaspoons cinnamon
- ¼ teaspoon nutmeg
- 1 teaspoon baking soda
- 2 teaspoons baking powder
- 1 teaspoon salt
- ½ cup canola oil
- 2 teaspoons vanilla
- 1 cup sugar
- ½ cup brown sugar
- 2 cups zucchini, *grated*
- ½ cup crushed pineapple, *drained*
- ½ cup walnuts or pecans, *chopped*
- ½ cup dried currants or raisins

Preheat oven to 375°F (190°C). Prepare two bread pans or 4 mini bread pans or a muffin pan with cooking spray.

Combine milk with vinegar and set aside. Mix dry ingredients in a bowl, combining flour, cinnamon, nutmeg, baking soda, baking powder and salt.

In another bowl, mix oil, milk mixture, vanilla, and sugars. Add in zucchini and pineapple. Then combine wet ingredients with dry ingredients but do not over mix. Stir in nuts and currants.

Divide into pans and bake for 30-40 minutes. Check with toothpick, inserted in the center, making sure it comes out clean. Do not over bake. Move to cooling rack for 10 minutes and then remove from pan to let cool. You could add a Glaze (page 336).

Hint:

Currants are produced from a small variety of grapes; these dried fruits resemble tiny raisins but have a stronger, tarter flavor. Raisins are easily a substitute for currants.

Oatmeal

Don't forget oatmeal! It is a simple and healthy way to start off the morning. If you are a regular user—good for you—if not revisit it!

½ cup old fashioned or cut oatmeal makes 1 cup cooked oatmeal
1 cup water for each ½ cup oatmeal
Sprinkle salt *(or not)*

Cook on medium-low or low, depending on if you are watching closely or not. Bring to a boil for a couple of minutes until it is nice and thick.

Put in a bowl and top with your favorite topping
- *Brown sugar*
- *Honey*
- *Agave syrup*
- *Maple syrup*
- *Molasses*
- *Blueberries*
- *Bananas*
- *Raisins*
- *Currants*
- *Nuts*
- *Ground flaxseed (great way to start off the morning!)*
- *Any fruit you have on hand*

Rusty's Silver Dollar Pancakes

This is in memory of our Grandmother Coco's pancakes without the buttermilk and bacon grease!

1½ cups all-purpose flour
1 teaspoon baking powder
1 teaspoon salt
½ teaspoon baking soda
1 tablespoon apple cider vinegar
2 cups unsweetened almond milk
1 ripe banana
2 tablespoons maple syrup
Small amount canola oil, *for pan*

In a medium bowl, mix flour, baking powder, salt and baking soda in a bowl. In a separate bowl, mix vinegar and milk, then set aside.

Mash banana in another bowl, and add maple syrup and mix to a smooth consistency. Add to milk mixture and mix until smooth. Stir and add liquids and banana to dry ingredients, using a whisk to smooth out any lumps.

Heat a nonstick pan or griddle on medium-high heat and add a thin layer of canola oil. When water sizzles on the pan, it is ready for the pancakes. Use a serving spoon that holds about 2 tablespoons of batter and make each pancake with one spoonful. Cook until bubbles form. Flip and cook another few minutes on the other side. The pan is the right temperature when pancakes quickly cook to a golden brown color. Adding a small amount of canola oil to pan for cooking is optional but does help with sticking. This recipe makes about 30 – 3" diameter pancakes.

If you like thicker pancakes, use less milk.
Serve with maple syrup or fruit

Banana Muffins with Walnut Topping

Scrumptious!

1½ cups unsweetened almond milk
2 teaspoons apple cider vinegar
2½ cups all-purpose flour or whole-wheat pastry flour
1½ teaspoons baking powder
½ baking soda
1 teaspoon salt
1 teaspoon cinnamon
⅓ cup vegan butter
1 cup evaporated cane sugar or regular sugar
1 container plain yogurt, *soy or coconut milk*
1 teaspoon vanilla
2 large bananas, *fully ripe, mashed*

Topping
½ cup pecans or walnuts, *chopped*
¼ cup brown sugar
½ teaspoon cinnamon

Preheat oven to 350°F (175°C). Coat muffin pan with cooking spray or fill with paper liners.

Mix milk and vinegar together and set aside. Mix together flour, baking powder, baking soda, salt and cinnamon. In separate bowl, beat vegan butter and sugar until fluffy in mixer. Add yogurt, milk mixture and vanilla. Pour wet mixture into dry ingredients and mix then stir in bananas.

For topping mix walnuts, brown sugar and ½ teaspoon of cinnamon together.

Spoon batter into paper liners in muffin pan and fill ⅔ full. Bake 10 minutes. Remove and add brown sugar mixture to top. Cook another 15 minutes or until toothpick comes out clean. Remove and place on cooling rack.

Hints:
◊ Instead of a large spoon, try using an ice-cream scoop to fill muffin and cupcake pans.
◊ A light mixing of batter creates a tender muffin.
◊ One pound of bananas equal 3 medium or 1¼ cup mashed or 2 cups sliced or 2¼ cup diced.

Blueberries & Oatmeal Breakfast Muffins

Warm, tender muffins that almost melt in your mouth. You will love them!

1 cup oatmeal
1 cup plain yogurt, *soy or coconut milk*
½ cup unsweetened almond milk
2 teaspoons apple cider vinegar
1 cup brown sugar
1 cup all-purpose flour
1 teaspoon salt
1 teaspoon finely ground flaxseeds
1 teaspoon baking soda
2 teaspoons baking powder
½ teaspoon cinnamon
3 tablespoons canola oil
1 teaspoon vanilla
1 cup fresh or frozen blueberries

Preheat oven to 400°F (205°C). Spray muffin pan with cooking spray or use paper liners.

Soak oatmeal in yogurt for 3-5 minutes. Mix almond milk with vinegar. Using an electric mixer or by hand, mix the sugar with the milk and oatmeal mixture and beat well.

In a small bowl, combine flour, salt, flaxseeds, baking soda, baking powder and cinnamon together then add to batter. Add oil and vanilla and beat well.

Stir blueberries into batter by hand.
Fill each cup ⅔ full in the muffin pan with the batter. Bake for 15 to 20 minutes, until toothpick comes out clean from center.

Hints:

◊ For the freshest flaxseeds buy finely ground flaxseeds by Spectrum® or 365 Brand® that are usually located in the vitamin section. Keep in the refrigerator to keep fresh longer.
◊ If you are using frozen berries, stir into batter without thawing, or their juice will turn the muffins purple.

Oatmeal & Chocolate Chip Muffins

Quite honestly, these should really be called cupcakes and in the dessert section. We just always make them for breakfast or brunch.

1 cup of oatmeal
1 cup of plain yogurt, *soy or coconut milk*
½ cup of unsweetened almond milk
2 teaspoons of apple cider vinegar
1 cup of brown sugar
1 cup of flour
½ teaspoon of salt
1 teaspoon of ground flaxseeds
1 teaspoon of baking soda
2 teaspoons of baking powder
3 tablespoons of canola oil
1½ teaspoons of vanilla
1 cup of vegan chocolate chips
½ cup walnuts, *chopped*

Preheat oven to 400°F (205°C). Spray muffin pan with cooking spray or use paper liners.

Soak oatmeal in yogurt 3 to 5 minutes. Mix almond milk with vinegar and set aside.

Mix milk mixture and oatmeal mixture with sugar and beat well. In small bowl, combine flour with salt, flaxseeds, baking soda, and baking powder and add to batter and mix. Next, add oil and vanilla. Mix well.

Lastly, stir in chocolate chips and nuts in by hand. Fill each cup in the muffin pan ⅔ full with the batter. Bake for 15 to 20 minutes, until toothpick comes out clean when inserted in the middle of a muffin. Remove and cool on cooling rack.

Hint:

When mixing the batter be careful and do not over mix—it overdevelops the flours gluten and creates toughness.

Peanut Butter Bread Mini Loaves

Fantastic for breakfast or a snack!

½ cup unsweetened almond milk
2 teaspoons ground flaxseed
4 medium bananas, *ripe*
3 tablespoons peanut butter
1 container plain yogurt, *soy or coconut milk*
1 cup sugar
1½ teaspoons vanilla
½ cup peanuts, *chopped*
1½ cup all-purpose flour
1 teaspoon salt
1 teaspoon baking powder
1 teaspoon baking soda

Preheat oven to 350°F (175°C). Lightly coat four mini loaf (or 2 regular) bread pans with cooking spray.

In a small bowl, mix flaxseed into almond milk and set aside.

Mash bananas with a fork or a potato masher in a medium-sized bowl. Add peanut butter, yogurt, sugar, vanilla, peanuts, and flaxseed mixture to bananas and mix well.

In a small bowl, mix salt, baking powder, and baking soda into flour. Fold banana batter into dry ingredients until well mixed without overworking the batter.

Divide batter into the loaf pans. Bake for 35–45 minutes and remove when toothpick inserted in middle of bread comes out clean and they are golden brown. Do not overcook but make sure the middle is not mushy.

Cool on cooling rack for 10 minutes before removing from pan. The top can be sprinkled with powdered sugar.

Fresh Strawberry Mini Muffins

These muffins are moist and sweet, with a fresh strawberry flavor.

1 tablespoon fine ground flaxseed
½ cup unsweetened almond milk
3 cups flour
1 cup sugar
1 teaspoon cinnamon
1 teaspoon salt
1 teaspoon baking powder
1 teaspoon baking soda
¼ cup canola oil
1 container plain yogurt, *soy or coconut milk*
1½ teaspoon vanilla
1 cups strawberries, *sliced, dried off with paper towels*
¾ cup pecans, *chopped*
Powder sugar for top muffins

Preheat oven to 350°F (175°C). Lightly spray muffin pan with cooking spray.

Mix flaxseeds with almond milk and set aside. Combine flour, sugar, cinnamon, salt, baking powder, and baking soda in large bowl and mix together well.

Stir in oil, yogurt, vanilla, and flaxseeds with milk to flour mixture. Gently stir in strawberries and pecans. Do not over stir strawberries. Fill muffin pans ¾ full. Bake for 20 minutes until tester comes out clean. Cool 5 minutes before removing muffins from tins. Sprinkle with light coating of powdered sugar.

Hints:

◊ If your strawberries need to be washed, do it at the last minute. Once the stems are gone they absorb water and turn mushy pretty fast. Always dry off with paper towels before gently adding to a recipe.
◊ A sweet crumble topping adds a crunchy crust. You can top with coarse sugar crystals or cinnamon sugar. Sprinkle over top after you have filled the muffin cups with batter. For cinnamon sugar mix ¼ cup of sugar with one teaspoon of cinnamon.

Chapter Eleven

Fruits and Desserts

Kitchen Tips

FLOURS AND CORNMEALS—Bob's Red Mill® coarse or medium ground cornmeal has great corn flavor and texture. Or, Arrowhead Mills® regular yellow cornmeal is preferred for texture and taste. Masa Harina De Maiz® is flexible to use for tortillas, to thicken soups or for masa dumplings. For baking, King Arthur bleached or unbleached all-purpose and whole-wheat pastry flour seems to work best, often mixing the two in equal parts.

BAKING POWDER—Make sure to look for a double-acting aluminum-free baking powder, like Rumford.

BAKING SODA—Not just for baking, baking soda can be used for cleaning and refreshing a freezer or refrigerator. Arm and Hammer is an old stand-by, but Bob's Red Mill Aluminum Free Baking Soda works just as well.

CORNSTARCH—This grain starch, made from ground corn kernels, has a cloudy appearance when added to water and a cereal-like taste when cooked. Use it to thicken soups, puddings and gravies.

ARROWROOT—Extracted from the roots of the arrowroot plant, this tuber starch stays clear when added to water and has a neutral taste. Good for puddings and cakes. It gives a silky gloss to the appearance of food.

CHOCOLATE—Ghirardelli® unsweetened is great for cocoa and semi-sweet or Double Chocolate chips for baking. Use Ghirardelli® Hot Chocolate in Mocha or Double Chocolate for a smooth, rich taste. Ah!laska Chocolate syrup® works well for topping ice cream or desserts.

VANILLA EXTRACT—Mexican vanilla extract is a favorite due to its consistent and strong flavor. Try Citlali brand, which has a complex depth of flavors.

Egg Substitutes

The hardest ingredient to substitute in baking is eggs, but don't give up. There are many options available.

GROUND FLAXSEEDS—One tablespoon of ground flaxseeds plus two tablespoons of water replaces one egg. Beat together with a fork until it becomes gooey, much like an egg white. It works best in things like pancakes, whole-grain items such as cornbread, oatmeal cookies, apple cakes or hearty breads. Flaxseeds have an earthy, nutty taste. Whole Foods sells bags of ground flaxseed (either 365 or Spectrum) in the area where vitamins are sold.

SILKEN TOFU—One-fourth of a cup of blended, silken tofu equals one egg. Blend in blender to smooth and cream. Usually requires a bit of non-dairy milk to smooth the texture. Silken tofu works best in dense cakes and brownies. It is also great in creamy pies and puddings. If you are trying it in a new recipe, go light at first as to not weigh the recipe down with too much of a tofu-like taste. Silken tofu is good if the recipe has strong flavored seasonings, but be cautious in using when recipe has a light, delicate flavor!

BANANA—One-half of a mashed banana equals one egg. Bananas work well as an egg replacer making things nice and moist. Of course, they have a banana flavor so they work best in breads, muffins, cakes and pancakes. Make sure bananas are ripe and are not green. This works best when used with baking powder or baking soda in a recipe.

BAKING POWDER—Baking powder is also a good egg replacer. 1½ teaspoons of baking powder equals one egg. This is an easy way to replace eggs in many recipes on most occasions. However, you must usually add a little more oil or liquid to the recipe to make it work.

ARROWROOT—Two tablespoons arrowroot plus ¼ cup of water equals 1 egg. This is another good way to replace an egg in baked goods.

PLAIN YOGURT, SOY OR COCONUT MILK—One-half of a cup of yogurt equals one egg. Using yogurt as an egg substitute does work and works well. Use this in recipes for a neutral taste and a creamy, richness.

ENER-G EGG REPLACER—Mix it up at the beginning of your recipe. It needs a few minutes to get foamy. Product can be inconsistent.

SOY FLOUR—One tablespoon of soy flour with 1 tablespoon of water can act as an egg substitute. Practice caution in using with delicate-tasting recipes as soy flour may have a strong taste that can be overpowering in some recipes.

APPLESAUCE—Use 3-4 tablespoons in baked goods. This can work well if the flavor works in your recipe.

Dairy Alternatives

Many non-dairy options are available: yogurts, cream cheeses, whipped creams, creamers, half-and-half, sour creams and puddings. Just check the labels to ensure that the product is vegan.

BUTTERMILK—The following is a simple recipe substitution for buttermilk that can be used to create light, moist and tender baked goods. Use 1 cup of unsweetened non-dairy milk and add one tablespoon of apple cider vinegar to mimic buttermilk. Let set for a few minutes before adding to your recipe.

MILK—Unsweetened ALMOND MILK is creamy and smooth in taste. The 365 Brand almond milk from Whole Foods has a great thickness for baking. Rice Dream Original rice milk is thinner than almond milk, but works well in some batters, like Okra Cakes (page 128). Avoid sweet or flavored milks which can change the taste of baked goods.

BUTTER & OIL—Earth Balance vegan butter has a nice, neutral taste. To substitute oil for butter, use one-third cup of oil for one half cup of butter. Using canola oil, try to use the least amount possible in a recipe to achieve the desired result. Another substitution for oil or butter in baked goods is pureed prunes or

apples. Just buy a jar of pureed baby food and use to replace fat in a recipe. This substitution only works best if prune or apple flavors enhance the recipe (e.g., cakes and breads).

WHIPPED CREAM—Healthy Top by Mimic Creme is a brand which has a creamy texture and taste. Unfortunately, it is often difficult to find in the stores, but it can be ordered online.

CREAM CHEESE—There are many different brands of good tofu cream cheese. Tofutti is good with a consistent texture and flavor.

Sweeteners

There are several alternatives to white sugar, including: organic cane sugars, such as beet or cane sugar, raw sugar, brown sugar, maple syrup, agave nectar, molasses, barley malt and brown rice syrup. Some refined white sugar products can be processed with animal bones, so be sure to do your research.

AGAVE NECTAR is a natural sweetener that comes from the agave cactus. It is low in sucrose and has a low glycemic index. It has slightly more calories than sugar by volume but is 25% sweeter, so you use less. Use it in desserts or your morning oatmeal.

BARLEY MALT is a low sucrose sweetener that comes from whole barley.

BROWN RICE SYRUP, as the name implies, is a natural sweetener made from fermented brown rice.

BROWN SUGAR is really just refined sugar with a little bit of molasses added. Once again, check your brands to determine if product is vegan friendly.

MAPLE SYRUP is great for baking and for pancakes.

MOLASSES is a thick robust-tasting syrup produced during the refining of sugarcane or sorghum, varying in color from light to dark brown. Great for baking, but a little goes a long way. Sorghum molasses is versatile while Blackstrap can sometimes have a bitter taste.

CANE and **EVAPORATED CANE SUGAR** for baking. Vegan refined cane sugar is available at natural food stores. Although a little less sweet, evaporated sugar is similar to white sugar with less processing.

CONFECTIONERS' SUGAR OR POWDERED SUGAR is a combination of ground sugar and cornstarch useful for making icing. Be certain your brand is vegan.

STEVIA—A powdered extract from the stevia plant, stevia is a zero-calorie sugar substitute. It is much sweeter than sugar. Some brands can have an aftertaste but many do not. One-half of a cup of sugar equals 3½ tablespoons of stevia.

TURBINADO SUGAR is a coarse, unrefined sugar sprinkled on cookies or cupcakes for a sweet crunch.

Fruit is Truly the Perfect Dessert

Sweetened with its own sugars, refreshing, light and oh so healthy.

My daughter-in-law's father always peeled and sliced an apple, pear or other fruit and passed it around the table at the end of each meal. This is such a beautiful tradition to create with your children; making a routine of finishing off meals with something a little sweet but with a strong, healthy statement that leaves everyone at the table satisfied.

Fruit Plates

Make individual fruit plates for family or guests. Use the fruits in season and be creative. It does not have to be a fruit salad of sorts, just sliced fruit on a plate with a few berries scattered around. I believe dinner guests appreciate having a healthy dessert instead of a richer, calorie-dense one.

You can even have a beautiful small platter of fruit, peaches, apricots, seedless grapes, pears, figs, raspberries, strawberries, and pass it around the table. Exotic varieties are also fun to try. It allows the conversation to continue and people love it. The choices are endless and there is nothing to cook.

- Bananas
- Blackberries
- Blueberries
- Boysenberries
- Currants
- Gooseberries
- Loganberries
- Raspberries
- Strawberries
- Coconuts
- Figs
- Grapes
- Grapefruit
- Kiwi
- Kumquats
- Mangos
- Cantaloupe
- Honeydew melons
- Watermelons
- Nectarines
- Oranges
- Papaya
- Peaches
- Pears
- Persimmon
- Pineapples
- Pomegranate
- Tangerines

Fruit Kabobs

This is a simple dessert to make, but kids of all ages seem to love it, perhaps because the fruit has been peeled and cut into perfect bite-sized pieces. Perfect for outdoor barbecues, picnics, snack times, or even birthday parties. Sometimes it is easy to forget the simple basics. Alternate fruit on bamboo skewers for a fun presentation.

- Grapes
- Strawberries
- Pineapple
- Apples
- Melon chunks
- Tangerine segments
- Bananas
- Pears
- Kiwis
- The list goes on.

Mom's Baked Apples

The wonderful aroma of this dessert baking reminds me of my mother and grandmother, who both adored baked apples. Always the finicky eater, my mother had to coax me into discovering how good they really are. She would be proud to see this recipe here.

4 large apples, *cored with the skin peeled around the top*
1 cup water
1 cup apple juice
¼-½ cup brown sugar
4 teaspoons vegan butter
Sprinkle cinnamon
4 teaspoons raisins or currants *(optional)*
4 teaspoons pecans, *finely chopped (optional)*
Brown sugar to sprinkle over top

Preheat oven to 375°F (190°C). Lightly oil baking dish or pan.

Place apples upright in cooking dish or baking pan. Mix water, apple juice, and cinnamon and brown sugar together. Down the center of each apple, distribute the liquid mixture evenly among the four apples, and then add a teaspoon of butter, a teaspoon of raisins or currants, and a teaspoon of pecans. Lightly sprinkle the peeled tops of the apples with brown sugar.

Bake 30-45 minutes until tender but not falling apart. Baste the apples with the juices as they are baking to prevent apples drying out before fully cooked. Remove and serve warm.

Basic Fruit Cobbler with Oatmeal Topping

You can use almost any fruit you want: peaches, blueberries, strawberries, blackberries, plums or nectarines fresh or frozen. Adjust the flavor of the preserves to go with the fruit or combine different flavors for a little zip to this dessert.

- 4 cups sliced fruit or berries
- ½ cup matching preserves
- A sprinkle cinnamon or nutmeg can be nice, *depending on fruit*
- 3 teaspoons lemon juice
- 4 tablespoons all-purpose flour
- ¼ cup brown sugar
- ¾ cup quick cooking oatmeal
- ¼ cup brown sugar or 2 tablespoons maple syrup or both
- 2 tablespoons vegan butter, *room temperature (optional)*
- ¼ cup sliced almonds, *chopped walnuts or pecans*

Preheat oven to 350°F (175°C). Lightly oil a 9"×9" baking pan or dish.

Place fresh fruit or berries in a medium bowl. Combine preserves, cinnamon, and lemon juice. Pour mixture over fruit and gently toss trying not to mash fruit. Sprinkle flour and ¼ cup brown sugar over mixture and toss. Spread fruit mixture evenly in the bottom of a baking dish.

In a large mixing bowl, combine oats, sugar or maple syrup and vegan butter. Crumble the oat mixture and nuts over top of the fruit. Place pan in oven and bake until light golden brown in color (about 20-25 minutes). Remove and serve warm or room temperature.

Peach Cobbler *with Biscuit Topping*

Peach season is a special time for Texans, and this dish is hard to beat. The smells of fresh peaches and hot sugar-coated biscuits are just heartwarming. Blueberries, blackberries, strawberries, figs, plums or apples can be used in this recipe. The berries and peaches work well frozen if they are out of season.

Biscuit Topping

- 1½ cups all-purpose flour
- 4 tablespoons sugar
- 2 teaspoons baking powder
- 1 teaspoon salt
- 5 tablespoons vegan butter, *melted*
- ½ cup unsweetened almond milk
- 1 tablespoon sugar for sprinkling on top

Preheat oven to 375°F (190°C). Lightly oil a 9"×9" baking dish or pan.

Combine flour, sugar, baking powder and salt. Add melted vegan butter and milk and stir until the dough is sticky. Set aside.

Create filling (below). Then spread evenly on bottom of baking dish.

Using a tablespoon, scoop out spoonfuls of dough and cover the top of the peaches. Leave the dough in biscuit-like mounds. Sprinkle top with sugar. Bake for about 30 minutes, until top is golden brown. Serve warm or room temperature.

Hint:

You can buy peach nectar in most grocery stores. It is usually located in the fruit section and it comes in a can. There are different fruit flavors. It is a good product to use to add more flavors to fruit dishes.

Filling

- 4 cups peaches, *peeled, thinly sliced, fresh or frozen*
- ½ cup sugar (¾ cup for tart fruit)
- Sprinkle cinnamon
- ½ cup peach nectar
- 2 tablespoons all-purpose flour

Combine peaches with sugar, and a sprinkle of cinnamon and put into baking dish. Mix the flour with the peach nectar and pour over the peaches.

Blueberry Treat

This is an *old* family favorite that has been around forever; it works just as well with peaches or any fresh or frozen berries.

2 cups blueberries, *fresh or frozen*
¾ cup sugar, *divided*
2 tablespoons vegan butter
¾ cup all-purpose flour
2 teaspoons baking powder
½ teaspoon salt
¾ cup unsweetened almond milk
1 teaspoon vanilla extract

Preheat oven to 350°F (175°C). Lightly oil 8"×8" baking dish or pan.

Mix blueberries with 2 tablespoons sugar and set aside.

Put vegan butter in baking dish and place in oven to melt.

Combine ½ cup sugar, flour, baking powder, salt, milk and vanilla to make batter.

Remove pan from oven and pour batter into pan but do not stir. Evenly distribute blueberries over the top of the batter, but do not stir or mix them in. Bake for 45-60 minutes or until bubbly and golden brown on top. Serve warm.

Apple Crisp

Fruit crisps are easy to throw together with fruit you have on hand and you can control the amount of oil and sugar that goes into each one. Everyone seems to enjoy this dessert piping hot out of the oven.

4 medium apples, *peeled, chopped*
2 tablespoons raisins, *dried red currants or dried blueberries*
½ teaspoon cinnamon
⅛ teaspoon nutmeg
¼ teaspoon salt
¼ cup brown sugar
½-1 cup apple juice

Preheat oven to 350°F (175°C). Spray canola cooking spray on a 10"×10" or 9"×13" baking dish or pan.

Toss apples and raisins with cinnamon, nutmeg, salt and brown sugar. Pour in apple juice and mix. Pour into baking dish or pan. With your fingers, crumble topping (below) over apples.

Bake 30-45 minutes until bubbly and golden brown. Serve warm.

Crisp Topping

1 cup oatmeal
¼ cup all-purpose flour
2-3 tablespoons vegan butter, *room temperature*
¼ cup brown sugar
½ teaspoon cinnamon
¼ teaspoon salt
½ cup pecans, *chopped*
4 tablespoons maple syrup

Using your hands, combine oatmeal, flour, vegan butter, brown sugar, cinnamon, salt, pecans and maple syrup together in a mixing bowl until coarse crumbles are formed.

Plum & Nectarine Crisp

A perfect paring of summer fruit.

4 plums, *pitted, sliced*
4 nectarines, *pitted, sliced*
¼ cup sugar
¼ cup brown sugar
½ teaspoon cinnamon
1 teaspoon lemon or orange zest
1 teaspoon flour

TOPPING
¾ cup all-purpose flour or whole wheat
¼ cup sugar
¼ cup vegan butter, *or any non-dairy butter*
¼ teaspoon salt
½ teaspoon cinnamon

Preheat oven to 375°F (190°C). Lightly oil a 9"×9" baking dish or pan.

Toss fruit with white and brown sugar, cinnamon, lemon zest and 1 teaspoon of flour. Pour into baking dish or pan. Combine all topping ingredients and mix with your fingers. Then crumble over top of fruit mixture.

Bake for about 30 minutes, until bubbly and top is lightly brown. Serve warm.

Cherry Crisp

Fresh cherries give this crisp a delightful color and tartness. This is a delicious crisp and a perfect way to use fresh cherries when they are in season.

1 pound cherries, *stemmed and pitted*
2 tablespoons vegan butter, *melted*
¼ teaspoon salt
¼ cup sugar
½ teaspoon vanilla extract

CRISP TOPPING
¾ cup all-purpose flour or whole wheat or combination
¼ cup sugar
¼ cup vegan butter, *room temperature*

Preheat oven to 375°F (190°C). Lightly oil a 9"×9" baking pan.

Combine cherries, melted vegan butter, salt, sugar and vanilla. Pour into baking dish or pan. With your fingers, crumble topping over cherries.

Bake for 20 minutes or until top turns light brown in color. Serve warm.

Wonderful topped with your favorite non-dairy vanilla ice cream or vegan whipped cream.

Combine with fingers and crumble over crisp.

Kettle Corn

My grandchildren prefer this to the real buttery mix at the farmers market on Saturdays.

½ cup popcorn kernels
2 tablespoons canola oil
½ cup sugar
1 teaspoon salt

Heat a large, deep pot to medium-high heat. Add oil and popcorn. Cover tightly with lid and cook until kernels just begin to pop, 3-4 minutes. Give pot an up and down shake every 30 seconds or so. When popping has almost stopped, remove pot from heat. Turn heat to low and add sugar and salt to popcorn. Return pot to heat until the sugar has melted, shake 5 or 6 times in an up and down motion to coat the popcorn. The sugar should be melted and beginning to caramelize. Take a long wooden spoon and mix popcorn to make sure it is separate kernels from bottom of the pot. Pour into a large bowl and serve.

Pie Crust

Making a great pie crust gets easier with practice. For the perfect pie crust, work the dough as little as possible and refrain from using too much flour. The big question is whether to use vegetable shortening, oil or vegan butter. Shortening makes a flakier crust, but vegan butter tastes better even though it is more difficult to handle and requires more practice. The key to success is to have all of the ingredients as cold as possible and to place the dough in the refrigerator between each step to keep the mixture firm. There are other great crusts in this cookbook that are easier to make if you prefer fewer steps and less preparation time.

One single crust for a 9" pie plate
6 tablespoon vegan butter stick
1 cup all-purpose or whole-wheat pastry flour
½ teaspoon salt
3 tablespoons ice cold water

Two crusts (top and bottom) for a 9" pie plate
2 cups all-purpose flour or whole-wheat pastry flour
1 teaspoon salt
12 tablespoons vegan butter stick
5 tablespoons ice cold water

Preheat oven to 425°F (220°C)

Take one vegan butter stick, and use the markings on the wrapper as a guide to cut into six one-tablespoon slices. Cut each slice into 4 pieces and spread the pieces on a small plate. Place plate in the freezer for 30 minutes.

Stir flour and salt together in a large bowl. Cut all the pieces of butter into the mixture with a fork or pastry cutter or use your hands and work the mixture until the texture is like a bowl of small English peas. Add ice water one tablespoon at a time, stirring with a fork until mixture will hold together when you make a ball. The ball should look a little rough in texture and not smooth. If you are making the double recipe, divide the dough in half, forming each half into a flat, round disk-like shape about 5" in diameter and 1" thick. Wrap each disk with plastic wrap. Put both wrapped disks of dough into the freezer for one hour.

Remove one of the disks from the freezer and let it stand until the disk becomes pliant enough that you can roll it out. Place 2 sheets of wax or parchment paper on a hard surface and lightly flour the surface of the paper. Place the disk of dough on the paper. Starting in the middle of the dough, use a rolling pin to push outward in all directions until you form a circle. Do not roll out too thin, especially around the edges. Roll dough 3" wider than your pie pan or plate.

Flour your rolling pin to keep the dough from sticking. If sticky dough is a problem for you, then place dough in the middle of two floured sheets of wax paper and roll the dough that way.

When you are ready to place the dough into a pie plate or pan, loosely wrap the dough around the rolling pin and then unroll it into the pan or fold the dough in half and move it to the pan. Press the dough into the pan and trim edges, but

don't worry about fluting them at this point.

If you are baking a single crust, place the pan and dough into the freezer for 30 minutes. Remove the pan with the dough from the freezer, flute the edges and take a fork and prick the dough all over on the bottom of the pan. Then line the dough with parchment paper and fill with dried beans. The dried beans will help the dough bake evenly. Bake for 15 minutes or until the sides and edges are golden brown.

If you are using a top and bottom crust, then placing the dough and pan into the freezer is not necessary. Fill the bottom crust in the pie pan with filling. Place top crust on pie and pinch or flute top and bottom crusts together. Prick the top with a fork or cut out a center design. Bake until golden brown on top and edges. If you notice that the edges are browning too fast, then cover the edges of the pie pan with a 3" strip of aluminum foil. Remove the foil for the last 15 minutes of baking time for the pie. Place pies in a 425°F (220°C) preheated oven and then lower the temperature setting to 350°F–375°F (175°C–190°C) for baking.

Nut & Medjool Date Crust

2 cups almonds, *pecans, pistachios or walnuts*
1 cup Medjool® dates
½ teaspoon salt

In a food processor, pulse the nuts until coarsely chopped. Add dates and salt and continue to pulse the food processor until the mixture is not wet but holds together when squeezed. Press the mixture into a pie or tart pan and evenly cover the bottom and sides of the pan. This does not need to be baked before using.

Graham Cracker Crust

Preheat oven to 350°F (175°C).

1½ cup crushed vegan graham crackers
2 tablespoons sugar
½ teaspoon cinnamon *(optional)*
¼ cup pecans, *finely chopped (optional)*
6 tablespoons vegan butter, *melted*

Combine all ingredients by gently pulsing in a food processor until the mixture holds together when squeezed. Press the mixture into a pie, tart or spring form pan and evenly cover the bottom and sides. Bake 15 minutes or until crust is lightly brown and let cool before adding filling.

Ginger Snap Crust

You can really use any of your favorite cookies in this easy recipe. Be creative.

1½ cup ginger snaps, *broken*
3 tablespoons sugar
6 tablespoons vegan butter

Preheat oven to 350°F (175°C)

Combine all ingredients by gently pulsing in a food processor until the mixture holds together when squeezed. Press the mixture into a pie, tart or spring-form pan and evenly cover the bottom and sides. Bake 10 minutes or until crust is lightly brown and let cool before adding the filling.

Walnut Pie Crust

This pie crust can be used for tarts or non-baked pies. It is a nice alternative to a regular crust.

1 cup of walnuts
1 cup of all-purpose or whole wheat pastry flour
½ teaspoon of salt
¼ cup of maple syrup
¼ cup of vegan butter, *melted or coconut oil*

Preheat oven to 350°F (175°C).

Combine walnuts, flour, and salt in a food processor and pulse until a fine meal is formed. Add maple syrup and butter and pulse until the dough is well mixed with the nuts a medium coarse texture. Place the dough in a pie or tart pan and press around until the inside of the pan is evenly covered with the dough. Bake for 15-20 minutes, until lightly browned. Let cool before filling.

Grapenut Pie Crust

This simple crust has been around forever but is good, easy and has no oil or butter. A good crust for any pudding filling.

2 cups of Grape Nut® brand cereal
½ cup of apple juice concentrate, *thawed*

Preheat oven to 375°F (190°C).

Mix cereal and apple juice together in a bowl. Press the mixture into the bottom and sides of a pie pan. Bake for 15 minutes, if you are using a no-bake filling. For other recipes, pour in the filling and bake per recipe.

Angela's Apple Pie

Angela's apple pies are wonderful in taste and aroma.

- 6 Braeburn apples (or 4 cups)
- 1 tablespoon of lemon juice
- 1 cup of sugar
- ½ teaspoon of cinnamon
- ¼ teaspoon of nutmeg
- 2 tablespoons of flour
- 1 tablespoon of vegan butter *(optional)*

Preheat oven to 425°F (218°C).

Prepare basic pastry for double pie crust.

Peel, core and thinly slice apples and toss with lemon juice. In a separate bowl, mix dry ingredients together and add mixture to apples. Gently toss mixture to coat apples.

Transfer to prepared crust and dot top with butter. Add top crust and cinch together edges of crust and cut 2-4 small openings in top crust for venting. Bake for 45 minutes or until golden brown and bubbly.

Remove from oven and cool.

Hint:

To prevent pie crust from over-browning, cover the crust edge with 3-inch strip of aluminum foil. Remove foil during last 15 minutes of baking.

Easy Blueberry Pie

Blueberries are more frequently available at grocery stores year-round, so you can have this anytime. For a more adventurous recipe, add a mixture of berries to this or use a different berry all together.

4 cups blueberries, *fresh or frozen*
½ cup sugar
3 tablespoons cornstarch or arrowroot
½ teaspoon cinnamon
2 tablespoons lemon juice
2 tablespoons vegan butter, *diced*
2 pie crusts, to use for top and bottom pie, *homemade or bought (page 306)*
Vegan butter, *sliced (optional)*
Sugar *(optional)*

Preheat oven to 350°F (175°C).

If using pre-packaged pie crusts, remove them from packaging and place on a lightly floured surface. Roll homemade or store bought bottom crust, placing the pie crust in a 9" pie plate. Roll second crust and prepare it for placement on top of pie.

Mix filling by combining sugar, cornstarch, and cinnamon together in a medium bowl. Drizzle lemon juice over blueberries in a separate bowl and then toss with the sugar mixture and vegan butter.

Add berries to pie plate with bottom crust and cover with top crust. Top the crust with 2-4 butter slices and a sprinkle of sugar, if desired.

Bake for 45 minutes or until bubbly and golden brown. Remove and cool.

Hint:

Cook juicy pies by placing a pie pan on a baking sheet; therefore, if the juices overflow, you will not have a big oven mess.

Creamy Coconut Pie

This delicious coconut filling can also be used as a pudding. This recipe calls for vanilla extract, but use coconut extract if you want a stronger coconut flavor.

- 1 bottom pie crust, *homemade (page 306), or store-bought or make a Graham Cracker Crust (page 308)*
- ¾ cup shredded coconut, *sweetened or unsweetened*
- 2 cups coconut milk
- 1 cup unsweetened almond milk
- ½-1 cup sugar, *depending on sweetness of coconut*
- ¼ teaspoon salt
- 1 tablespoon of agar flakes
- ⅓ cup cornstarch or arrowroot
- 1½ teaspoon vanilla or coconut extract
- ½ cup sweetened, toasted coconut, *for the top pie*
- ⅓ cup water

Preheat oven to 350°F (175°C).

Prepare pie crust and bake in a 9" pie plate. Set aside to cool. Spread ½ cup of coconut on a baking sheet and toast until golden brown. Set aside.

In a sauce pan, add coconut milk, almond milk, remaining ¼ cup of coconut, sugar, salt and agar flakes and bring to medium-low heat. Stirring constantly, bring mixture to a boil. In a separate bowl, mix in water to the cornstarch and add to coconut mixture. Lower the heat and simmer for 5-8 minutes until smooth and free of lumps. Once thickened, remove from heat and add vanilla extract. Mix in well.

Pour mixture into pie crust. After pie cools for 15 minutes, sprinkle toasted coconut around on top of pie. Let cool for 15 minutes and then place in refrigerator one to four hours.

Rustic Fruit Pie

This is a wonderful dessert that fills the kitchen with rich, fruity aromas. Use any combination of fruit you prefer. If your follow the steps carefully, this recipe is easier than you'd expect.

1¼ cup all-purpose flour
1 tablepoon sugar
¼ teaspoon baking powder
¼ teaspoon cinnamon
½ teaspoon salt
⅓ cup chilled vegan butter
1 tablespoon vanilla extract
⅓ cup ice cold water
Rustic Pie Filling *(below)*

Preheat oven to 375°F (190°C).

In medium bowl, mix together flour, one tablespoon of sugar, baking powder, cinnamon and salt to make crust. Using pastry cutter, or by pulsing in a food processor, blend vegan butter into flour mix until mixture has a crumbly consistency. The goal is to work quickly so the vegan butter does not melt. Add vanilla and one tablespoon of ice water and mix with a wooden spoon. Add additional water one tablespoon at a time, until dough just holds together. Wrap the dough in plastic wrap and form into a disc shape. Refrigerate for 10 minutes.

Remove dough and roll out between two layers of lightly floured parchment paper. Once is about ½" thick, refrigerate dough in parchment paper for 10 minutes. While dough is chilling, mix pie filling in a separate bowl.

Once the dough is cool, remove parchment paper and roll dough onto a lightly-oiled baking sheet in a rough circle about a ½" thick.

Assemble the pie by placing thinly-sliced apples in an overlapping circular pattern on the dough, leaving a 2" to 3" border of dough around the outside of the circle. Pour the liquid from the pie filling over the top of apples. Fold the border dough up to top the fruit filling. The dough will not cover all of the apples, thus giving the pie a rustic appearance. Dough does not need to be perfectly round. Place baking sheet with pie in the refrigerator for 15 minutes.

Remove pie from refrigerator and lightly brush edges and top of fruit filling with maple syrup. Sprinkle extra sugar over dough and fruit. Bake for 35 minutes until crust is lightly brown. Remove from oven and serve warm.

Rustic Pie Filling

6 tablespoons brown sugar
2 tablespoons flour
¼ teaspoon cinnamon
1 teaspoon vanilla
2 apples, *peeled, pitted and thinly sliced (or your choice fruit)*

¼ cup maple syrup
2 teaspoons sugar to top pie

In medium bowl, whisk together sugar, flour, cinnamon and vanilla to make filling. Toss apples in mixture.

Lemon Tart

This fresh and mouth-watering recipe is a family favorite.

- 1 cup sweetened coconut
- 1 cup all-purpose flour
- 3-4 tablespoons vegan butter
- 3 tablespoons sugar
- 1 tablespoon agave nectar or honey
- ½ teaspoon salt
- Lemon Tart Filling *(below)*
- Vegan whipped cream *(optional)*
- Lemon wedge *(optional)*

Preheat oven to 350°F (175°C).

Stir coconut, flour, butter, sugar, agave nectar and salt together. Press into lightly oiled tart pan with removable bottom. Bake for 20 minutes until golden brown. Remove from oven and let cool. Place tart pan onto baking sheet pan to catch any overflow.

Assemble tart filling and pour into the tart pan. Cool at room temperature for 30 minutes. Place in the refrigerator for at least one hour and chill until firm. Serve chilled with a dab of vegan whipped cream or a slice of lemon in the center for decoration.

Lemon Tart Filling

- 1 (14 oz) can coconut milk
- 1 cup water
- 1 cup sugar
- 1 teaspoon salt
- Sprinkle of turmeric *(for color)*
- 3 tablespoons agar flakes
- ½ cup lemon juice
- 2 tablespoons lemon zest
- ¼ cup arrowroot or cornstarch
- 1 cup plain yogurt, *soy or coconut milk*
- 1 vanilla bean, *split down the center, scoop out the seeds*

In a saucepan over medium heat, combine milk, one cup of water, sugar, salt, turmeric and agar flakes. Stirring constantly, bring mixture to a boil. Lower heat and simmer until mixture is smooth and creamy, about 5-8 minutes. Add lemon juice and zest. Continue to stir and bring to a boil. Mix arrowroot with ½ cup of water and stir into saucepan and cook until mixture thickens, about 2 minutes. Remove from heat and stir in vanilla bean and yogurt. Stir until smooth and well mixed.

Hint:

One half of a vanilla bean is equal to one teaspoon of vanilla extract. A few reasons to use a vanilla bean instead of vanilla extract are; first it will not add color to your light pudding and fillings. Second, the tiny seeds add a unique appearance. Third, most of the pastry chefs use vanilla beans only. Fourth, it has a lovely vanilla taste and smell.

Key Lime Tart

You will have a difficult time refusing seconds with this dessert. Great for a summer party.

1½ cup crushed vegan graham crackers
½ cup almonds, *roasted, chopped*
4 tablespoons vegan butter
1 tablespoon agave nectar or honey
3 tablespoons sugar
Key Lime Tart Filling *(below)*
Vegan whipped cream *(optional)*
Fresh berries *(optional)*

Preheat oven to 350°F (175°C).

Place graham crackers, almonds, butter, agavr nectar and sugar in a food processor. Pulse until texture resembles coarse cornmeal. Press into a lightly oiled tart pan with removable bottom.

Bake for 20 minutes until light golden brown. Remove and let cool. Place tart pan on baking sheet pan so when filling is added the bottom pan will catch the overflow.

Create filling and pour over crust in tart pan and cool at room temperature for 30 minutes. Place cooled tart in the refrigerator and chill until firm, typically 1-2 hours. Serve chilled with a dab of vegan whipped cream or with thinly sliced rounds of lime. Raspberries, strawberries or blueberries placed in the center the tart add a finished look.

Key-Lime Tart Filling

1 (14 oz) can coconut milk
1 cup water
1 cup sugar
Sprinkle of turmeric *(for color)*
1 teaspoon salt
3 tablespoons agar flakes
½ cup key lime juice, *regular lime will work*
2 tablespoons lime zest
¼ cup arrowroot or cornstarch
1 cup plain yogurt, *soy or coconut milk*
2 teaspoons vanilla

In a saucepan over medium heat, combine milk, one cup of water, sugar, turmeric, salt and agar flakes. Stirring constantly, bring mixture to a boil. Lower heat and simmer until mixture is smooth and creamy, about 5-8 minutes. Add lime juice and zest. Continue to stir and bring to a boil. Mix arrowroot with the ½ cup of water and stir into mixture until it thickens, about 2 minutes.

Remove from heat and stir in yogurt and vanilla and until smooth and well mixed.

Hint:

Agar, a natural see vegetable gelatin, is sold in powder form or in flakes. Flakes are the easiest to use. Just stir into the liquid in your recipe and bring to a boil for 5-8 minutes to dissolve.

Puff-Pastry Pies

Use leftover apple pie filling or any fruit filling you wish. Peach is wonderful. This recipe makes eight muffins.

- 3 large peaches, *peeled, pitted and cut into ½" chunks*
- ¼ cup sugar
- 1 tablespoon cornstarch
- 1 teaspoon vanilla extract
- 2 (9"×16") pieces frozen puff pastry, *thawed but very cold*

Preheat oven to 400°F (205°C).

In large bowl, add peaches, sugar, cornstarch, and vanilla extract and toss to combine.

Cut puff pastry in half, place on a sheet of parchment paper and roll into a 10" square. Using a cookie cutter or standard drinking glass, cut pastry into 4½" circles. Use the circles to line muffin pans, leaving the extra edges in place.

Spoon peach pie mixture evenly into each muffin cup. Roll out another puff pastry sheet and cut out 3" circles to place over the top of each muffin cup. Fold the edges of the bottom pastry over the top and pinch tightly to seal each pie.

Bake pies for approximately 25-35 minutes until they are puffed and golden brown. Immediately after removing the pan from the oven, carefully run a small knife between the edges of each pie and the muffin pan to loosen the pastry from the pan. Transfer pastries to a platter to cool.

These can be served warm or room temperature, but they are best when fresh.

Fresh Strawberry Yogurt Pie

Light and refreshing, this is a wonderful pie that is versatile in taste when you change the type of fresh fruit you choose for the topping. Strawberries and blueberries are especially yummy.

- 10 graham crackers
- ¼ cup raw almonds
- 3 tablespoons oil, *vegan butter or apple juice*
- 1 tablespoon honey or agave nectar
- Yogurt filling *(below)*
- ½-1 cup fresh strawberries, *sliced or your choice fresh fruit*

Preheat oven to 350°F (175°C).

Combine graham crackers and almonds in food processor. Drizzle in oil, mixing thoroughly. Add a tablespoon of honey or agave nectar. Make sure you do not get mixture too wet or too dry. Add a little at a time. Press crust mixture into a 9" pie plate or pan. Bake 15 minutes or until crust is lightly brown and let cool and chill before filling.

Make yogurt filling (see recipe below).

Pour yogurt filling into chilled crust. Return to refrigerator for at least 3 hours, or until set.

Create a topping for pie by mixing strawberries (or other fruit) with 1 teaspoon of honey or agave nectar. The fruit tends to get too juicy if you add it to the top of the whole pie, so it generally works best to top each slice of pie individually with the fruit when serving. In those circumstances where the whole pie will be eaten immediately and presentation is important, the fruit topping can be poured over the top of the pie before serving.

Yogurt Pie Filling

- 1 cup plain yogurt, *soy or coconut milk*
- 8 ounces non-dairy cream cheese *softened*
- ¼ cup sugar
- 1 tablespoon honey or agave nectar
- 2 teaspoons vanilla extract

Mix yogurt, cream cheese, sugar, honey and vanilla until very smooth. Add additional sugar if desired.

Brownies

Making a perfect brownie can be challenging. This is one of the best crowd pleasers around.

¾ cup unsweetened almond milk
1 teaspoon apple cider vinegar
6 tablespoons canola oil
2 teaspoons vanilla
1 cup flour
1 cup sugar
½ cup brown sugar
½ cup unsweetended cocoa, *Ghirardelli*®
2 teaspoons finely ground flaxseed
1 teaspoon baking powder
1 teaspoon salt
1 cup pecans or walnuts, *chopped*
1 cup non-dairy chocolate chips

Preheat oven to 350°F (175°C). Lightly spray 8"×8" or 9"×9" baking pan with canola cooking spray.

Combine almond milk with apple cider vinegar and set aside. Then combine oil, milk mixture, and vanilla. Whisk until well mixed.

In a separate bowl, combine, flour, sugars, cocoa, flaxseed, baking powder and salt. Fold the flour and milk mixtures together but do not over mix. Fold in nuts and chocolate chips.

Pour into pan and bake for 20-25 minutes, until surface cracks appear but brownies are not quite set. Do not over bake. The brownies will set while they are cooling. Cool completely before cutting. Enjoy.

Hint:

To chop nuts, spread the nuts in a single layer on a cutting board. Using a chef's knife, carefully chop the nuts with a gentle chopping motion.

Chocolate Chip Cookies

Excellent cookies. If baked properly, these chocolate chip cookies are a perfect combination of being crunchy with a softer center.

2¼ cups all-purpose flour
1½ teaspoon baking powder
1 teaspoon baking soda
½ teaspoon arrowroot
1 teaspoon salt
½ cup white sugar
½ cup brown sugar
¾ cup vegan butter
1½ teaspoon vanilla
¼ cup unsweetened almond milk
2 cups vegan chocolate chips
1 cup nuts, pecans or walnuts, *chopped*

Preheat oven to 375°F (190°C).

Mix flour, baking powder, baking soda, arrowroot, and salt together in small bowl.

Beat sugars together with butter and vanilla in mixer. Slowly add flour mixture to batter. Milk can be added at this point to keep mixture from being too dry. Stir in nuts and chocolate chips.

Using a large tablespoon, drop dough onto ungreased cookie sheet. Cook for 10-15 minutes or until golden brown around the edges. Remove and cool.

Hints:

◊ To give cookies you baked a couple of days ago that just-out-of-the-oven appeal, put them on a baking sheet pan, put in a 350°F (175°C) oven and heat for 3-5 minutes.
◊ Arrowroot adds a crisp texture to cookies.

Coconut Pecan Cookies

A light, simple recipe that is fun for children to help make.

¾ cup vegan butter
½ cup sugar
½ cup brown sugar
1½ cups all-purpose flour
½ teaspoon salt
2½ teaspoons vanilla extract
½ cup sweetened shredded coconut
½ cup pecans, *finely chopped*
¼ cup unsweetened almond milk, *if needed*
Pecan halves for top cookies
Powdered sugar for sprinkling *(optional)*

Preheat oven to 350°F (175°C).

Cream butter and sugar together until fluffy. Add flour, salt, and vanilla. Stir in coconut and pecans. This makes thick cookie dough that can be hard to stir so use your hands if necessary. If dough is too dry and will not hold together, add one tablespoon of almond milk at a time until desired consistency is achieved.

Roll into small balls and place on cookie sheet 2" apart. Flatten with fork or spoon and place a pecan half on top. Bake cookies for 14-17 minutes until lightly brown on the edges.

Cool cookies then sprinkle with a light coating of powdered sugar or a light drizzle of melted chocolate across top.

Mexican Wedding Cookies

A traditional recipe that vegans can enjoy.

1 cup vegan butter
¼ cup sugar
1½ teaspoons Mexican vanilla extract
¼ teaspoon salt
2 cups all-purpose flour
1 cup pecans, *finely chopped or any nut your choice*
2-3 cups powdered sugar

Preheat oven to 350°F (175°C). Line parchment paper on cookie sheet.

Mix butter, sugar, vanilla and salt until fluffy. Add flour. Stir in pecans. Using a teaspoon, spoon batter into balls that are small enough to be eaten in a single bite, placing each on baking sheet about 1" apart.

Bake 15-20 minutes until cookie balls are set and beginning to lightly brown around bottom. You can test readiness by opening one up to see if inside the dough it is uncooked. Remove from oven.

Place powdered sugar in large bowl. Add warm cookies and toss around to coat. Remove and place on wax paper or clean baking pan. Wait 2-5 minutes until the cookies are cooler. Then, toss in powdered sugar again for a final coating.

Yummy Peanut Butter Cookies

Although these scrumptious cookies are delicious without chocolate, the dough works well with chocolate chips. If you really need a chocolate fix, drizzle melted chocolate over them.

- 1½ cup all-purpose flour
- 1 teaspoon finely ground flaxseed
- 1 teaspoon salt
- ½ teaspoon baking soda
- ½ teaspoon arrowroot
- 1 teaspoon baking powder
- ½ cup vegan butter
- ½ cup brown sugar
- ½ cup white sugar
- 1 cup natural peanut butter, *crunchy or smooth*
- 1 teaspoon vanilla extract
- ⅛ cup unsweetened almond milk
- ½ cup oatmeal *(optional)*
- ½ cup vegan chocolate chips *(optional)*
- ½ cup peanuts, roasted and chopped *(optional)*

Preheat oven to 375°F (190°C).

Mix flour, flaxseeds, salt, baking soda, arrowroot and baking powder together. Set aside.

Using a mixer, combine butter with white and brown sugar until fluffy. Add peanut butter and vanilla and continue to mix. One large tablespoon at a time, add flour mixture to mixing bowl containing sugars. Add one tablespoon of almond milk at a time, to thin out dough if it is too dry. Mixture should be moist and easily hold together; do not add too much milk. For a crunchier cookie, stir in oats or peanuts by hand. Add chocolate chips if you like.

Roll dough with your hands into small balls and placed on a cookie sheet. Flatten with fork. Dip fork into water to keep from sticking to dough. Bake 12-15 minutes or until slightly brown on edges. Place on cooling rack until room temperature.

Simple Banana Pudding

This is so easy and tasty. Your family will be begging for it all the time. My mom always made a variation of this for all Easters and her grandchildren could not get enough.

2 boxes vegan vanilla pudding
4 cups unsweetened almond milk
1½ cup crushed vegan graham crackers
3 bananas, *ripe, sliced*
1 cup finely crushed graham crackers for top
(optional)

Prepare the pudding according to package instructions using almond milk. Let pudding cool in refrigerator for 30 minutes.

After the pudding has cooled, add several spoonfuls to the bottom of a 13"×9" dish. Next, add a layer of graham crackers, then a layer of bananas. Top with a layer of pudding. Repeat layers ending with a layer of pudding on top. Sprinkle for 1-2 hours crushed graham crackers on top. Refrigerate until serving time.

Hint:

This doesn't really keep well in the refrigerator past a couple of days. It gets mushy as the crackers soak up the pudding.

Chocolate Pudding or Pie

A simpler nor more delicious recipe may not exist. Your guests will love it, and you can garnish with fresh raspberries for a more sophisticated presentation.

½ cup cocoa, *Ghirardelli® unsweetened*
1 cup sugar
⅓ cup cornstarch
¼ teaspoon salt
2½ cups unsweetened almond milk
1 teaspoon vanilla extract

Whisk unsweetened cocoa, sugar, cornstarch, salt and milk in a medium saucepan. Bring to a boil over medium-low heat, stirring consistently until it thickens. Remove from heat and add vanilla. Pour into bowl and cover with plastic wrap. Refrigerate for at least 3-4 hours.

To make this into a pie, pour pudding into a pre-baked pie crust instead of the bowl and then refrigerate.

Pie crusts that complement this fully are: Graham Cracker (page 308), Walnut Crust (page 309) or the Ginger Snap Crust (page 308). For a traditional chocolate pie, prebake one regular pie crust before adding the pudding mixture. Garnish top of pie with a few raspberries, shavings of dark chocolate, or a dollop of vegan whipping cream.

Coconut Pudding

This pudding makes a simple, light but satisfying dessert. This can be made into a pie by pouring it over a precooked homemade pie crust (page 306) or store-bought one.

¼ cup sweetened coconut for top
1½ cup coconut milk
1 cup unsweetened almond milk
1 cup sugar
⅓ cup cornstarch
¼ teaspoon salt
1 teaspoon vanilla or coconut extract

Preheat oven to 375°F (190°C).

Spread ¼ cup of coconut evenly on a baking sheet and toast until golden brown. Set aside.

Place coconut milk, almond milk, sugar, cornstarch and salt in saucepan on medium-low heat. Stir constantly so mixture will be smooth and creamy, allowing 5-8 minutes for mixture to thicken. When thick, remove from heat and stir in vanilla and mix well. Pour into dish or dishes and sprinkle toasted coconut on the top of each dish. Refrigerate for at least 1 hour.

Hint:

Canned coconut milk is not the milk from the coconut; it is actually an extract made from shredded fresh coconut.

Fresh Apple Cake *with Walnuts*

This is one of those scrumptious, moist cakes everyone loves.

- 1 large Granny Smith apple, *peeled, diced*
- 1 teaspoon cinnamon
- 1 cup brown sugar
- 1 teaspoon lemon juice
- 1½ cup all-purpose flour or whole-wheat pastry flour
- 3 teaspoons baking powder
- 1 teaspoon baking soda
- ⅛ teaspoon nutmeg
- ½ teaspoon salt
- ⅓ cup canola oil
- 1 cup unsweetened applesauce
- ¼ cup unsweetened almond milk
- 1 teaspoon vanilla extract
- Vegan cream cheese frosting, *optional*
- ½-1 cup walnuts, *chopped*

Preheat oven to 350°F (175°C). Oil lightly or use a cooking spray on a 9"×9" cake pan.

Toss apple with cinnamon, 1 tablespoon of the sugar and the lemon juice.

Mix flour, baking powder, and baking soda, nutmeg and salt together. Mix remaining sugar, oil, applesauce, unsweetened almond milk and vanilla on low speed. When mix is smooth add dry ingredients in small batches then turn to medium speed until combined.

Fold in apples and walnuts by hand. Pour into baking pan and bake for 25-30 minutes or until toothpick comes out clean when inserted in the middle of cake. Remove and cool in pan.

Serve plain or covered with Cream Cheese Frosting (page 337) or Butter Frosting (page 334) with a few added chopped walnuts.

Carrot Cupcakes

Children love these. Icing can be added, but a sprinkle with a little powdered sugar or cinnamon sugar added right before cooking is enough.

- 1 tablespoon finely ground flaxseeds
- ¾ cup unsweetened almond milk
- 1½ cups all-purpose unbleached flour or whole-wheat pastry flour
- ¾ cup sugar
- ¼ cup brown sugar
- 1½ teaspoons baking powder
- 1 teaspoon baking soda
- 1 teaspoon salt
- ⅛ teaspoon freshly grated nutmeg
- 1½ teaspoon cinnamon
- 1 container plain yogurt, *soy or coconut milk*
- 1½ teaspoon vanilla
- ¼ cup oil
- 2 cups carrots, *peeled, grated (2 large carrots)*
- ½ cup shredded coconut
- ½ cup crushed pineapple, *drained*
- ½ cup dried currants or raisins
- ½ cup pecans or walnuts, *chopped (optional)*
- Cinnamon Sugar *(below)*

Preheat oven to 350°F (175°C). Lightly coat muffin pans with cooking spray or use liners.

In a medium bowl, mix flaxseed with almond milk and set aside. Stir together flour, white and brown sugars, baking powder, baking soda, salt, nutmeg and cinnamon in bowl. Whisk together yogurt, vanilla, oil, and milk mixture and then stir into the flour mixture. Then fold in carrots, coconut, pineapple, currants and nuts.

Spoon into muffin cups and bake for 25 minutes or until toothpick comes out clean when inserted in the middle. Remove and let cool. Top with Cinnamon Sugar (below), Cream Cheese Icing (page 337), or Butter Icing (page 334).

Cinnamon Sugar

Mix ¼ cup of sugar and 1 teaspoon of cinnamon together and sprinkle on cupcakes right before you put them in the oven.

Hint:

Buy whole nutmeg and use a fine zester to grate the amount you need. Then keep the nutmeg nut in a small container with your other spices. It keeps a long time and adds a fresher flavor than jarred.

Simple Chocolate Cake or Cupcakes

Great for birthdays. This recipe makes a wonderful, moist cake or cupcakes. It will become your basic go-to. Make two complete recipes if making a two or three-layer cake. Do not just double the recipe. Use any icing from a chocolate, peanut butter and chocolate or vanilla butter cream but it is also delicious plain.

- 1 cup unsweetened almond milk
- 2 teaspoons apple cider vinegar
- 2 cups all-purpose flour
- 1 cup sugar
- ½ cup brown sugar
- 1 teaspoons baking soda
- 1 teaspoon salt
- 2 teaspoons baking powder
- ⅓ cup cocoa plus 2 tablespoons
- 1 container plain soy or coconut milk yogurt
- ½ cup canola oil
- 2 teaspoons vanilla

Preheat oven to 375°F (190°C). Spray cake pan or muffin pans with canola cooking spray. This recipe makes one 9"×9" pan; one 8"-9" round pan; one Bundt pan; or 8-10 cupcakes.

Mix almond milk with vinegar and set aside. In a separate bowl, mix dry ingredients, combining flour, white and brown sugars, baking soda, salt, baking powder and cocoa.

In a second bowl, mix the milk mixture with the yogurt, oil and vanilla. Combine the milk/yogurt mixture with dry ingredients, mixing by hand, but do not over mix.

Spoon into desired pan for 30-35 minutes or until toothpick comes out clean when inserted in the middle of cake. Cool completely before icing with Coconut Butter Icing, next page.

Coconut & Banana Nut Cupcakes

This might be one of the best cupcakes ever. Moist, tender and delicious.

- 1½ cup unsweetened almond milk, or 1 cup coconut milk
- 2 teaspoons apple cider vinegar
- 2½ cup all-purpose flour
- 1½ teaspoon baking powder
- ½ teaspoon baking soda
- 1 teaspoon salt
- 5 tablespoons vegan butter
- 1 cup sugar
- ½ cup vanilla soy or coconut milk yogurt
- 1¼ teaspoon vanilla
- ½ cup sweetened coconut *(if using unsweetened coconut you might need a little more sugar)*
- 2 large bananas, *ripe, mashed*
- ½ cup pecans or walnuts, *chopped*

Preheat oven to 375°F (190°C).

Mix unsweetened almond milk and apple cider vinegar then set aside. If using coconut milk do not add vinegar.

Mix flour, baking powder, baking soda, and salt together. In a separate bowl, beat vegan butter and sugar together in mixer until fluffy. Add yogurt and vanilla to milk mixture. Pour wet ingredients into dry ingredients and mix together by hand. Stir in coconut, bananas and nuts.

Spoon batter (use an ice cream scooper) into lightly oiled baking pan (or liners). Bake 25 minutes or until toothpick comes out clean when inserted in the middle of cake. Cool before icing (recipe below).

Coconut Butter Icing

- 2 cups confectioners' sugar
- 4 tablespoons vegan butter, *softened*
- ¼ cup unsweetened almond milk or coconut milk
- 1 teaspoon vanilla
- ½ cup shredded coconut, *sweetened or unsweetened*

Mix sugar and vegan butter with mixer on medium speed until fluffy, adding milk a little at a time until the desired smoothness is reached. Add vanilla. Stir in coconut by hand. Refrigerate until needed.

Hint:
Using cupcake liners is a good way to skip using cooking oil, but many times the cake will stick to the liner.

Hummingbird Cake

This is an old recipe that my mom always made when I was a kid, so I was thrilled when I was able to adapt it to being vegan. The pineapple makes it tropical in taste and smell. Hope you enjoy it.

1 cup unsweetened almond milk
1 tablespoon apple cider vinegar
3 cups all-purpose flour
¾ cup sugar
½ cup brown sugar
2 teaspoons baking powder
1 teaspoon baking soda
1 teaspoon salt
1 teaspoon ground cinnamon
1 container plain yogurt, *coconut milk or soy*
½ cup canola oil
1½ teaspoon vanilla
1 (8 oz) can crushed pineapple, *with liquid*
2 ripe bananas, *chopped*
1 cup pecans, *chopped*
Cream Cheese Frosting (page 337)

Preheat oven to 350°F (175°C). Spray cooking spray onto three 9" cake pans or a 9"×13" pan or 2 muffin pans. Cupcake liners can be used in muffin pan instead cooking spray.

Begin by adding a tablespoon of vinegar in the milk and setting to the side.

Combine flour, white and brown sugars, baking powder, baking soda, salt, and cinnamon in large bowl. To the flour, add milk mixture, yogurt and oil, stirring by hand until dry ingredients are moist. Do not beat. Stir in vanilla, pineapple, bananas and pecans.

Spoon batter into baking pans. Bake 25-30 minutes or until toothpick comes out clean when inserted in the middle of cake. Cool in pans for 10 minutes. Remove and let cool completely before icing.

Lemon Cupcakes

These are lemony, moist and delectable.

1⅓ cup all-purpose flour
1½ teaspoon baking powder
1 teaspoon baking soda
½ teaspoon salt
5 tablespoons canola oil
1 cup sugar
1 container plain yogurt, *soy or coconut milk*
½ cup unsweetened almond milk
1½ teaspoon vanilla
¼ cup fresh lemon juice
1 tablespoon lemon zest
Lemon Zest Icing *(below)*

Preheat oven to 365°F (185°C). Lightly spray muffin pan with canola cooking spray or use liners.

Mix together flour, baking powder, baking soda, and salt. In another bowl mix the canola oil, sugar, yogurt, almond milk, vanilla, lemon juice and zest together. Combine with dry mix and stir until well blended.

Fill cups to ⅔ full in muffin pan and cook for 20 minutes or until the edges are beginning to turn golden brown and a toothpick comes out clean when inserted in the middle of cake. Remove cupcakes from pan and cool completely before icing.

Lemon Zest Icing

¼ cup vegan butter
2 cups powdered sugar
⅛ cup unsweetened almond milk
3 tablespoons lemon juice
½ teaspoon vanilla
1 tablespoon lemon zest

Mix vegan butter, sugar, almond milk, lemon juice, vanilla, and lemon zest together with mixer. Refrigerate until ready to use. You will need to remove mixture from the refrigerator a few minutes before it is time to ice cupcakes so it will be easier to spread.

Oatmeal Cake

This cake has been around for years and it was always one of my family favorites. It's been adapted so we can still enjoy it. Great cake because it stays so moist.

1½ cup hot water
1 cup oatmeal, *regular*
1 tablespoon ground flaxseeds
½ cup unsweetened almond milk
5 tablespoons canola oil
½ cup brown sugar
½ cup white sugar
1 teaspoon vanilla
1½ cup all-purpose flour or whole-wheat pastry flour
1 teaspoon baking soda
2 teaspoons baking powder
1 teaspoon salt
1 teaspoon cinnamon
Brown Sugar Icing *(below)*

Preheat oven to 350°F (175°C). Use a 9"×13" baking dish that has been lightly sprayed with cooking oil.

Pour hot water over oats and let stand about 15 minutes. Mix flaxseeds with almond milk and set aside.

Separately, cream the canola oil and white and brown sugars together, add vanilla and flaxseed mixture.

Mix flour with baking soda, baking powder, salt and cinnamon. Combine flour mixture to sugar mixture, then add oatmeal and blend well.

Pour into baking dish. Bake for 30-35 minutes or until toothpick comes out clean when inserted in the middle of cake. Ice the warm cake with the following icing.

Brown Sugar Icing

2 tablespoons vegan butter
¼ cup unsweetened almond milk
½ cup brown sugar
1 teaspoon vanilla
1 cup coconut
1 cup chopped nuts

Mix butter, unsweetened almond milk and sugar together in small saucepan over medium heat and bring to a boil for 1 minute. Remove from heat and add vanilla, coconut and nuts. Spread over the top of cake. Place iced cake under broiler until bubbles appear and icing is slightly brown. Watch carefully.

Vanilla Cake or Cupcakes

Perfect vanilla cake. This cake is so moist with great texture and flavor. Frost with any flavor icing you choose.

1 cup unsweetened almond milk
2 teaspoons apple cider vinegar
2½ cups all-purpose flour
3 teaspoons baking powder
½ teaspoon baking soda
1 teaspoon salt
½ cup vegan butter, *melted*
1¼ cups sugar
1 cup plain yogurt, *soy or coconut milk*
1½ teaspoons vanilla
Butter Frosting (page 334) or Chocolate Butter Frosting (page 335)

Preheat oven to 375°F (190°C). This recipe makes one 9"×9" cake or one dozen cupcakes. To make stacked cake see Hint below. Spray with cooking oil to prepare pans or use cupcake liners.

Combine milk with vinegar and set aside. In medium bowl combine flour, baking powder, baking soda and salt.

In a large bowl, cream the butter and sugar together. Add the milk mixture, yogurt, and vanilla. Then combine with flour mixture and beat until mixed.

Fill pan or cupcake liners half-way and cook for 25-30 minutes or until toothpick comes out clean when inserted in the middle of cake. Let cool before icing.

Hints:

◊ Hide treats inside muffins or cupcakes such as fruit jams or chunks of ripe summer fruit. Fill muffin cup half-way and dab jam in the center of each cup. Then add more batter to conceal jam or fruit.
◊ To make a stacked cake, use three to four cake pans and make thin layers. If the layers are too thick, cake has difficulty cooking through to the center.

Chocolate Ganache

- 1 cup vegan semi-chocolate chips *(use the best chocolate you can find)*
- ¼ cup coconut milk
- 2 tablespoons canola oil
- ½ cup sugar

Melt chocolate chips with coconut milk, oil and sugar over a double boiler or in the microwave oven on medium heat. Whisk mixture until smooth. The easiest way to ice cupcake using this frosting is to dip the top of the cupcake into the hot chocolate mixture, being careful not to dip too far. This makes a very rich, chocolate icing for cupcakes.

Butter Frosting

If the coconut flavor works for your recipe, you can use coconut milk instead of almond milk.

- 2 cups powdered sugar
- ½ cup vegan butter, *room temperature*
- 1½ teaspoons vanilla extract
- 2 tablespoons unsweetened almond milk or coconut milk

Combine sugar, vegan butter and vanilla with mixer. Beat with mixer on medium-high speed until combined. With the mixer running, add one tablespoon of almond milk at a time until desired consistency is reached.

Can be stored in refrigerator for 3 or 4 days.

Hint:
For lemon cupcakes, add a little lemon zest to frosting or sprinkle lemon zest on top icing.

Cream Cheese Frosting with Pecans

1 (8 oz) container of non-dairy cream cheese, *softened*
1 tablespoon vegan butter
2 cups powdered sugar
1 teaspoon vanilla
Unsweetened almond milk to thin
½ cup chopped pecans

Combine cream cheese and butter, beating until smooth. Add powdered sugar and the vanilla, and then beat until light. Add a couple of tablespoons of milk at a time to thin. By hand, stir pecans into mixture. Refrigerate until needed.

> *Hint:*
> Always add solid ingredients, nuts or fruits, at the end of mixing and gently mix in by hand.

Chocolate Butter Frosting

2 cups powdered sugar
½ cup vegan butter, *room temperature*
⅓ cup cocoa
1 teaspoon vanilla extract
2 tablespoons unsweetened almond milk

Combine sugar, vegan butter, cocoa and vanilla with mixer. Beat on medium-high until combined. Slowly add one tablespoon of almond milk at a time until desired consistency is reached.

Refrigerator for up to 4 days.

Glaze

A glaze can be added to the top of baked breads or muffins when they are removed from the oven to add a touch of sweetness.

1 cup powdered sugar
1 tablespoons orange or lemon juice
2 teaspoons orange or lemon zest
Pinch salt

Whisk all ingredients together. If the glaze seems too thick, add a couple of drops of juice. Brush over muffins or bread while still warm.

Peanut Butter & Chocolate Icing

The only difference in this recipe and the regular chocolate icing recipe is that you are replacing the vegan butter with the peanut butter.

½ cup peanut butter, *smooth or crunchy*
⅓ cup cocoa, *Ghirardelli® unsweetened*
¼ cup unsweetened almond milk
2 cups powdered sugar
¼ teaspoon salt
1 teaspoon vanilla extract

Mix all ingredients together in a mixer until light and fluffy. Refrigerate until needed. Remove icing from refrigerator a few minutes before cupcakes are ready to be iced.

Cream Cheese Frosting

8 ounces of non-dairy cream cheese
1½ cups of powdered sugar
1 teaspoon of vanilla extract

Mix together all ingredients until smooth and creamy. Refrigerate until needed. Remove from refrigerator a few minutes before you are ready to ice cupcakes.

Index

ALMONDS
Edamame Pesto, 192
Fresh Strawberry Yogurt Pie, 317
Green Beans w/ Almonds & Mushrooms, 119
Key Lime Tart, 315
Lemon Tart, 314
Miso & Sun-Dried Tomato Pesto, 205
Nut & Medjool Date Crust, 307
Nutty Miso Dressing, 262
Rice Pilaf, 178
Roasted Almonds, Walnuts, Cashews or Peanuts, 266
Sun-Dried Tomato Pesto, 194

APPLES
Angela's Apple Pie, 310
Apple Crisp, 302
Fresh Apple Cake w/ Walnuts, 326
Jen's Apple Spice Bread, 277
Mom's Baked Apples, 298

ASPARAGUS
Asparagus, Spinach & Leeks, 101
Grilled Asparagus, 146
Roasted Asparagus, 102
Skillet Asparagus, 103

ARUGULA
Arugula Salad, 26
Arugula w/ Roasted Garlic Hummus Dressing, 27
Penne Pasta w/ Green Beans & Arugula, 47
Pistachio Pesto, 199

ASIAN SAUCES & Marinades
Chili Marinade, 230
Chili Peanut Dip, 264
Marinade w/ Garlic, 230
Nutty Miso Dressing, 262
Sesame Sauce, 259
Sesame Grilling Marinade, 151
Spicy Marinade, 223
Tamari Sauce, 259

AVOCADOS
Avocado Jalapeno Yogurt Dip, 266
Guacamole, 258
Romaine & Avocado Salad w/ Classic French Dressing, 31
Spicy Avocado Dressing, 57
Spinach Salad w/ Oranges, Avocados & Red Wine Vinaigrette, 35
Tomato, Avocado & Red Onion Sandwich, 94

BALSAMIC VINEGAR
Balsamic Maple Vinaigrette Dressing, 36
Baked Red Potatoes w/ Onions & Balsamic Vinegar, 167
Garbanzo Bean Salad, 45
Green Beans w/ Balsamic Brown Butter, 119
Roasted Brussels Sprouts, 111
Roasted Garlic Hummus Dressing, 27

BANANA
Banana Muffins w/ Walnut Topping, 287
Banana Bread w/ Coconut & Pistachios, 278
Simple Banana Pudding, 323

BARLEY
Basic Barley, 184

BEANS
Baked Beans, 237
Bean & Chili Pasta Bake, 212
Black Beans, 238
Black Bean Layer Dip, 263
Black Bean Salsa, 254
Black Bean Soup, 61
Black Bean Tostadas, 84
Butter or Large Lima Beans, 241
Chickpea Sandwich Spread, 86
Country Lentil Soup, 66
Deb's Pinto Beans, 242
Easy BBQ Beans, 240
Farfalle w/ Red Beans & Chiles, 193
Garbanzo Bean Salad, 45
Red Beans & Broccoli, 244
Red or Kidney Beans, 243
Red Beans & Rice, 245
Refried Black Beans, 239
Roasted Edamame, 267
Spicy Black Bean Burger, 96
Spinach, Beans & Bowtie Pasta, 201
Three Bean Chili, 62
Quick Penne & Beans, 210
Quinoa & Pinto Beans Salad, 52
White Beans, 244
White Bean & Kale Soup, 63
White Bean Spread, 85

BEETS
Basic Beets, 104
Romaine Lettuce w/ Beets & Cashews & Shallot Vinaigrette Dressing, 30
Steamed Beets w/ Dressing, 106
Tossed Roasted Beets, 105

BLUEBERRIES
Blueberries & Oatmeal Breakfast Muffins, 288
Blueberry Treat, 301
Easy Blueberry Pie, 311

BOK CHOY
Steamed Bok Choy w/ Dressing, 106

BREADS
Banana Bread w/ Coconut & Pistachios, 278
Cornbread, 280
Cornbread Dressing, 281
Easy Biscuits, 279
Homemade Breadcrumbs, 270
Homemade Croutons, 270
Lemon Bread, 282
Jen's Apple Spice Bread, 277
Masa Dumplings, 271
Peanut Butter Bread Mini Loaves, 290
Pita Toasts, 272
Simple Bread, 283
Zucchini Bread, 284

BREAKFAST
Also see **MUFFINS** & **BREADS**
Blueberry & Oatmeal Breakfast Muffins, 288
Easy Biscuits, 279
Rusty's Silver Dollar Pancakes, 286
Oatmeal, 285
Potato & Veggie Sausage Bake, 221
Veggie Sausage with Cream Gravy, 260

BROCCOLI
Broccoli Salad w/ Nuts & Raisins, 39
Cream of Broccoli Soup, 64
Fettuccine w/ Broccoli & Lemon Pesto, 195
Penne Pasta w/ Broccoli, Capers, Green Olives & Pine Nuts, 198
Red Beans & Broccoli, 244
Red Pepper Broccoli, 109
Roasted Broccoli, 109
Steamed Broccoli, 108
Soba Noodle Salad, 50

BROCCOLINI & BROCCOLI RABE
Broccolini or Broccoli Rabe' w/ Lemon, 107

BRUSSELS SPROUTS
Boiled Brussels Sprouts, 110
Roasted Brussels Sprouts, 111
Sautéed Brussels Sprouts, 110
Steamed Brussels Sprouts, 111

BURGERS
Mushroom & Nut Burger, 97
Spicy Black Bean Burger, 96

CABBAGE
Braised Red Cabbage, 112
Cabbage Slaw, 41
Skillet Cabbage w/ Veggies, 113
Steamed Cabbage, 112

CAKES OR CUPCAKES
Also see **MUFFINS** & **BREADS**
Carrot Cupcakes, 327
Coconut & Banana Nut Cupcakes, 329
Corn Cakes, 157
Fresh Apple Cake with Walnuts, 326
Hummingbird Cake, 330
Lemon Cupcakes, 331
Oatmeal Cake, 332
Simple Chocolate Cake or Cupcakes, 328
Vanilla Cake or Cupcakes, 333

CAPERS
Fried Capers, 268
Penne Pasta w/ Broccoli, Capers, Green Olives & Pine Nuts, 198
Tomatoes, Olives & Capers w/ Pasta, 207

CARROTS
Carrot Cupcakes, 327
Grated Carrots, 114
Sautéed Carrots, 115
Steamed Carrots, 115

CASHEWS
Cashew Cream, 252
Nutty Miso Dressing, 262
Roasted Almonds, Walnuts, Cashews & Peanuts, 266
Romaine Lettuce w/ Beets & Cashews & Shallot Vinaigrette Dressing, 30
White Bean Spread, 85

CASHEW CREAM
Cashew Cream, 252
Creamy Potato Leek Soup, 70
Fast Corn Chowder, 65
Creamy Tomato Soup, 72

CASSEROLES
Baked Pasta Casserole, 217
Bean & Chili Pasta Bake, 212
Brown Rice & Vegetable Casserole, 222
Garden Bake, 138
Macaroni Casserole, 216
Potato & Veggie Sausage Bake, 221
Spicy Potato Casserole, 166
Squash Casserole, 136
Sweet Potato Casserole, 171
Tofu & Vegetable Lasagna, 213
White & Sweet Potato Casserole, 173
Wild Rice Casserole, 183

CAULIFLOWER
    Cauliflower w/ Curry Butter and Rice, 117
    Mashed Cauliflower w/ Caramelized Onions, 116
    Roasted Cauliflower, 117
    Steamed Cauliflower, 117

CHERRIES
    Cherry Crisp, 304

CHICKPEAS (garbanzos)
    Garbanzo Bean Salad, 45
    Chickpea Sandwich Spread, 86
    Pasta w/ Chickpeas & Cherry Tomatoes, 191
    Roasted Vegetables w/ Chickpeas, 141

CHOCOLATE
    Brownies, 318
    Chocolate Butter Frosting, 335
    Chocolate Chip Cookies, 319
    Chocolate Ganache, 334
    Chocolate Pudding or Pie, 324
    Oatmeal & Chocolate Chip Muffins, 289
    Peanut Butter & Chocolate Icing, 336
    Simple Chocolate Cake or Cupcakes, 328

COBBLERS & CRISPS
    Apple Crisp, 302
    Basic Fruit Cobbler with Oatmeal Topping, 299
    Blueberry Treat, 301
    Cherry Crisp, 304
    Peach Cobbler w/ Biscuit Topping, 300
    Plum & Nectarine Crisp, 303

COCONUT
    Banana Bread w/ Coconut & Pistachios, 278
    Coconut & Banana Nut Cupcakes, 329
    Coconut Butter Icing, 329
    Coconut Pecan Cookies, 320
    Coconut Pudding, 325
    Creamy Coconut Pie, 312

COOKIES
    Brownies, 318
    Chocolate Chip Cookies, 319
    Coconut Pecan Cookies, 320
    Mexican Wedding Cookies, 321
    Yummy Peanut Butter Cookies, 322

COOKING TECHNIQUES
    Blanching or Parboiling, 39
    Julienne, 139

CORN
    Corn Cakes, 157
    Fast Corn Chowder, 65
    Grilled Corn, 146
    Grilled Veggie Salad w/ Spicy Pepper Dressing, 42
    Kettle Corn, 305
    Mom's Creamed Corn, 158
    Mixed Cream Corn, 159
    Potato Corn Soup, 69
    Roasted Corn On The Cob, 159
    Succotash, 160

CORNBREAD
    Cornbread, 280
    Cornbread Dressing, 281

COUSCOUS
    Basic Couscous, 185

CREAM CHEESE (vegan)
    Cream Cheese Frosting, 337

CRUDITE'S (raw vegetables)
    Raw Vegetables, 25

CRUSTS
    Ginger Snap Crust, 308
    Graham Cracker Crust, 308
    Nut & Medjool Date Crust, 307
    Pie Crusts, 306
    Walnut Pie Crust, 309

CUPCAKES
    See **CAKES**

DIPS
    Avocado Jalapeno Yogurt Dip, 266
    Black Bean Dip, 264
    Black Bean Layer Dip, 263
    Chili Peanut Dip, 264
    Chive Aioli Dip, 265
    Cucumber Walnut Yogurt Dip, 265
    See **HUMMUS**
    See **SALSAS**
    Guacamole, 258
    Pico de Gallo, 258

DESSERTS
    See **FRUITS**
    See **CAKES** & **CUPCAKES**
    See **PUDDINGS**
    See **PIES**

DRESSINGS
    Balsamic Maple Vinaigrette Dressing, 36
    Basic Vinaigrette Dressing, 56
    Champagne Vinaigrette Dressing, 37
    Chili-Spice Vinaigrette Dressing, 29
    Classic French Dressing, 31

Cornbread Dressing, 280
Garlic Vinaigrette Dressing, 34
Lemon Vinaigrette, 56
Nutty Miso Dressing, 262
Peanut Butter Dressing, 223
Raspberry Maple Vinaigrette Dressing, 28
Red Wine Vinaigrette, 35
Roasted Garlic Hummus Dressing, 27
Shallot Vinaigrette Dressing, 30
Sherry Vinaigrette Dressing, 32, 33
Spicy Avocado Dressing, 57
Spicy Pepper Dressing, 42

EDAMAME
Edamame Pesto w/ Soba Noodles, 192
Edamame Salad, 43
Roasted Edamame, 267

ENCHILADAS
Enchilada Sauce, 251
Spinach & Mushroom Enchiladas, 214
Also see Enchilada Fillings, 215
Verde Sauce, 261
Ranchero Salsa, 255

EGGPLANT
Grilled Eggplant, 147

EXTRAS
Deb's Seasonings, 269
Deb's Taco Seasonings, 269
Fried Capers, 268
Homemade Croutons, 270
Kettle Corn, 305
Masa Dumplings, 271
Pita Toasts, 272
Tortilla Strips, 272

FENNEL
Romaine w/ Fennel, Carrots & Edamame w/ Sherry Vinaigrette Dressing, 33

FRUIT
Also see **COBBLERS**
Fruit Kabobs, 297
Fruit Plates, 297
Mom's Baked Apples, 298
Summer Fruit Salad, 44

GARLIC
Grilled Garlic, 147
Roasted Garlic Hummus Dressing, 27
Roasted Garlic Hummus, 87
Whole Roasted Garlic, 118

GLAZES
BBQ Sauce Glaze, 96
Glaze (for cakes), 336

GRAINS
Basic Barley, 184
Basic Couscous, 185
Basic Quinoa, 184
Oatmeal, 285
Quinoa Pilaf, 186
Quinoa & Pinto Bean Salad, 52
Quinoa Sauté, 187

GRAVIES
Caramelized Onion Gravy, 251
Mushroom Gravy, 253
Quick Peanut Sauce, 254
Vegetable Gravy, 253
Veggie Sausage & Cream Gravy, 260

GRILLED
Grilled Asparagus, 146
Grilled Corn, 146
Grilled Eggplant, 147
Grilled Leeks, 147
Grilled Portobello Mushrooms, 148
Grilled Mushrooms on Skewers, 148
Grilled Red Bell Peppers, 149
Grilled Okra, 149
Grilled Onions, 149
Grilled Sweet Potatoes, 150
Grilled Squash, 150
Grilled Tofu Sandwich, 93
Grilled Vegetable Sandwich, 95
Grilled Veggie Kabobs, 145
Grilled Vegetables, 144
Grilled Vegetables w/ Sesame Marinade, 151

GREEN BEANS
Garlic Green Beans w/ Almonds & Mushrooms, 119
Green Beans w/ Balsamic Brown Butter, 119
Green Beans w/ Easy Caper Sauce, 120
Penne Pasta w/ Green Beans & Arugula, 47
Simple Green Beans, 118

GREENS
Collard Greens, 122
Kale w/ Peanut Dressing, 124
Kale, Zucchini & Tomatoes, 124
Sautéed Greens, 120
Sautéed Kale, 123
Skillet Chard Greens, 121
Steamed Kale, 123
Tomato Rice soup w/ Greens, 74

GUACAMOLE, 258

HUMMUS
- Artichoke & Hummus Open Faced Sandwich, 83
- Chipotle Hummus, 88
- Hummus Quesadillas, 88
- Red Bell Pepper Hummus, 87
- Roasted Garlic Hummus, 87
- Roasted Garlic Hummus Dressing, 27
- Spinach Quesadillas, 89
- Veggie Wraps, 98

ICINGS & FROSTINGS
- Brown Sugar Icing, 332
- Butter Frosting, 334
- Chocolate Butter Frosting, 335
- Chocolate Ganache, 334
- Cinnamon Sugar, 327
- Coconut Butter Icing, 329
- Cream Cheese Frosting, 337
- Cream Cheese Frosting w/ Pecans, 335
- Glaze, 336
- Lemon Zest Icing, 331
- Peanut Butter & Chocolate Icing, 336

KALE
- Baked Acorn or Butternut Squash w/ Kale, 132
- Kale w/ Peanut Dressing, 124
- Kale, Zucchini & Tomatoes, 124
- New Potato, Tomato & Kale Soup, 71
- Sautéed Kale, 123
- Steamed Kale, 123
- Tofu w/ Kale & Carrots & Peanut Dressing over Brown Rice, 223
- White Bean & Kale Soup, 63

LEEKS
- Grilled Leeks, 147

LEMON
- Lemon Bread, 282
- Lemon Cupcakes, 331
- Lemon Pesto, 195
- Lemon Tart, 314
- Lemon Vinaigrette Dressing, 56
- Lemon Zest Icing, 331

LENTILS
- Country Lentil Soup, 66

MARINADES
- Basic Marinade, 230
- Chili Marinade, 230
- Create your own marinade, 231
- Marinade with Garlic, 230
- Sesame Grilling Marinade, 151
- Spicy Marinade, 223
- Tomato Marinade, 230

MUFFINS
- Banana Muffins w/ Walnut Topping, 287
- Blueberries & Oatmeal Breakfast Muffins, 288
- Fresh Strawberry Mini Muffins, 291
- Oatmeal & Chocolate Chip Muffins, 289

MUSHROOMS
- Grilled Mushrooms on Skewers, 148
- Grilled Portobello Mushrooms, 148
- Grilled Portobello Mushroom Sandwich w/ Spicy Mayonnaise, 90
- Mushroom Gravy, 253
- Mushroom & Nut Burger, 97
- Mushroom Stir-Fry, 126
- Sautéed Mushrooms, 125
- Sautéed Mushrooms & Tofu w/ Rice Noodles, 224
- Spinach & Mushroom Enchiladas, 214
- Stuffed Portobello Mushrooms, 127

NOODLES
- Edamame Pesto w/ Soba Noodles, 192
- Fettuccine w/ Broccoli & Lemon Pesto, 195
- Peanut Noodle Salad, 46
- Sauteed Mushrooms & Tofu w/ Rice Noodles, 224
- Soba Noodle Salad, 50
- Spicy Noodles, 197
- Spaghetti w/ Chile Pesto, 204
- Spinach Linguine w/ Zucchini, Peas & Carrots, 202
- Stir-Fry w/ Soba Noodles, 225

OKRA
- Grilled Okra, 149
- Okra Cakes, 128

ONIONS
- Caramelized Onions, 116
- Caramelized Onion Gravy, 251
- Grilled Onions, 149
- Pickled Onions, 47

PANCAKES
- Pop Pop's Silver Dollar Pancakes, 286

PASTAS
- Baked Pasta Casserole, 217
- Bean & Chili Pasta Bake, 212
- Edamame Pesto w/ Soba Noodles, 192
- Farfalle w/ Red Beans & Chiles, 193
- Farfalle w/ Sun-Dried Tomato Pesto & Zucchini, 194

Fettuccine w/ Broccoli & Lemon Pesto, 195
Fusilli & English Peas w/ Pistachio Pesto, 199
Kid-Friendly Spanish Spaghetti (Fideo), 203
Macaroni Casserole, 216
Macaroni & Peanut Butter, 196
Old Fashion Macaroni Salad, 45
Olive Pesto With A Kick, 206
Pasta w/ Chickpeas & Cherry Tomatoes, 191
Pasta Primavera Sauce, 200
Peanut Noodle Salad, 46
Penne Pasta w/ Broccoli, Capers, Green Olives & Pine Nuts, 198
Penne Pasta w/ Green Beans & Arugula, 47
Quick Penne & Beans, 210
Rus & Niki's Fresh Pasta Sauce w/ Vegetables, 209
Sauteed Mushrooms & Tofu w/ Rice Noodles, 224
Soba Noodle Salad, 50
Spaghetti w/ Chile Pesto, 204
Spicy Noodles, 197
Spinach, Beans & Bowtie pasta, 201
Spinach Linguine w/ Zucchini, Peas & Carrots, 202
Stir-Fry w/ Soba Noodles, 225
Tofu & Vegetable Lasagna, 213
Tomatoes, Olives & Capers w/ Pasta, 207
Whole-Wheat Penne Pasta w/ Miso & Sun-Dried Tomato Pesto, 205

PEACH
Summer Fruit Salad, 44
Peach Cobbler w/ Biscuit Topping, 300

PEANUT
Chili Peanut Dip, 264
Kale w/ Peanut Dressing, 124
Macaroni & Peanut Butter, 196
Peanut Butter Bread Mini Loaves, 290
Peanut Butter & Chocolate Icing, 336
Peanut Noodle Salad, 46
Roasted Almonds, Walnuts, Cashews or Peanuts, 266
Yummy Peanut Butter Cookies, 322

PEAS
Black-eye Peas, 246
Black-eye Pea Salsa, 256
Crowder or Cream Peas, 247
Fusilli & English Peas w/ Pistachio Pesto, 199
Split Pea Soup, 67

PECANS
Apple Crisp, 302
Brownies, 318
Hummingbird Cake, 330
Jen's Apple Spice Bread, 277
Maple Glazed Pecans, 271
Mom's Baked Apples, 298
Spinach & Romaine Salad w/ Balsamic Maple Vinaigrette, 36
Sweet Potato Casserole, 171

PEPPERS
Avocado Jalapeno Yogurt Dip, 266
Grilled Red Bell Peppers, 149
Grilled Veggie Salad w/ Spicy Pepper Dressing, 42
Potatoes & Pepper Fajitas, 220
Red Pepper Broccoli, 109
Red Bell Pepper Hummus, 87
Roasted Red Bell Pepper, 129
Sautéed Peppers, 130
Stuffed Red Bell Peppers, 129

PESTO
Chile Pesto, 204
Edamame Pesto, 194
Lemon Pesto, 195
Miso & Sun-dried Tomato Pesto, 205
Olive Pesto with a Kick, 206
Pistachio Pesto, 199
Sun-Dried Tomato Pesto, 194

PIES
Angela's Apple Pie, 310
Chocolate Pudding or Pie, 324
Creamy Coconut Pie, 312
Easy Blueberry pie, 311
Fresh Strawberry Yogurt Pie, 317
Ginger Snap Crust, 308
Graham Cracker Crust, 308
Grapenut Pie Crust, 309
Key Lime Tart, 315
Lemon Tart, 314
Nut & Medjool Date Crust, 307
Pie Crusts, 306
Puff Pastry Pies, 316
Rustic Fruit Pie, 313
Walnut Pie Crust, 309
Veggie Pot Pie, 219

PINE NUTS
Lemon Pesto, 195
Olive Pesto With A Kick, 206
Penne Pasta w/ Broccoli, Capers, Green Olives & Pine Nuts, 198
Toasted Pine Nuts, 267
Tofu & Vegetable Lasagna, 213
Romaine Salad & Pine Nuts w/ Garlic Vinaigrette, 34
Veggie Pasta Salad w/ Pine Nuts, 51
Zucchini Cakes, 142

PISTACHIOS
Banana Bread w/ Coconut & Pistachios, 278
Pistachio Pesto, 199
Penne Pasta w/ Green Beans & Arugula, 47
Roasted Brussels Sprouts, 111

PIZZA
Matt's Pizza, 218

PLUMS
Plum & Nectarine Crisp, 303

POSOLE (hominy)
Mexican Red Posole Soup, 68

POT PIE
Veggie Pot Pie, 219

POTATOES
Also see **SWEET POTATOES**
Baked Red Potato Slices, 168
Baked Red Potatoes w/ Onions & Balsamic Vinegar, 167
Baked Stuffed Potatoes, 161
Creamy Garlic Potato Slices, 168
Creamy Potato Leek Soup, 70
Crispy Red Potatoe w/Sweet Roasted Garlic, 167
Easy Potato Salad, 48
Grilled Potatoes, 150
Mushrooms & English Peas over Mashed Potatoes, 164
New Potato, Tomato Kale Soup, 71
Oven Fries, 165
Potato Sandwich, 92
Potato Corn Soup, 69
Potatoes & Pepper Fajitas, 220
Potato & Veggie Sausage Bake, 221
Red New Potatoes, 169
Rusty's Mashed Potatoes, 162
Smashed Potatoes, 163
Spicy Potato Casserole, 166
Warm Potato & Baby Spinach Salad, 49
White & Sweet Potato Casserole, 173

PUDDINGS
Chocolate Pudding or Pie, 324
Coconut Pudding, 325
Simple Banana Pudding, 323

QUESADILLAS
Hummus Quesadillas, 88
Spinach Quesadillas, 89

QUINOA
Basic Quinoa, 184
Quinoa & Pinto Bean Salad, 52
Quinoa Pilaf, 186
Quinoa Saute', 187

RICE
Basic Brown Rice, 174
Basic White Rice, 174
Brown Rice Salad, 40
Brown Rice & Vegetable Casserole, 222
Easy Spanish Rice, 180
Fresh Salsa Rice, 179
Green Rice, 176
Hot Rice w/ Fresh Vegetables, 175
Lemon Rice, 177
Mexican Rice Salad, 53
Orzo & White Rice w/ Fresh Salsa, 178
Red Beans & Rice, 245
Rice Pilaf, 178
Simple Vegetable & Rice Soup, 77
Spinach Rice, 181
Tofu Stir-Fry, 226
Tofu w/ Kale & Carrots & Peanuts Dressing over Brown Rice, 223
Wild & Brown Rice Casserole, 183
Wild & Brown Rice Pilaf Salad, 55
Wild & Brown Rice w/ Corn, 182

SALSAS
Black Bean Salsa, 254
Black-eye Pea Salsa, 256
Corn Salsa, 257
Pico de Gallo, 258
Ranchero Salsa, 255

SALADS
Arugula Salad, 26
Arugula w/ Roasted Garlic Hummus Dressing, 27
Artichoke, Hearts of Palm & Olive Salad, 38
Baby Spinach w/ Walnut & Raspberry Maple Vinaigrette Dressing, 28
Black Bean Salsa, 254
Black-eye Pea Salsa, 256
Broccoli Salad w/ Nuts & Raisins, 39
Brown Rice Salad, 40
Cabbage Slaw w/ Vinaigrette Dressing, 41
Corn Salsa, 257
Easy Potato Salad, 48
Edamame Salad, 43
Fresh Raw Vegetables, 25
Garbanzo Bean Salad, 45
Grilled Veggie Salad w/ Spicy Pepper Dressing, 42
Guacamole, 258
Mexican Rice Salad, 53
Old Fashioned Macaroni Salad, 45
Peanut Noodle Salad, 46

Penne Pasta w/ Green Beans & Arugula, 47
Pickled Onions, 47
Pico de Gallo, 258
Quinoa & Pinto Bean Salad, 52
Red Leaf Lettuce w/ Water Chestnuts and Chili Spice Vinaigrette Dressing, 29
Romaine Lettuce w/ Beets & Cashews & Shallot Vinaigrette Dressing, 30
Romaine & Avocado Salad w/ Classic French Dressing, 31
Romaine w/ Frisee & Sherry Vinaigrette, 32
Romaine w/ Fennel, Carrots & Edamame w/ Sherry Vinaigrette Dressing, 33
Romaine Salad & Pine Nuts & Garlic Vinaigrette, 34
Spinach Salad w/ Oranges & Avocados & Red Wine Vinaigrette, 35
Spinach & Romaine Salad w/ Balsamic Maple Vinaigrette Dressing, 36
Romaine Salad w/ Champagne Vinaigrette Dressing, 37
Soba Noodle Salad, 50
Summer Fruit Salad, 44
Veggie Pasta Salad w/ Pine Nuts, 51
Waldorf Salad, 54
Warm Potato & Baby Spinach Salad, 49
Wild & Brown Rice Pilaf Salad, 55

SANDWICHES
Artichoke & Hummus Open Faced Sandwich, 83
Black Bean Tostadas, 84
Chickpea Sandwich Spread, 86
Chipotle Hummus, 88
Fried Green Tomato Sandwich w/ Creole Mayo, 91
Grilled Portobello Mushroom Sandwich w/ Spicy Mayo, 90
Grilled Tofu Sandwich, 93
Grilled Vegetable Sandwich, 95
Hummus Quesadillas, 88
Mushroom & Nut Burger, 97
Potato Sandwich, 92
Red Pepper Hummus, 87
Roasted Garlic Hummus, 87
Spicy Black Bean Burger, 96
Sloppy Joes, 92
Spinach Quesadillas, 89
Tomato, Avocado & Red Onion Sandwich, 94
Veggie Wraps, 98
White Bean Spread, 85

SAUCES
Chili Peanut Dip, 264
Enchilada Sauce, 251
Fresh Tomato Sauce, 208
Nutty Miso Dressing, 262
Pasta Primavera Sauce, 200
Peanut Butter Dressing, 223
Quick Canned Tomato Sauce, 208
Quick Peanut Sauce, 254
Ranchero Salsa, 255
Sesame Sauce, 259
Spicy Soy Sauce, 139
Tamari Sauce, 259
Verde Sauce, 261

SEASONINGS
Deb's Seasoning, 269
Deb's Taco Seasoning, 269

SOUPS
Basic Stock, 78
Black Bean Soup, 61
County Lentil Soup, 66
Cream of Broccoli Soup, 64
Creamy Potato Leek Soup, 70
Creamy Tomato Soup, 72
Deb's Vegetable Soup, 76
Fast Corn Chowder, 65
Hearty Tomato Soup, 73
Mexican Red Posole Soup, 68
New Potato, Tomato & Kale Soup, 71
Potato Corn Soup, 69
Roasted Tortilla Soup, 75
Simple Vegetable & Rice Soup, 77
Split Pea Soup, 67
Three Bean Chili, 62
Tomato Rice Soup w/ Greens, 74
Tomato Stock, 79
White Bean & Kale Soup, 63

SPINACH
Asparagus, Spinach & Leeks, 101
Baby spinach & Walnuts w/ Raspberry Maple Vinaigrette, 28
Sautéed Spinach, 131
Spinach, Beans & Bowtie Pasta, 201
Spinach & Mushroom Enchiladas, 214
Spinach Quesadillas, 89
Spinach Salad w/ Oranges, Avocados & Red Wine Vinaigrette, 35
Spinach & Romaine Salad w/ Balsamic Maple Vinaigrette Dressing, 36
Warm Potato & Baby Spinach Salad, 49

SPREADS
Chipotle Hummus, 88
Chive Aioli Dip, 265
Creole Mayo, 91
White Bean Spread, 85
Red Pepper Hummus, 87
Spicy Mayo, 90
Roasted Garlic Hummus, 87

SQUASH
Baked Acorn or Butternut Squash w/ Kale, 132
Baked Butternut Squash, 134
Boiled Yellow Squash, 136
Grilled Squash, 150
Sauteed Yellow Squash w/ Onions, 137
Squash Casserole, 136
Steamed Summer Squash, 137
Stuffed Acorn Squash, 133
Stuffed Yellow Squash, 135

STRAWBERRY
Fresh Strawberry Mini Muffins, 291
Fresh Strawberry Yogurt Pie, 317

STIR-FRY
Mushroom Stir-Fry, 126
Stir-Fry w/ Soba Noodles, 225
Tamari Sauce, 259
Tofu Stir-Fry, 226
Zucchini Stir-Fry, 143

STOCKS
Basic Stock, 78
Tomato Stock, 79

SWEET POTATOES
Baked Sweet Potato Dinner, 170
Cajun Sweet Potato Fries, 165
Candied Yams, 172
Grilled Sweet Potatoes, 150
Steamed Sweet Potatoes, 170
Sweet Potato Casserole, 171
White & Sweet Potato Casserole, 173

TARTS
Lemon Tart, 314
Key Lime Tart, 315

TOFU
Baked Tofu, 229
Battered Tofu, 236
Broiled Tofu, 232
Cornmeal-Crusted Tofu, 232
Crumbled Tofu, 233
Grilled Tofu, 230
Grilled Tofu Sandwich, 93
Sauteed Mushrooms & Tofu w/ Rice Noodles, 224
Sauteed Tofu, 235
Sloppy Joes, 92
Stir-Fry w/ Soba Noodles, 225
Tofu Stir-Fry, 226
Tofu w/ Kale & Carrots & Peanut Dressing over Brown Rice, 223
Tofu w/ Teriyaki Sauce, 234
Tofu & Vegetable Lasagna, 213

TOMATO
Creamy Tomato Soup, 72
Fresh Tomato Sauce, 208
Fried Green Tomato Sandwich w/ Creole Mayonnaise, 91
Hearty Tomato Soup, 73
Pasta w/ Chickpeas & Cherry Tomatoes, 191
New Potato, Tomato & Kale Soup, 71
Tomato, Avocado & Red Onion Sandwich, 94
Tomatoes, Olives & Capers w/ Pasta, 207
Tomato Rice Soup w/ Greens, 74
Tomato Stock, 79

VEGETABLE DISHES
Also see the Individual Category for each Vegetable
Garden Bake, 138
Steamed Julienne Vegetable Medley, 139
Steamed Vegetables w/ Spicy Soy Sauce, 139
Roasted Vegetables, 140
Grilled Vegetables, 144
Grilled Veggie Kabobs, 145
Grilled Vegetables w/ Sesame Marinade, 151
Vegetable Packets for the Grill, 152
Veggie Pot Pie, 219

WALNUTS
Baby Spinach & Walnuts w/ Raspberry Maple Vinaigrette Dressing, 28
Banana Muffins w/ Walnut Topping, 287
Coconut & Banana Nut Cupcakes, 329
Fresh Apple Cake w/ Walnuts, 326
Mushroom & Nut Burger, 97
Nut & Medjool Dale Crust, 307
Nutty Miso Dressing, 262
Roasted Almonds, Walnuts, Cashews & Peanuts, 266
Walnut Pie Crust, 309

WILD RICE
Wild & Brown Rice w/ Corn, 182
Wild & Brown Rice Pilaf Salad, 55
Wild & Brown Rice Casserole, 183

YOGURT
Avocado Jalapeno Yogurt Dip, 266
Blueberries & Oatmeal Breakfast Muffins, 288
Cornbread, 280
Cucumber Walnut Yogurt Dip, 265
Lemon Bread, 282
Potato & Veggie Sausage Bake, 221
Vanilla Cake or Cupcakes, 333
Fresh Strawberry Yogurt Pie, 317

ZUCCHINI
Farfalle w/ Sun-Dried Tomato Pesto & Zucchini, 194
Kale, Zucchini & Tomatoes, 124
Spinach Linguine w/ Zucchini, Peas & Carrots, 202
Steamed Julienne Vegetable Medley, 139
Zucchini Bread, 284
Zucchini Cakes, 142
Zucchini Stir-Fry, 143

Trademark Credits

The TOBASCO® marks, bottle and label designs are registered trademarks and servicemarks exclusively of McIlhenny Co., Avery Island, LA 70513

RO*TEL® is a registered trademark of International Home Foods, Inc.

Wildwood Garlic Aioli®

365 Brand®

Spectrum®

Whole Foods®

Ghirardelli®

Ah!laska Chocolate syrup®

Masa Harina De Maiz®

Not-Chick'n Natural Bouillon Cubes by Edward & Sons®

Simply Organic Vegetable Seasoning®

McCormick Spicy Steak®

Tony Chachere's Original Creole Seasoning®

Burritos® and Old El Paso Taco Seasonings®

Sky Valley Sriracha® sauce by Organicville®

Sambal Oelek® chili paste

The Wizards® Worcestershire Sauce

Muir Glen®

Veganaise®

French Nicoise®

Greek Kalamata®

MedJool®

Grape Nut®

www.ingramcontent.com/pod-product-compliance
Lightning Source LLC
Chambersburg PA
CBHW080917170426
43201CB00016B/2172